Speech Behavior
and Human Interaction

Date Due

30 AVR. '91			
NOV 1 1 1991			

Speech Behavior
and Human Interaction

George A. Borden Associate Professor of Speech
Richard B. Gregg Associate Professor of Speech
Theodore G. Grove Assistant Professor of Speech

The Pennsylvania State University

Prentice-Hall, Inc.
Englewood Cliffs, New Jersey

174559

PRENTICE-HALL INTERNATIONAL, INC., *London*
PRENTICE-HALL OF AUSTRALIA, PTY. LTD., *Sydney*
PRENTICE-HALL OF CANADA, LTD., *Toronto*
PRENTICE-HALL OF INDIA PRIVATE LTD., *New Delhi*
PRENTICE-HALL OF JAPAN, INC., *Tokyo*

Library of Congress Catalog Card Number 69–11570.
Printed in the United States of America.

Current printing (last digit)
10 9 8 7 6 5 4 3 2 1

Preface

For 5000 years researchers have been studying the communication process. They have given this study different names in various eras—*rhetoric* in ancient times, *elocution* in the past two centuries, and *public speaking* in the twentieth century—but they have always tried to help the student toward better self-expression and better understanding of communication in general. In recent years researchers have begun to investigate communication phenomena by scientific means, thereby producing new explanations and conceptualizations. It is time for the college student to consider these developments.

In many institutions of higher learning, students must take a basic speech course to help them develop a skill they will use throughout their lives. At present, most of these are predominantly how-to-do-it courses geared to the public-speaking goals of the first half of the century. However, the growing trend in colleges and universities is toward making the student aware of the entire human communication process rather than just public speaking. In this text we set forth some of the major ideas concerning this process. In doing so we consciously refrain from giving instructions on how to communicate.

With these considerations in mind we have assembled in this book introductions to some of the many theories basic to speech behavior in human interaction. To do this we have drawn on knowledge from such diverse areas as neurology, psychology, linguistics, sociology, speech, journalism, and cybernetics. The reader will find that this is not a speech-making recipe book. And it is also not a psychology, sociology, or linguistics text. Rather, it is an introduction to speech behavior in human interaction.

The topics considered do not nearly exhaust all those that readers may feel are important to the communication process. The inclusions and omissions are the result of a selection process governed by criteria the authors imposed on the existing topics in the field of speech communication; the material reflects the authors' preferences for its inclusion in a study of speech behavior in human interaction. We expect that those who find this book useful either in the basic speech course or else-where will exert another selective influence—supplementing some and de-emphasizing other topics to serve the demands of a particular course goal and of the unique perspective of their own field.

The material in this book divides into three major parts. Each is complete within itself but also builds toward the total picture presented in conjunction with the others. In the first part we look at a person in isolation and try to establish the process of communication as it occurs within him. With some understanding of what is going on inside one's self, one may understand why certain things happen as they do when two or more individuals come together to communicate for a specific purpose. We consider interpersonal communication in the second part. The third part expands the communication process to the most general level by presenting some of the theories about what has traditionally been called public communication.

Although all three authors worked on the entire manuscript, each au-thor was primarily responsible for a particular part of the book: Dr. George Borden for Part I; Dr. Theodore Grove for Part II; and Dr. Richard Gregg for Part III. The following individuals merit special thanks for their contributions to this volume: Dr. Theodore Clevenger, Jr., for his extensive comments during several of the manuscript stages; Dr. Robert Kibler for his perceptive critique during the final stages of preparation; the many students who provided comments on various parts of the manuscript, especially Miss Wendy Weber, whose thoughtful criticisms led to meaningful changes; Charolette Gregg for her careful preparation of the index. Errors and weaknesses in the book are the responsibility of the authors, not the persons mentioned above, who gave so generously of their time. Finally we would like to thank Mr. James H. Clark (speech editor) for his patience, persistence, and the fine working relationship we enjoyed with Prentice-Hall because of him.

GEORGE A. BORDEN
RICHARD B. GREGG
THEODORE G. GROVE

University Park, Pennsylvania

Contents

Speech Behavior
and Human Interaction

Introduction

In the preface to the book of readings *Interpersonal Dynamics*, the authors reflect that man's problems fall into two classes: noninteractional, or problems of man in relation to nature; and interactional, or man in relation to man. They note that stunning scientific progress has been made with regard to the first class of problems, but that the continuing nature and the intensity of national and international crises witness to human incompetence in the second category.

> The trouble is that these national and international conflagrations have their counterparts at every level of human intercourse: in small groups, in marriages, in friendships, among lovers and siblings, between teachers and students, between worker and boss. Unless the protagonists are famous, the tensions go unnoticed, to be registered indirectly and anonymously in divorce rates, homicides, and gang wars or often in the more pedestrian way civilized people live with their human problems: poison pen letters, petty jealousies, unproductive relationships, prejudices, practical "jokes," destructive fantasies, unstable careers, ulcerative colitis, "frayed nerves," tranquilizers, and sleeping pills.[1]

One of the primary ways by which a man establishes contact with his fellows and either achieves cooperation and mutual gain or falls into conflict and disarray is through the process of communication. Poor human communication is not the sole cause of a man's problems, and effective communication is not the panacea for his ills. But in both cases, communication usually is a party to the action.

John Horrocks notes in his foreword to Muzafer Sherif's essay *In Common Predicament* that ours is an age "when group is pitted against group, when misunderstanding is rife, and when the speed of communication makes for immediate confrontation of groups whose contacts were once insulated by distance and time."[2] He is referring here to the dramatic

---

[1] Reprinted by permission from Warren G. Bennis *et al.*, *Interpersonal Dynamics* (Homewood, Illinois: The Dorsey Press, 1964), p. ix.
[2] *In Common Predicament* (Boston: Houghton Mifflin Company, 1966), p. ix.

new dimension of communication created by the electronic mass dissemination of messages. And this new dimension of communication adds a new element to our daily lives. McLuhan says it well:

> Electric speed in bringing all social and political functions together in a sudden implosion has heightened human awareness of responsibility to an intense degree. It is this implosive factor that alters the position of the Negro, the teenager, and some other groups. They can no longer be *contained*, in the political sense of limited association. They are now *involved* in our lives, as we in theirs, thanks to the electric media.[3]

Finally, and to shift focus slightly, political scientist Karl Deutsch asserts the significance of human communication in the manipulation and control of human activity when he suggests that "it might be profitable to look upon government somewhat less as a problem of power and somewhat more as a problem of steering," and that "steering is decisively a matter of communication."[4]

These statements from established scholars in diverse academic disciplines exemplify the increasing preoccupation with the nature, purposes, and effects of human communication. If communication is as important as the statements quoted above indicate, it behooves us all to become acquainted with ourselves as communicating beings.

THE THEORETICAL STRUCTURE

When we think of human communication, we naturally dwell on the social situations in which we as individuals talk, read, or listen. We may think of such diverse examples of communication as talking to a friend on a Friday night date, watching T.V., attending classes, speaking before a social club, or reading a newspaper. The list is almost endless. However, if we analyze each of the above situations, we begin to see a pattern that may help us to understand what this phenomenon is all about. One immediate observation is that human communication involves people—individuals like you and me. Since this is the case, perhaps we should take a closer look at the individual human being in our attempt to understand the human-communication process.

If we begin our investigation with the individual, our first question should be, "What does the individual do in a communication situation that makes him essential to it?" There are any number of answers to

[3] Marshall McLuhan, *Understanding Media: The Extensions of Man* (New York: McGraw-Hill Book Company, 1965), p. 5.
[4] *The Nerves of Government* (New York: The Macmillan Company, 1963), p. ix.

this question. One may be that he reads, listens, or watches, i.e., receives information from those who make up the communication situation. Another may be that he talks or acts, i.e., transmits information, in such a way as to obtain and maintain the attention of the others involved in this communication situation. If these two types of individual behavior occur in the communication situation, and they do, then perhaps we should investigate more thoroughly those facets of the individual which enable him to behave in this way. Figure 1 is a schematic representation of the individual, depicting the two types of behavior mentioned above. The arrows indicate that these two functions may be pictured as revolving about a structure within the individual which enables him to receive and transmit information. The first part of this book investigates the individual's communication system, i.e., those characteristics of a human being which enable him to communicate.

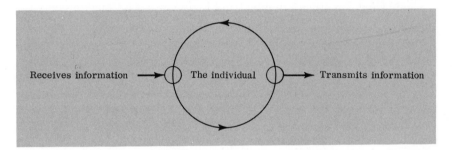

Fig. 1. The individual as a system of receivers and transmitters revolving about an inherent structure.

Regardless of how engrossed we become with the individual and his inherent communication system, we must realize that it is unnatural for an individual to exist for any length of time without some interaction with other human beings. Some individuals can tolerate isolation better than others, but no one can maintain himself either physically or mentally without contact with others. You can see the social nature of individuals in the many situations in which two or more people are united in a group effort. Marriage and family relations, church and school organizations, political and social activities all call upon the individual to interact with other individuals to gain a desired goal. This process of interaction is commonly called *interpersonal communication;* we may picture it in much the same way as we pictured the individual's communication system above. The interaction of two or more individual communication systems in turn produces its own system, which is schematized in Fig. 2. The arrows do not mean that each individual may receive informa-

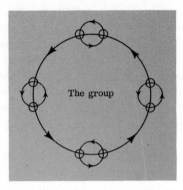

Fig. 2. The group as a system of individuals revolving about an inherent structure.

tion only from one other individual and may transmit information only to another; they indicate the structural bond which ties all the members of a given group together so that they function as a system. The communication process which evolves under conditions of high personal involvement and in face-to-face settings is the subject matter for the second part of this book. The emphasis is still on the individual and on why he exhibits the communicative behavior that he does.

Though we are all members of various groups, or perhaps because we are all members of various groups, we realize that something beyond the group affects us as individuals. We know that many of our actions are tempered by the attitude of the group we are functioning in, but that, in the same way, the actions of the group are affected by the temperament of society. However, in both these cases, the individual is the basic unit for the interaction. Thus, groups behave as they do only because individuals voice their opinions, in one way or another. In turn, though group thinking may influence one's opinions, society takes the stands it does on various issues only because individuals voice their opinions. Therefore, when we consider the rise of the Nazi party in the 1930s, or the repeal of slavery in the 1860s, or the rise of Christianity in the first three centuries A.D., we ultimately have to consider the communicative behavior of various individuals. In each case we find various groups, each with its own spokesmen, interacting with one another with varying degrees of cooperation—from outright hostility to complete agreement. Figure 3 illustrates the interaction of such groups. Again we must point out that the arrows do not indicate the direction of the flow of information; they indicate that groups are bound together in such a way as to establish a communication system peculiar to the structure of a particular society. It should also be made clear that the interaction of groups in this social setting is dependent upon the reception and transmission of information by group members. The process of communication involved when a member of a group seeks to influence the attitudes of society is the subject matter of the third part of this book. It should be apparent that the individual is still the center of the communication process.

In this introduction we have tried to build for you an increasingly more complex schema of the human-communication process. The focal point of this schema is the individual and his communicative behavior. We have indicated that Part I of this book is concerned with the individual's internal communication system, which enables him to receive and transmit information. Part II is concerned with the communication system that evolves when two or more individuals interact in the process of receiving and transmitting information. And Part III is concerned with the communication process involved when one individual strives

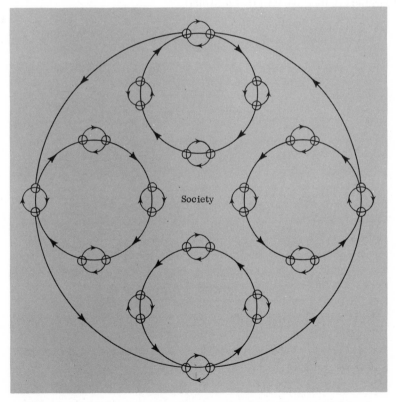

Fig. 3. Society as a system of groups revolving about an inherent structure.

to influence the attitudes of society in a public-communication situation.

You should keep several things in mind while reading the pages which follow. In effect, we have put together in this book three distinct essays. Each essay sustains its own perspective, discusses concepts in light of its perspective, displays a unique style, and ultimately stands on its own as a unitary treatment. Hence, you may progress in any order you choose. But, taken in its entirety, the book strives to present a fairly holistic picture of the human being as a sender and receiver of oral messages. This is not to say that the theories and explanations presented are final, complete, or completely integrated. We are a long way from final answers; indeed systematic studies of some aspects of human communication have just begun. But many teachers and researchers are hard at work, and we have tried to provide some of the fruits of their labor. If the book helps you to better understand your own communicative behavior and that of others, if you are stimulated to probe more deeply into the unexplored and unanswered problems the researchers detect, we will feel gratified.

I

The Individual's Communication System

In this part of the book we shall consider the individual as a self-contained, self-regulating unit. That is, we shall look at him as a system that is entirely separated from the outside world. Perhaps you may tend to think of him as a robot who has certain channels into which information can be fed and certain ways in which he may react to this information after it has been processed through his internal circuitry. However, we would rather you think of this individual as "you," a real, live individual who sees, hears, feels, smells, and tastes; who learns, remembers; thinks, and makes decisions; and who then talks, gestures, and behaves in such a way as to make "you" unique. To help you understand the various aspects of your communication system and how they are integrated to make you communicate the way you do, we shall present a very simple, rather mechanical description of this system.

The general process of communication implied above consists of receivers, a processing unit, and transmitters. For our purposes here the receivers are your five senses, the processing unit is your central nervous system, and the transmitters are your facilities for speaking, writing, gesturing, and behaving in a way that will transmit a signal from you to someone else. The receiving and transmitting phases are more familiar to most of us (though we may not understand all we know about them) than is the processing phase. For this reason we shall continue to subdivide the processing phase into the various areas of interest delimited by researchers: storing information (memory), learning, thinking, and recalling (remembering). We may schematize this oversimplified description of the human-communication process on the individual level as in Fig. 4. This figure shows that the human-communication process

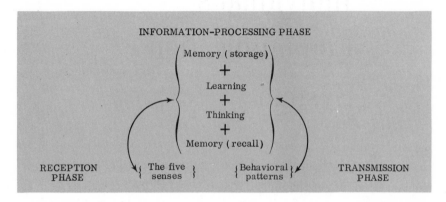

Fig. 4. The RIPT descriptive schema of the individual's communication process.

has three phases—reception, information-processing, and transmission—referred to as RIPT. It further indicates that the five senses pick up information, which is then assimilated into our mental makeup through the processes of storing, learning, thinking, and recalling (all of which are intertwined and occur simultaneously). This processing phase may then lead to some communicative behavior. The double-headed arrows between the three phases indicate that all three are interdependent. That is, the state of any one materially affects the functioning of the other two. If one is defective, it will adversely affect the others. Thus, if you have lost the total or partial use of one of your senses or if your central nervous system has been damaged in some way or if you have a physiological defect in any of the organs by which you transmit messages, your communicative behavior is materially affected. This is not to say that your ability to communicate is necessarily hindered. You can probably think of people who have overcome tremendous obstacles in any one or all three of these phases to become very effective communicators.

We immediately recognize that the individual's communication system is extremely complicated. It involves the reception of a signal; the processing of the information contained in this signal, i.e., the development of a message (meaning) in light of our past experiences through decoding (taking meaning out of the code in which the signal was received) and encoding (formulating a message which may be transmitted via the appropriate code); and then the transmission of the appropriate signals. While this process is going on, our central nervous system is constantly monitoring itself, to keep track of our physical and mental condition (called *internal feedback*) and also the condition of the communication situation we are in (called *external feedback*). The messages it receives from these two monitoring processes are an integral part of the total communication situation.

Our brain, then, functioning as the information-processing unit, is processing several distinct messages simultaneously. If it were active only in interpersonal communication (communication among individuals), the system would be much less complicated; but, when we realize that this mass of cells must also regulate our internal processes, we realize that the problems increase astronomically. You are probably experiencing some of these internal processes right now. Do you feel sleepy, hungry, sick, or sexy? Do you have a pain here or there that interrupts your concentration? Such autonomic and proprioceptive stimuli continually bombard the brain and are often prime factors in our ability to communicate effectively.

The brain, being the data-processing center for both external and internal stimuli, has an extremely difficult job. It must, if it is really effective, separate these stimuli sufficiently to keep one set from affecting the processing of the other set. Couple with this the fact that we also have memories and imaginations active in this center, and you begin to see the complexity of the human-communication process. It is not surprising that we can handle only a limited amount of information per unit of time, and that, if we are pressured to handle more, our nervous system breaks down.

The complexity of the communication process may be realized by meditating on the purely mechanical properties of this process. However, the fact that this process is not really mechanical can be seen in that we do not always act in a reasonable manner. A machine operates on well structured principles and never deviates from them. We are not machines. We marry too young, drive too fast, eat too much, and sleep too little. It is almost safe to say that the majority of our actions are unreasonable. Add to this the fact that the response one person gives to a certain stimulus may be completely different from that of someone else, and you can see that we are much more than machines.

However, the approach taken in the first part of this book is mechanical in nature because the information we have to disseminate fits very well into such a model. The nature of our neurological system and the fact that our brain is analogous in many respects to an electronic computer make the mechanistic approach vital for your understanding of the information contained in the first part of this book. The remaining two parts will show the nonmechanical nature of human communication much more clearly. Thus, you should keep in mind that we use mechanistic terms here primarily for the clarity they provide while you are trying to understand some of the principles of the human-communication process internal to the individual.

We do want you to realize, however, that even in a mechanical sense we may think of ourselves as self-regulating systems; that is, we are in control of our own communicative behavior. Since our brain is able to interpret our own internal as well as external stimuli and to have us react to them in purely personal ways, we are much more than robots programed by society. Though we have mentioned the autonomical and proprioceptive stimuli, we shall not dwell on them to any extent in what follows. Our main goal is to explicate the internal processes activated when we communicate with others. Each individual is unique in all the phases covered in this part of the book. Therefore, we can speak only in general terms. What you do in each of these phases should be subsumable under the general theory presented. We hope that you will be able to supply many of your own experiences to help clarify various points throughout the text.

The Collection of
Information

Let us begin with an example.

Millie had always loved her grandmother—really. But some things about her gave Millie a feeling of distaste. That funny smell that surrounded her reminded Millie of the overwhelming, sweet smell that came through her window when the honeysuckle bush was in full bloom. But she supposed that, when she grew up, she would smell that way too.

Other things bothered Millie about her grandmother—that red stuff, for instance, that came off her cheeks whenever Millie kissed her. It tasted so icky. Millie wondered whether her skin would start peeling off when she got that old. Yet, why should her grandmother's cheeks be peeling when they felt so soft to her lips when she kissed her? Millie wondered how old you had to be before you started to crumble that way.

She thought back to the last time her grandmother had come to visit and remembered again how funny she had looked in the dress that was obviously too big for her. It just seemed to hang on her, and it came six inches below her knees. Maybe her grandmother had a disease that was slowly eating away her body. This could account for her skin's flaking off when she was kissed and for the fact that she tried to hide as much of her legs as possible. Millie finally decided that one of the signs which told you whether a woman had this disease was those bright red spots on her cheeks.

She was brought quickly out of her thoughts by a kind, pleasant voice at her door saying, "Millie, I'm here." Immediately she knew why she liked her grandmother so much. It was the sound of her voice, which always said, "Millie, I love you," no matter what words she was saying at the time.

This example shows how a little girl uses her five senses to get her own mental picture of reality. Obviously, Millie's picture will change as she matures and becomes acquainted with the world of cosmetics. You might stop here and reflect on the information children gather through the five senses. They touch things to see what they feel like because they do not trust their eyesight.   They taste many more things than adults do because adults have learned that humans do not eat paper, dirt, or grass.   Only with training do they learn what are the good and the bad smells.   And their hearing is attuned as much to outside noises as it is to words.   Our senses, then, are our only true contact with reality.   Perhaps we should take time to acquire a better understanding of the part they play in the human-communication process.

THE SENSE ORGANS

The precise way in which we gather data remains a mystery, although, in our ever increasing desire to know ourselves, we have made some important progress toward understanding this phenomenon.   Most people are aware of the physiology of the five natural senses; and they realize that their proper functioning is essential to the development of the whole person.   The child is born with fully developed sense receptors; it remains for him to use these receptors to a degree commensurate with his vocational activities.   Each sense has its own particular area of specialization and thus its own relative importance to the individual.

Even though we probably gather more external information through our sense of sight than through any of the others, we are conditioned to forget much of this information.   How much of what you see do you remember?   One of the distinguishing characteristics of a painter is that he learns to recall the minute details we all see but fail to remember. The same can be said of the musician with respect to hearing, the finisher of fine furniture with respect to touch, the wine taster with respect to taste, and the perfume manufacturer with respect to smell.

As we noticed in the example at the beginning of this section, Millie relied on all her senses to give her a total picture of her grandmother. This picture had many dissonant features, yet, somehow they all fitted together to give her the feeling of her grandmother which she enjoyed. The sense of hearing was the one that gave her the most important part of this mosaic.   This reliance on the sense of hearing as the major information-gathering sense develops as a child becomes more language conscious.   The more highly structured the language is in his culture, the more he will consciously rely on this sense to give him the information he is seeking.

Even though, in most communication situations, we have learned to subordinate all other senses to the auditory sense, we find that messages which we might consider extraneous are being picked up by the other senses.   Our brain uses these messages to "flavor" the main message received by our ears, e.g., "Your lips tell me no! no!, But there's yes! yes!

in your eyes."[1] The fact that all the senses are active in giving man the information he is to process is made quite evident by the loss of any one of these senses. Since sight, hearing, touch, and smell are the most active senses in the everyday communication situation, you should be aware that these senses are gathering information at any given time, and you should be able to sort out the various messages received and make a proper evaluation of each.

All of us should be aware of the part our various senses play in the communication process. We see pretty girls or handsome men and desire to meet them. After we meet them, we may find that the messages our other senses collect reinforce the first impression we had of these individuals, i.e., their conversation may be charming and their cologne enticing. On the other hand we may get entirely different messages from our other senses (now even your best friends will tell you) and thus lose interest in these people. The important things to remember are that all our senses are at work continuously and that the messages each one sends to the brain exert some influence on the meaning obtained from each particular communicative act.

It is not important at this time that the reader understand exactly how each sense organ works, i.e., how it picks up a stimulus and transforms it into a neural impulse which is transported to the brain. Suffice it to say that with the senses of sight, taste, and smell a chemical transformation originates the neural impulse, while with the senses of touch and hearing a mechanical transformation of pressure stimuli performs this function. The receptor cells for each sense are different, of course; they are specialists and are designed specifically for the one function they perform[2] and for the certain types of stimuli they receive. The stimulus itself goes no farther than the receptor cell, where the transmission of data begins with a transformation of the stimulus into a neural impulse. The mysterious part of the act of sensing is that all the neural impulses are the same regardless of which sense organ they come from. Their destinations in the brain are different, to be sure, but the interpretation of these impulses as to intensity and variation of stimuli is still a great mystery.

The transformation of information from stimulus to neural impulse is analogous to the transformation taking place when someone presses a teletypewriter key or speaks into a microphone. The stimulus received changes into an electrical impulse and goes on its way. As long as the teletypewriter or microphone is turned on, it performs this transforma-

---

[1] Copyright 1924 by Jerome H. Remick & Company. Used by permission of Warner Bros.–Seven Arts, Inc.

[2] See Wolfgang Von Buddenbrock, *The Senses* (Ann Arbor, Michigan: The University of Michigan Press, 1958), for a complete analysis of this concept.

tion regardless of the intent of the originator of the incoming stimulus. However, there is a threshold below which it will not function. Sense receptors are similar to teletypewriters or microphones. They are turned on whenever we are conscious, and they perform their transformations as long as the incoming stimuli are above their natural threshold. Thus, sense receptors are like great sponges; they soak up all stimuli in their media and above their natural threshold. This being the case, one can see how much information is available to a person and also how much is extraneous to the intended message of a given communication situation.

NEUROLOGICAL INHIBITION

The process by which the impulse gets from the sense organs to the brain has been investigated at some length using present technology, with its emphasis on chemical and electrical reactions; even with these limited tools some explanation is possible. We can detect electric impulses in the nerve fibers leading from the sense organs to the brain and can measure these impulses with electronic equipment. Nevertheless, we cannot assume complete understanding of this process.[3]

Nerve networks, or systems, are composed of many nerve cells working together to transmit messages to and from the higher centers of the nervous system. The shortest nerve circuit is the reflex arc; the longest may involve much of the spinal column and many parts of the brain. The part of this system of special importance to us at this time is the juncture of these nerve cells (the point of contact of one cell with another) and particularly that of the sensory nerve fiber. It is at this juncture (called the *synapse*) that the nerve impulse may be stopped or propagated depending on the triggering threshold of the cell. At each synapse the impulse must be re-created in the adjoining nerve cell. If this re-creation does not take place, the stimulus reacted to by the receptor cell is not reported to the communication center (the brain).

Thus there is a natural threshold below which messages are not conveyed. The impulse from the receptor cell must be of sufficient strength to trigger the next nerve cell into re-creating this impulse and sending it along communication routes to the center for which it is intended. An important aspect to keep in mind is that the impulse does not fade out as it proceeds along this neural pathway. As each cell is triggered, it re-creates a like impulse of equal magnitude and sends it on its way. Thus, each nerve cell may be likened to a relay station which receives and

---

[3] Sir John Eccles, "The Synapse," *Scientific American*, 212 (January 1965), 56–66; and, Bernhard Katz, "How Cells Communicate," *Scientific American*, 205 (September 1961), 209–20.

transmits signals. Only signals above a certain amplitude are received, but, after they are received, they are transmitted to the next station with the same amplitude. This is true of the networks operating from all five sense organs.

The communication circuit outlined above is, of course, overly simplified. To make our explanation more precise, we must mention another important aspect of the process. If the nervous system worked only as described above, its degree of efficiency and the reception by the brain of messages from the outside world would be dependent only on the natural thresholds of the sense receptors and nerve cells. This is not the case, however, for researchers have found that present at each junction in the neural system are nerve fibers that carry inhibitory impulses. That is, these nerve fibers can raise the threshold of the nerve cell to a point where re-creation of an incoming impulse is not possible.[4]

To simplify the inhibitory process for the present discussion we may state that the inhibitory fiber carries an impulse which causes the chemical content of the nerve-cell body to be so altered that the impulse from the excitatory nerve fiber is not of sufficient amplitude to activate the nerve cell. Because this complicated chemical process is just now being partially understood, we must be satisfied at this time to report that the threshold of a nerve cell may be raised above its natural level by the action of impulses supplied to it over inhibitory nerve fibers.

The implications of such a refinement of the nervous system on the collection of data by the human mind are significant. If the reception threshold of nerve cells can be raised by impulses sent to them from other nerve cells, does this mean that we have some "real" control over our sensory activities? Is it true then that our brain is not a repository for all the stimuli that bombard our sensory organs? Can we turn these receivers "on" and "off"? Is it possible that all the maladjustments in people who act differently from us originate not only in the way they interpret the data they receive but also in the amount they receive and in the way they receive it? The implications of these questions for human communication should be apparent.

You should not confuse this ability to modify or stop the flow of information to the brain with the physiological impairment of sense organs. Certainly, a person whose hearing has become impaired or whose eyes have been damaged is physically unable to receive all the data presented to him in any given communication situation; but it may be equally possible for a person to fail to receive certain stimuli because of neural inhibitions. And evidence also indicates that at least some of our sense receptors have the ability within themselves to limit the amount of information passed on by them.

4 Eccles, "The Synapse," 56–66.

Although the reception threshold of a nerve cell may be modified at any juncture, we have evidence that the major modification of a neural impulse takes place in the spinal cord.[5] Interacting stimuli from different senses also may inhibit or modify the message reaching the brain. Further sources of inhibition or modification are certain drugs which cause specific areas of the brain or spinal cord to fail to function properly and thus interrupt the flow of impulses along these fibers. So it should be clear that the central nervous system, a vastly complex network, is able to interact with itself in a neurological way to control the messages received by the brain.

We might assume that in a normal person the neurological apparatus is kept open and is operating at full efficiency at all times. Even if this is the case, however, we still do not collect all the information available to our sense organs. If they pass on to the brain all the stimuli they are capable of receiving, much of it still is never available for the brain to interpret. This phenomenon is caused by another small neurological organ called the *reticular formation*.[6] When impulses come from the various sense organs to the brain, they branch at a particular point in the nervous system. Some of them enter the reticular formation, and the rest go to their respective places in the cortex of the brain. If the reticular formation ignores these impulses, the rest of the brain also fails to perceive the stimuli generating the impulses. Thus the reticular formation has the specific duty of awakening the brain so that it will perceive the incoming impulses. The reticular formation does not modify the existing message, but rather it sprays the brain with impulses to activate it so that it may receive impulses coming from any one of the sense organs.

This unique apparatus is able to learn which stimuli are important and which are not for it may allow you to sleep regularly in a house beside an active railroad while awakening you at the sound of a baby's cry. This formation is also the one which controls your ability to concentrate for it shuts out all stimuli but those upon which the brain is concentrating. Anesthetics can block the flow of impulses to this part of the brain. However, when the anesthesia wears off, the impulses again flow through the reticular formation, and the person is able to perceive the stimuli originating these impulses. The reticular formation has some control too over the activity of the entire nervous system; reflex actions are considerably fewer when it is deactivated.

Thus the reticular formation is the "high command" of the central nervous system. It tells the brain which of the information passing

[5] Ronald Melzack, "The Perception of Pain," *Scientific American*, 204 (February 1961), 41–49.
[6] J. D. French, "The Reticular Formation," *Scientific American*, 196 (May 1957), 54.

through it it can perceive, and it is active in inhibiting the flow of information over the entire nervous system. Perhaps each of us should insert a small electrode in our reticular formation and attach a generator so we can keep ourselves alert and attentive when we need to communicate effectively.

PSYCHOLOGICAL CONSIDERATIONS

Because we have introduced the inhibitory nerve fiber into this discussion of sensation, we may now investigate the possibility that psychologically activated inhibitory mechanisms may prohibit evidence of stimuli from reaching the brain, where they can be interpreted and responded to. It is very possible that the interpretation of a specific experience may set in motion a neurological circuit which will prohibit the brain from ever receiving such a message again. In the process of setting this circuitry in motion, the brain or the circuit itself may inadvertently block the reception of other messages as well. As Melzack states, we know that the mechanism for establishing such restrictions exists.

> Investigators in a number of countries have recently demonstrated the presence of systems of nerve fibers that run from the higher areas of the brain downward to make connection with the message-carrying nerve pathways in the spinal cord. Electrical activity induced in these higher brain areas is capable of suppressing or modifying the message; it may never get beyond the lower levels of the central nervous system or an entirely different message may reach the brain.
>
> There is no longer any doubt that these message-modifying fibers exist; it has been found that electrical stimulation of widespread regions of the brain is able to modify the messages transmitted through every major sensory system. The origins and terminations of these message-controlling fibers have not yet been fully established. But even at this stage it is reasonable to speculate that the fibers provide the mechanism whereby higher brain activities such as memories, thoughts, and emotions can modify the sensory messages after injury. We can assume, moreover, that this modification can occur throughout the entire axis of the central nervous system, at every junction at which nerve messages are relayed from one neuron to the next in the course of their ascent to the highest areas of the brain. If this view is right, we have a conceptual physiological model to account for the fact that psychological events play an essential role in determining the quality and intensity of the ultimate perceptual experience.[7]

[7] From Melzack, "The Perception of Pain," p. 44. Copyright © 1961 by Scientific American, Inc. All rights reserved.

It is not very difficult to understand how the psychological results of a traumatic experience may lead to the planned, conscious act of imposing mind over matter. The characteristics of the central nervous system mentioned above give us a neurological basis for all kinds of psychological set (a learned bias that affects our communication process). If our mind has the ability to block or modify the signals sent to it from the sense organs, and it does, what are the implications for our view of reality and the possible causes of communication breakdown?[8] In a very real sense our psychological makeup plays an important role in the collection of data for our brain to interpret.

The psychological characteristics of an individual may affect his collection and subsequent interpretation of data in another way—the way in which his mind weighs one sense against another. When the information received by the brain from two or more senses conflicts, the brain must choose which sense it is going to trust the most before it begins to react to these data. When you are talking to someone, do you put more trust in what your ears hear him say or in what your eyes tell you from the expression on his face or from his general behavior? This interaction of various senses has been investigated and some pertinent results have been recorded.[9]

At this point we shall make you aware of the levels of sensation. We are able to differentiate among at least three such levels. That is, there are three separate thresholds below which we cannot do specified things with the information collected. The first is the detection threshold. At this point a person is able to say only that a stimulus did or did not occur. He is unable to interpret anything from the stimulus except the fact of its occurrence. Perhaps, after talking to someone, you have felt that he reacted differently from what you had expected. You could not really say what it was that was different, but you definitely received a cue from him that was different from the one you expected. We sometimes attribute this feeling to intuition. More often than not it is the result of detecting a stimulus but not being able to recognize it.

The second threshold is that of recognition. At times we are primed to hear certain sounds, or to see certain objects or colors, or to use any of our other senses in some particular way to recognize a given stimulus among other stimuli. The very fact that we have been primed lowers our threshold and thus makes our sensory acuity much sharper. We may liken this priming to mentally setting up a pattern of signals with which we immediately compare all incoming signals. When the correct pattern appears, we say that we recognize the stimulus. This is usually what

8 Melzack, "The Perception of Pain," 41–49.
9 Herman A. Witkin, "The Perception of the Upright," *Scientific American*, 100 (February 1959), 50.

happens when we jump to conclusions. We communicate with someone in such a state of mind (psychological set) that, the moment we receive a cue that we recognize as favorable or unfavorable to our position, we immediately draw the conclusion that this person is for or against us. It is at this level that we make the most mistakes in our communication process. Because the mind is able to prime itself to recognize certain stimuli, it often acts too quickly, not waiting for all the information to be processed before it decides what the message means.

The third threshold is that of identification and is much higher than detection or recognition. A person must have a great deal more information fed into his brain to identify a stimulus than to detect or to recognize it. Because we attempt in the process of identification to put together a coherent picture of a stimulus, we must have sufficient information to conceptualize the stimulus. The identification process depends to a great extent on our past experiences and on the type of information stored in our brain. It calls on us to use our memory, and it indicates the importance of memory to the communication process. At this point you should be aware that identification differs from recognition in that the subject must identify a stimulus without being primed.

We realize that we slipped over into the information-processing phase of communication in the identification of the three preceding thresholds. This shift was necessary in order for you to realize that the ability to sense stimuli depends somewhat on the purpose for which they are being sensed and thus on the condition of the nervous system at the time of sensation. We may conclude then that the brain actually controls the threshold level. And, since it does, do we even receive all the sensations of familiar stimuli or do we stop the flow of information to the brain as soon as they are recognized? The latter appears to be the case with many people. We have all known those who cut into the middle of what we are saying with perfect knowledge of what we were going to say. This auditory phenomenon is somewhat connected with the visual phenomenon in which figures do not appear to us in their entirety but rather as segments which are put together by the brain. Perhaps, when the brain has enough information to make an intelligent guess at what the figure will be, it stops its input and proceeds to the output stage of communication.

If this is the case, it seems that the brain is continuously asking for trouble for it receives signals not only from its sense organs concerning the stimulus under investigation but also from other stimuli which it must do something with. We usually think that these other signals mask the desired signals and thus interfere with the communication process. However, some extraneous stimuli aid the nervous system in its efforts to sense the desired stimulus. This is true for extraneous stimuli occurring in the same sense as well as for those occurring in other senses. For example, certain sounds (pitches and harmonics) enhance the taste of food; and no one need be reminded what different seasonings do to the taste of a sizzling steak. The same observation holds for the odors that go with certain foods—without them our taste identification threshold would be much higher. Perhaps we are fortunate that no sensation takes place completely isolated from all others.

In summary, the brain is continually receiving from all the sense organs a barrage of signals which it must sort and store or discard. In the process of maturing we learn to use more and more of these signals in the organization of our perceptual world. As we have seen, people have a much lower threshold for stimuli they are primed to receive. Thus our psychological set (our predetermined [learned] attitude toward a stimulus) has much to do with the reception of sensory information about a stimulus.

The complexity of the sensory phase of the communication process is further increased by the fact that, while the brain is receiving signals from the five external sense organs, it is also receiving signals from the autonomic or proprioceptive systems or from both. All these data must be interpreted and in some way controlled by the brain. Is it any wonder that the excess weight of unsolved problems sometimes causes this nervous system to break down? Just the physical act of receiving and discharging so many signals staggers the imagination. In some cases, however, repeated stimulation of the sense organs may cause them to become inhibited in their ability to receive this stimulation and to transmit it to the brain. This may be the brain's way of overcoming a condition that could well ruin it. On the other hand, repeated stimulation can sometimes make a sense organ much more receptive to a given stimulus. Again, this is an activity that is controlled by the brain and that is usually done for a specific purpose.

The Storage of
Information

As we have shown, the sense organs are the major gatherers of information. After the information is collected, either consciously or unconsciously, and the central nervous system allows it to reach the brain, the reticular formation determines whether it should be stored. The storage we designate *memory,* and it is only because we have the ability to remember things that we are able to communicate effectively. However, the phenomenon of memory also causes much of the difficulty in the communication process.

The ability to remember what we have sensed enables us to use these data for future communicative behavior. We shall see, as we continue to unfold the human-communication process, that memory plays an important role in each phase of this process. We have already pointed out that the various perception thresholds are dependent to a great extent on what is stored in memory. We shall now present the basic ideas about the concept of memory as we will refer to it throughout the remainder of this part of the book.

We build up a vast supply of memories throughout our lifetime. Without these memories we would be unable to function for these are our ties to the past and our foundation for the future. The present is that era in time which makes it possible to have memories, and it is even affected by the memories of the past. Yet past memories may be easily forgotten. For example, men in Homer's *Odyssey* were sent out to see what the lotus-eaters were like. After eating some of the lotus and finding the results pleasant, they decided to stay, promptly forgetting their once fond memories of their homeland.

The same phenomenon is at work in prisoner-of-war camps where men have been persuaded to forsake their past affiliations and to begin a new life in the land of their captors. We call this *brainwashing*—a word well chosen for the effect it has. It is as though the brain is washed clean of the pleasant memories of the past and in their place are stored hopes for the future and exaggerated ill feelings of the past. The way in which this is done is only partially understood from both the psychological and the neurological points of view.

21

With a little reflection (which entails using memory) you may realize the importance of memory in the communication process. You may also realize that you are not too sure just what the concept of memory includes. An analysis of this concept reveals a number of ways of looking at it. Through the ages, theoreticians from Plato on have attempted to separate memory from other mental processes and to determine its importance in human communication. They have generally recognized that memory is in some way connected with the concept of time. Thus memory gives us our sense of time and allows us to build up our knowledge through the passage of time.

As our knowledge of the brain increases, we continue to learn more and more about the phenomenon of memory. Recently, memory has been given much attention by psychologists and neurophysiologists. And with this increased attention has come the desire to define the concept more precisely. Each definition, however, tends to stress the major interest of the investigator. Thus the neurophysiologist defines memory as involving "a modification of neural activity in the central nervous system or its output signals, as a function of exposure to previous events or 'experience'."[1]

A less specifically neurological approach is given by this definition:

> Memory, then, is the capacity of the brain to retain a record of all impressions and the capacity to recall them to awareness at will. The "impressions" include all sensory experiences, all motor performances, all associative experiences including thought, emotions, language; in brief, everything that makes an impression whether one is conscious of the impression or not.[2]

This definition reminds us that the memory process is a continuing one and that it develops a much more complete picture of reality than that which we are aware of. However, it also makes memory contingent upon the ability to recall these pictures of reality.

Another definition makes a distinction we would like to point out at this time. "'Remembering' can be defined thus: To 'remember' an item of knowledge is to be in a state of mind in which you can immediately reproduce the item if required to do so."[3] Thus we may make the distinction between remembering and memory. In remembering, we recall the thing that is in our memory. Yet there may be many things in our memory which we cannot recall, at least at a given time. We shall see

---

[1] Reprinted from Frank Rosenblatt, ed., *Principles of Neurodynamics* (Washington, D.C.: Spartan Books, 1962), p. 53.

[2] J. M. Nielsen, *Memory and Amnesia* (Los Angeles: San Incas Press, 1958), p. 15.

[3] Patrick Meredith, *Learning, Remembering and Knowing* (New York: Association Press, 1961), p. 9.

that both memory and remembering play a definite role in human communication but that they can and should be looked upon as separate processes.

What role does memory play in the human-communication process? To speak we have to have available in our memory not only the words but also the ideas we desire to express.   Ideas, as we shall see later, develop from an interplay of the many experiences we have had.   Thus, to communicate rationally we must have a memory system which will make our past experiences available for immediate use.   The vast majority of these experiences we have forgotten; yet they are still actively represented in our communicative behavior.

> To the average child many experiences leave memories of which he is unaware, yet which influence his future life.   These memories constitute what psychiatrists call "the unconscious."   That they are still recorded in the engram patterns is evident by their evocation through sodium amytal interviews or by other psychiatric techniques.   It is by virtue of such memories that persons are conditioned to respond in peculiar ways later in life.   The various phobias, obsessions, and compulsions are thus founded.[4]

It should be evident, then, that memory plays an important part in the human-communication processes in both conscious and unconscious ways.

If we realize that all our communicative acts, i.e., the words we use, the gestures we make, and the behavior patterns we produce, stem from the information we have stored in our memory, we begin to see the importance of knowing something about our memory system.   We may then realize why we are not able to communicate so effectively as we would like and also why we should be more tolerant of the communicative behavior of others.   We should be able to dismiss many of the communicative slips that result from a lapse in memory or which stem from the unconscious memories of past experiences.

We should understand something about the storage phase of memory if we are to comprehend the concepts of learning and meaning.   The material we have stored in our memory bank is the basis for meaningful learning (as opposed to rote learning).   New information is meaningful to us only if our brain is able to set up a substantive (nonarbitrary) relationship between this new information and our present cognitive structure.   Thus meaningfulness is an individual matter because it depends on the cognitive structure of the individual, and, as we shall see, the individual's cognitive structure is the result of the relationships he has established in his memory among all the pieces of information he has

[4] Nielsen, *Memory and Amnesia,* p. 36.

stored there.   Thus, if we understand something about the memory process, we may be able to understand why a particular piece of information is meaningful to some people but not to others.   In this way, meaningfulness has definite implications for our communicative behavior when we are trying to persuade or teach.

As we know, the sense receptors send a signal, created from the stimulus, to the brain.   The neurological nature of this signal has been discussed.   After the signal reaches the brain, one is aware of the original stimulus only for a limited time.   In other words, the memory of the signal has a very short life.   This has definite implications in the feedback received from your own speech (who has not been interrupted while speaking and then cannot remember where he was?) as well as in the responses we give to someone speaking to us.   If we cannot remember exactly what he said or did, it is difficult for us to respond intelligently.   This loss of memory occurs regardless of the rate at which information is received.

Memory interference is present almost every time we need to remember.   Yet this interference alone does not explain all the cases of "forgotten" information.   If you are given a list of groceries orally and told to go to the store to purchase them, chances are, if there are more than eight or nine items on the list, you will forget some of the items even before you hear the last one.   The brain has a built-in capacity for the number of things it can store in one sequence.   Furthermore, in such instances, you will usually remember the first few and the last two items but be unable to recall those in the middle.[5]

Some researchers hypothesize that memory consists of two parts: a short-term memory and a long-term memory.   Incoming information is immediately stored in short-term memory (STM), where it is soon forgotten unless it is rehearsed.   If it is rehearsed, it passes on to long-term memory (LTM), where it is permanently stored.   Other researchers believe that every impulse is permanently stored in the brain and that our future conscious use of this information is dependent only on our ability to recall it.   We shall discuss the recall problem at greater length later.   At this point we should make it clear that we are of the school that believes every impulse received by the brain is permanently stored.   The major implications of STM and LTM, then, are in the area of recall rather than of storage.

There are other ways of looking at memory other than in terms of remembering and forgetting over a period of time.   Suppose we were to interest ourselves in the different types of data which enter into our

[5] George A. Miller, "The Magical Number Seven Plus or Minus Two: Some Limits on Our Capacity for Processing Information," *Pyschological Review*, 63, No. 63 (1956), 81–97.

everyday experiences. We would soon find ourselves deluged by an unending list of categories into which we could try to place all knowledge. However, if we appealed to those who function in the world of mental disorders, we would find that the behavior of patients who have had memory losses has supplied just the categories we are looking for.

Dr. Nielsen,[6] through his work in the disease known as *amnesia*, is able to divide memory into two categories: personal experience and impersonal knowledge. Personal experience is, as one would expect, serially linked together as a chain of events, with time supplying the links. It is, therefore, chronologically ordered. Impersonal knowledge is intellectually acquired knowledge which, to be sure, was obtained at some period in time but which is not a function of that time. It is categorically ordered.

When one has temporal amnesia a certain portion of his life experience is blotted out, i.e., he may not be able to remember anything that happened in the past few days, weeks, months, or years. Thus he may not be able to remember that he once owned an orange grove, but he still remembers what an orange is and has no trouble in identifying one. On the other hand, when one has categorical amnesia, he loses his memory of impersonal knowledge and must "learn" all over again, e.g., he does not remember what an orange is. Though amnesia is really a disease involving recall, the fact that these two types of amnesia exist makes it imperative that we hypothesize two types of memory systems. In terms of the previously mentioned memory systems these two types are further divisions of long-term memory.

It may be, then, that our memory system has many subdivisions which function independently and yet cooperate in the function of memory. This idea is further substantiated by the fact that in learning a language a child forms a completely new set of "memories," recording sounds, letters, words, grammar, syntax, etc. Each of these memories not only works in conjunction with the others, since normal people are able to speak intelligibly, but also can be destroyed without harming the others. When brain damage affects speech (aphasia), one may recall sounds but not be able to put them together into words, or one may recall words but not be able to put them into intelligible sentences. Thus we hypothesize a third division of LTM—a linguistic system which is semantically ordered. We have then a number of memory subsystems whose recall abilities may collapse independently but which function collectively to enable man to communicate.

Having hypothesized these three memory systems—experience, concept, and linguistic—we must now give some indication as to how they combine to allow man to communicate. It should be evident to you

6 Nielsen, *Memory and Amnesia.*

(with a little reflection) that somehow, when we bring a particular experience or concept to mind, we immediately associate words with this recalled entity. It should also be clear that this phenomenon is not automatic or perfect. Many times we have had experiences or thoughts that we could not find words to express. Again, studies of mental disorders show that people may be able to recall concepts or experiences and also words but not be able to put them together.

Understanding the interconnections of these three memory systems is one of the major concerns of learning theory. As one matures, he continues to build up experience, concept, and linguistic memories. The sophistication of the interconnections of these memories determines the intelligence level of the individual. To communicate one must first choose the concept or experience he wishes to convey and then "find" the words in his linguistic memory by which he can best convey it. In this sense each linguistic memory trace may have several specific concept memory traces associated with it. It should be intuitively evident why we have said "several specific concept memory traces." In like manner, one concept memory trace may be associated with several linguistic memory traces.

The steps that take place may be described as follows: The stimulus signal approaches the brain on one or more incoming nerves. Depending on its strength, it goes into STM or LTM. If it is strong enough, it passes immediately into the appropriate section of long-term memory. If it stops in STM, we soon forget it since it is not associated with like traces; as we rehearse it, it becomes associated with like traces, and, as these associations build up, the information becomes more firmly imbedded in our memory. We say that information has been learned when its memory traces are associated with like traces in some definite order, i.e., categorically, chronologically, or semantically. Learning and thought processes develop the interconnections among both the memory traces for this information and the appropriate memory traces in the remaining two sections. The quantity and quality of memory traces in each of these three divisions plus the quantity and quality of the interconnections among the traces within each division and among the three divisions determine our level of intelligence.

The Processing of
Information

Now that we have given you some insight into the reception and storage phases of the communication process, we must regress briefly and delve into the structure of our mental processes to see how and why we communicate the way we do. We shall see how the structure of our mental processes has developed and how this structure affects our present behavior in communication situations.

Psychoanalysts tell us this about the development of our mental processes:

> During the first weeks of life, conscious perception, in the sense in which psychoanalysis defines the term, is not present. At this time practically all activities of the neonate are uncoordinated and undirected because a central volitional—that is, conscious—steering organization has not yet emerged. Physiological activities are the exception; they become increasingly coordinated and integrated into a functioning totality. But *intentional* skeletal musculature is not yet integrated under the direction of a *central steering and coordinating organization* and will only become so in the course of the subsequent months. It is this central steering organization to which we assign psychological functioning, both conscious and unconscious.[1]

This "central steering and coordinating organization" has been given the name *cybernetic,* a term with which college students are becoming increasingly familiar. Like other terms it has a number of definitions. You should keep in mind the one above as you encounter the term in this book.

The question we are really asking ourselves at this time then is just what is this cybernetic—this central steering mechanism? From a purely evolutionary viewpoint and in conjunction with the model of memory developed earlier, we may explain it this way. A child is born with

[1] This selection from Rene A. Spitz, "Ontogenesis: The Proleptic Function of Emotion," *Expression of the Emotions in Man,* ed. Peter Knapp (New York: International Universities Press, Inc., 1963), p. 43. Copyright 1963 by International Universities Press, Inc. and used with permission.

few if any memory traces. As he matures his sense organs collect information which his nervous system transmits to his brain. These sensory data are stored there, and the association process which forms the interconnections among these memory traces begins. We are still unable to give any scientific explanation of what "causes" the associations to develop as they do. Seemingly, a primary force starts the formation of associations and continues to direct the storage process. This primary force we call the *human cybernetic;* its presence is observable by the time the child is three months old.

As the child matures he continues to collect and store information from the outside world. Eventually he is able to manipulate his mind so that he not only stores data collected by his sense organs but also consciously associates two or more memory traces to form another. Thus, the child's cybernetic works through the unconscious association of sense data plus the conscious organization of this information. We may call this conscious association *thinking.* As the child grows older he is able to do more with his thinking than just organize sense data; he is also able (hopefully) to extrapolate this information into new concepts, and thus he develops the ability to think "creatively." The guiding force which stimulates these thought processes is his cybernetic.

To understand the workings of the human cybernetic, we must explore some of its ramifications. However, since the explication of the cybernetic is not the primary function of this book, we shall only sketch the relevant areas of this concept.

To begin, we must posit that the cybernetic is innate to the human being. Thus, a child born without any mental defects is thought to possess this basic mental force. Two of its primary functions are to discriminate among incoming sense data and to categorize them into basic mental states, e.g., desires, beliefs, and fears. As these mental states develop, all available information, whether external sense data or internally generated thoughts, is processed in the light of their present condition. Thus, as new information is processed, these mental states continue to develop, forming our attitudinal frame of reference.

One of the basic principles operating in the development of these mental states is that of equilibrium. The mind has a tendency to strive toward mental balance, which may be defined as the arrangement or weighting or both of our memory traces in such a way that mental pressure is kept to a minimum. Thus, the activity of the mind minimizes internal pressures or conflicts within our cognitive structure. The mind processes incoming information—a question to be answered, new data to be assimilated, or a message that stimulates us to review old memories— with a view toward bringing more coherence to our total knowledge of reality. Thus, all data are processed with our cybernetic continuously asking the question, "How does this information fit in with your overall view of reality?" We see the dynamics of this theory in that each time the brain processes another bit of information, it modifies its overall view of reality. Thus the fact that we rejected a date with a person last week because he was not the kind of person we chose to be seen with does not mean that we will reject the same offer next week. The frame of reference by which we evaluate such a proposal will have changed in this period of time, and one of the things that may cause the greatest change is the first offer.

The principle of mental balance is best exemplified by the theory of cognitive dissonance and the congruity principle. Both these ideas will be explicated in some depth later on. At present we must return to another basic concern of our cybernetic and develop it sufficiently to give us the necessary tools to consider the above two theories. This other concern of our cybernetic is its capacity for language acquisition. That is, one of its major concerns is that the human develop a symbol system by which he can readily acquire, process, and generate information.

As you read earlier, a child's cybernetic usually becomes apparent by the time he is three months old. One of its primary functions is to govern the structuring of the memory traces of all the information the child receives through his senses. As a child experiences love, anger, joy, fear, tension, etc., he also hears linguistic terms used. As these two types of memory traces, experiential and linguistic, are produced, their affinity for each other is structured to form the nuclei of concept memory traces. Since a child has no linguistic abilities at this time, we must conclude that most of his memory traces result from nonverbal stimuli. However, at some time in a child's life, language becomes his primary conscious means of communication. From that time on his whole world of meaning is linguistically structured. At that time also his concept memory begins to develop more rapidly by interconnecting language, concept, and experience traces. This learning process changes later on, when the primary acquisition of new concepts and words gives way to the refinement of existing concepts through the use of language.

OUR CONSCIOUS MENTAL CODE

Though we are unable to determine the exact extent to which we are language-dependent, language is the most essential product of our humanity. Man is the only animal we know of who is able to symbolize to the extent that he can learn from his ancestors and reflect on his own being. This symbolization in itself hints at a very elaborate and complex system, and indeed, after examining our language, we marvel that we are able to learn anything from it. Yet the fact that words may have more than one meaning is what makes communication possible, although it is also an inherent difficulty of any symbolization process.

At this point we should be sure that we understand what is meant by *symbol*. This term is usually used to some degree in association with the words *sign* and *signal*. It is unfortunate that these words have been confused and have been used in so many different ways by all too many experts in communication. This being the case, however, we must make clear what we expect you to understand when we use these terms.

A symbol is a perceivable stimulus which stands for, is associated with, or is used in reference to another object. The referent object may or may not be perceivable, but the symbol itself is never the re-ferent object. Thus words are symbols. They may stand for other things, be associated with other things, or be used to refer to other things. But, when they are used as the referent object, we become in-volved in what is called *metalanguage*, and that is beyond the scope of this book. The word *dog* stands for the domesticated, four-legged animal that barks, but it is not that animal. It also has many other meanings and thus portrays the true character of a symbol. When sym-bols are used in conjunction with other symbols, we call the result *lan-guage*, and we use it to evoke meaning in the minds of other people as well as in our own mind (thinking).

On the other hand, a sign is a necessary part or consequence of an action and is thus inseparable from that action. Smoke is usually a sign of fire. We may use it to signal (as the Indians did) and thus evoke some meaning other than fire. However, a sign is usually differentiated from a symbol in that a sign evokes the same meaning whenever it is encountered. Difficulty occurs only when people react to symbols as though they were signs, e.g., when, upon hearing the word *airplane*, a person becomes airsick. The interactions of these words, i.e., symbols, signals, and signs, may become very complex, and in many instances it is difficult or impossible to classify an object as one or the other, e.g., what is the sound of a siren—the word *stop* or the word *help?* The im-portant idea for you to grasp at this time is that, in dealing with symbols as we do in speaking, we must be aware that the symbol the speaker is using may not have the same referent for him as it does for the listener. This awareness should enable us to give the speaker extra consideration.

If we again return to the model of memory presented earlier, we see that linguistic symbols tie concepts and experiences together. Not only are memory traces intertwined among the words that we know, but they also connect many of the concepts and experiences that we have stored in our brain. These word memory traces develop as we mature and come into contact with our language—first in the auditory sense and then through the visual sense. To understand how closely these two senses work together one need only recall that he first learned what a dog was by seeing one and by having someone tell him that we call it a dog. Then a visual experience enabled him to learn that *dog* is the visual symbol for the auditory symbol dog. To facilitate this association, he was usually shown a picture of a dog with the word printed under it.

Obviously, as we mature, the number of our experiences increases, and thus we have to increase the symbols we need to refer to these experiences. If the correspondence between experiences and words were one-to-one, we would soon be overwhelmed by the mass of words we would have to remember. However, because this correspondence is not one-to-one, words develop a multiplicity of meanings as an increasing number of people begin to use them. Even the precise language used by mathematicians becomes adulterated when it comes into common usage or passes into another discipline, as the term isomorphic transformation has. Words have particular meanings to particular groups of individuals on both the technical and the informal levels. Thus, *communication* evokes visions of electronic systems to an engineer, of interpersonal interactions to a sociologist, of intrapersonal interactions to a psychologist, and of lines of command to a management specialist. So we see that the meaning one word can evoke may be extremely varied depending on the background of the receiver.

Yet, for us to communicate effectively it is absolutely essential that words be able to evoke these different meanings. This requirement seems strange when we observe that it is precisely this characteristic of words that causes most of the ambiguity in the process of human communication. One need only think for a minute to understand this necessity, and, if he is willing and has the time, he may want to try to develop a simple language in which there is one and only one meaning evoked by each word. He will soon find that it is impossible to have many, if any, abstract concepts.

Think back if you can to the time when you did not know what the concept *animal* or *fish* or *mineral* or *democracy* or *religion* or *love* meant. Can you determine exactly how you came to understand what someone was talking about when he used these words? Are you able to define each of these concepts now so that your classmates can understand exactly what you mean when you use them? Probably you cannot. But just as probable is the fact that you can define the first three better than you can the last three. To understand how we process information, we should understand how we formulate concepts and the implications of this process.

In the memory model presented earlier we stated that it was impossible to determine which came first, the concept memory trace or the word memory trace. There is some controversy about whether a person can know and understand a concept without knowing the word by which it is called. We are sure, however, that naming concepts or objects is an essential part of learning and, therefore, a primary concern of our cybernetic. As we have seen, one word may have many meanings; so too, one object or concept may have many names, depending on the approach one is taking at the time. Thus we call a large, four-legged animal which has horns and gives milk a *cow*. We may also call it an *animal, a quadruped, one of several cattle, farmer Brown's means of support, Bessie,* or some other name of endearment. One may differentiate among these many names for the same object by saying that they differ in their level of abstraction.

We usually suppose that the more we mature the more we are able to use abstract concepts. This assumption is not altogether correct. A child usually learns the words and concepts which are most useful to him. Although the abstractness of concepts may not be apparent to him until sometime later, he may use the words for concepts quite intelligently (in a limited sense) for some time before he actually understands the full content. For example, he may use the word *fish* correctly long before he does bass, trout, pike, and perch. He may use the word *car* before he can differentiate among Fords, Chevies, Plymouths, and Ramblers. The ability to differentiate among objects and to include them all under the appropriate concept usually develops between the ages of 6 and 12.

On the other hand we usually learn the names of the vegetables and fruits that we eat before we do the concept names. We also learn the names of our cousins, aunts, and uncles before we fit them all under the heading *relatives*. It is sometimes amusing to be with a child when he first finds a word which subsumes many others that he already knows. First graders learn to draw the correct set from a number of similar objects. By this process they learn to collect and categorize material into clumps, which allows for quicker and easier mental manipulations. Thus, when we have found one word which subsumes a whole group of objects under it or when we find that one of the words we are already using stands for many others, we begin to develop the interconnections among our memory traces that make it easier to process future information. However, this same process makes it easier to misunderstand a communicator and perhaps more difficult to get our own meaning into words.

Words exist in a particular language for everything that is essential in the culture which uses that language, and as the culture changes so does the language. We may carry this idea further and state that elaborate distinctions in a language among objects and activities reflect the importance of these objects and activities in the life of the people. Thus the Eskimo has at least nine words for the concept *snow* but no word that takes in the whole concept. In other words, people learn a language and its concepts for a utilitarian purpose. They must communicate with each other, and in order to do this they must use a common language. When one learns a foreign language, he immediately discovers that concepts take on different dimensions. This is nowhere more evident than when one learns English as a second language. The foreigner who has learned the words *hot* and *dog* is appalled when someone asks him if he would like a hotdog for lunch. It should be apparent then that concept names, regardless of how they developed, are arbitrary handles by which we, when we thoroughly understand them, are able to handle the information we process through our central nervous system.

OUR ATTITUDINAL FRAME OF REFERENCE

With the development of the interrelationships among our linguistic, conceptual, and experiential phases of memory comes the maturing of our mental states. That is, a sense of values develops to the extent that our parents feel it is safe to let us make our own decisions based on our evaluation of the information we have at hand. Thus we listen to a salesman, a politician, a preacher, or a friend, and, after processing the incoming data in light of all our desires, fears, and beliefs (collectively called our *attitudinal frame of reference*), we make a decision to do or not to do whatever they want us to. The development of this frame of reference has usually instilled in us some guidelines by which we measure both incoming data and outgoing messages. One author puts it this way:

> It is the nature of the conscious life of man to revolve around some concept of value. So true is this that when the concept is withdrawn or when it is forced into competition with another concept, the human being suffers an almost intolerable sense of being lost. He has to know where he is in the ideological cosmos in order to coordinate his activities. Probably the greatest cruelty which can be inflicted upon the psychic man is this deprivation of a sense of tendency. Accordingly every age, including those of rudest cultivation, sets up some kind of signpost. In highly cultivated ages, with individuals of exceptional intellectual strength, this may take the form of a metaphysic. But with the ordinary man, even in such advanced ages, it is likely to be

some idea abstracted from religion or historical speculation and made to inhere in a few sensible and immediate examples.[2]

The fact that we all have different value systems, or attitudinal frames of reference, is evident from even the barest information we may have about a person. We constantly hear the expression, "I don't see what he sees in her," or, "She should know better than to wear something like that to this sort of thing." You should be able to make an almost endless list of these expressions, which merely indicate that some difference in values exists between the speaker and the one spoken about. A shrewd listener can find out as much about the speaker by what he says as he can about the topic he is speaking on. That our basic values differ is apparent, and, we might add, would it not be a boring world if they did not? The main goals of this section are to make you understand why they differ and to make you aware of how they can differ.

When we look deeper into the development of our attitudinal frame of reference, we find that our cybernetic, being innate, governs the development of our mental states based on the information we receive and create, and, in so doing, it facilitates the development of our language system. However, since both our mental states and our language system are learned and thus are influenced by cultural and linguistic forces, the development of our attitudinal frame of reference is a continuous process, starting with the development of the brain and ending with death. It may be schematized as follows:

As we have stated, the basic principle involved in the development of our attitudinal frame of reference is that of mental balance. As data accumulate the mental states are continuously weighed against each other, and our attitudinal frame of reference develops. We should not look upon our attitudinal frame of reference as a static system against which we weigh decisions but rather as a dynamic system which continues to be molded each day of our life as we enter into new situations. Thus, our

[2] Richard Weaver, *The Ethics of Rhetoric* (Chicago: Henry Regnery Co., 1953), p. 235.

attitudinal frame of reference is a relatively stable, slowly evolving, highly complex value system against which we weigh each decision we make—consciously or unconsciously.

It should be immediately apparent how this idea fits in with our present attempt to illuminate the idea of interpretation. To interpret a message, we must have some standard or guide to refer back to. Thus our attitudinal frame of reference is a mental (cognitive) yardstick by which we can measure (obtain meaning from) a signal we have received and have stored in our memory. As we have indicated, this yardstick develops through experience and is dynamic—it is continuously being updated to fit our latest experience into our overall view of reality.

We may take another approach to the idea of a general, overall value system by stating that it is a *predisposition to action*. If we allow action here to be either overt or covert, an attitudinal frame of reference is our particular bias or predisposition to think or act in a way peculiar to us as individuals. It immediately becomes clear then that each person's value system differs from all others. Researchers attempt to discover what our value systems are by giving us personality tests or other psychological tests, hoping that we will reveal our true selves in this manner. It almost never happens. Psychiatrists and psychoanalysts attempt to get at the true self by letting us talk freely in their presence. They seem to have slightly better success, though they are now becoming very aware that their behavior may have more effect on the patient than they thought it did. The upshot is that one finds it very difficult to really know a person's true self. Because most of us unconsciously believe Shakespeare's comment that all the world is a stage and every man an actor, we tend to play the role which we think is expected of us in whatever situation we find ourselves. In fact, this tendency is one of the most basic predispositions to action that we have. Thus we go through life playing roles, hoping that someday we will find our true selves.[3]

To understand what a mental state is, we shall analyze our belief system. Milton Rokeach divides it into three subsystems:

1. A *central* region represents what will be called the person's "primitive" beliefs. These refer to all the beliefs a person has acquired about the nature of the physical world he lives in, the nature of the "self" and of the "generalized other."

2. An *intermediate* region represents the beliefs a person has in and about the nature of authority and the people who line up with authority, on whom he depends to help him form a picture of the world he lives in.

[3] See Erving Goffman, *The Presentation of Self in Everyday Life* (Garden City, New York: Doubleday & Company, Inc., 1959), for an analysis of this idea.

      3. A *peripheral* region represents the beliefs derived from authority, such beliefs filling in the details of his world map.[4]

We do not expect you to be able to classify all of your or someone else's beliefs into these three categories. However, we do expect you to better understand yourself and your fellow humans by recognizing that one may analyze beliefs in this manner.

    Rokeach refers to the central region, or core, of our belief system as our *primitive beliefs*. We may further refine this concept by saying that these beliefs stem directly from our sense perceptions. They pertain to color, size, shape, sound, space, time, etc. They show how we view the physical and social world—how we visualize ourselves as well as how we see others. We obtain these as well as the other beliefs by interpretation of sense stimuli in light of our past experiences; these beliefs however concern the dead-level reckoning of reality. Thus they become the very basis of our values, and we seldom if ever question them. If others do, we tend to doubt the sanity of the questioner rather than the validity of our belief.

    In our present state of knowledge we tend to put all scientifically derived "truths" in the category of primitive beliefs because we supposedly can prove that they are true. As the extensions of our senses increase, we relegate more beliefs to this area of our attitudinal frame of reference. However, if we look closely at many of these basic beliefs, we find that they are based not on sense data but on theories extrapolated from these data. We then must hypothesize a second-order basic belief system. In this system we consider such things as, "How many others believe as I do?" and "What is the probability of its being challenged?" The periodic excitement over Unidentified Flying Objects, for example, tests our second-order basic belief system. Group pressures can sometimes change these beliefs. We shall consider such pressures in another part of this book.

    The intermediate region of our belief system concerns our outlook on authority. You probably know someone who questions everything anyone says. Others believe everything anyone says. Most of us are somewhere in the middle. Some authorities we accept without any qualms; others we reserve acceptance of until we see how well they are accepted by our control groups; still others we tend not to believe regardless of what they say. Obviously, however, we must have some belief in authorities. Unless we are able to view the evidence ourselves, our acceptance of scientific theories is predicated on our belief that the men who formulated them were honest, sincere, knowledgeable, etc. Since most of the information we use to develop our own world view comes

[4] From *The Open and Closed Mind* by Milton Rokeach (New York: Basic Books, Inc., Publishers, 1960), pp. 39, 40.

from authorities and may be attributed to still other authorities, it is important that we examine our own beliefs in the intermediate region. What authorities do you accept without question? American students seem to have been brainwashed into believing that the professor is one such authority. In the political arena we tend not to believe anything the candidates from the opposing party say. Sometimes we believe what members of our peer group say, but we check it first.

In assessing authority figures then we run the complete continuum in our belief system from absolute belief in to absolute disbelief of. As an example, one of the authors knows an archconservative who has absolute belief in the Bible and absolute disbelief in the Communist Manifesto. Because of this belief system he can gain no insight into human behavior by reading the Communist Manifesto, and therefore when he attacks communism he does so on false assumptions; he also cannot tolerate any form of religion other than his own for he has believed himself into an infallible position. We usually call people with such an outlook *closed-minded*. They have taken some form of outside authority, assimilated this feeling of authority into their own belief systems (though usually they have not bothered to carry with it the content of the authority), and have thus created an authority figure in themselves which tends to be unmodifiable and carries them through their lives with a distorted view of reality. They refuse to consider new information.

The closed-minded person does not question his own beliefs with a view toward changing them to coincide more closely with reality. And he does not evaluate new information with a view toward modifying his present position to a more realistic one. Rather, he evaluates all data with the idea of accepting it if it agrees with his position and rejecting it if it does not. On the other hand, the open-minded person considers all information for what it can add to his knowledge of the subject. He has neither absolute belief nor disbelief but questions each message to see what he should do with it in light of his present belief system. He may reject it in the long run, but he first analyzes it with respect to other information he has. He thus accepts this new information as part of his experience and uses it to interpret future messages.

The final division of our belief system is the peripheral region, which contains all the beliefs derived from our primitive beliefs and from our beliefs in authority. That is, we abstract and extrapolate the data we receive and reunite them into new concepts. These new concepts become part of our belief system and thus we use them to interpret new incoming information. Through the active association of words, concepts, and experiences, our mind develops other concepts, words, and imaginary experiences which allow us to look beyond the world of sense experience. Some of this abstraction and extrapolation goes on in our unconscious for we are often hard put to find where we obtained an idea about some person or thing. We call this process *learning* for it changes our disposition or mental capability in such a way that information is retained and is further modified by new sense and mental experiences.

Thus, we learn our values. As we develop mentally, we modify our positions on various subjects and look at the world through continuously changing lenses. Those who refuse to regrind their lenses are closed-minded people; we often ridicule their false notions of reality. Those who are willing to consider new evidence, analyze it, and weigh it according to accepted standards are open-minded people; we are usually willing to spend our time helping them in this process. You should realize how close these two areas are to each other. You should also be able to see when it may be beneficial to be closed-minded, or, perhaps, that on certain subjects one may have more reason to be closed-minded than on others. If one were completely open-minded on all topics, he would be unable to consider all the vast amount of available information received on any one topic. Thus, to put it more realistically, each of us has degrees of open- or closed-mindedness, and the degree to which we fall in either category depends on the topic under discussion and the amount of knowledge we have on that topic. Of course it also depends on many other factors, not the least of which is our basic attitude toward learning in general.

Another way of looking at the closed-minded individual, though from a less derogatory point of view, is to consider the commitment one has to any given belief. If you find that your friend has a different belief than you have on, for example, one's responsibility to society, you may first want to know how firmly he is committed to this belief; but eventually, if there is to be any really intelligent understanding of each other, you will want to know why he takes the stand he does. Perhaps, if you were to reason from the same premises as he does, you would come to the same conclusion. A brief look at how or why one develops certain commitments to various beliefs will help us to understand how these beliefs play a part in our attitudinal frame of reference.

Needless to say, we could dismiss the whole topic of commitment by saying that it develops from our experience. This would not help us very much, although it would be a true statement. We shall gain more by treating commitment under three headings—enlightened, superstitious, and emotional. Before considering these three approaches, we must determine when one is committed to a given belief. Perhaps the best answer is the scientists' answer—when curiosity rests. When we are no longer curious enough about a topic to actively engage in research on it, we are committed to a certain extent to our present belief. This does not mean that when we are presented with new information on the topic we will not consider it and modify our belief accordingly. (The closed-minded person though would not.) Thus, if we were to take an inventory of our mind, we would find ourselves committed to partial beliefs or immature beliefs on many subjects mainly because we do not have sufficient knowledge to develop a reasonable position on those subjects. When we are interpreting information collected by our senses on a certain topic, however, we often find it difficult to realize that we may have an immature position on this topic. Too often we treat all our beliefs as though they were fully developed, knowledgeable positions.

One may say that our first category, enlightened beliefs, contains only those beliefs that are fully developed and rigorously supported. We shall not go that far, however, for many of our enlightened beliefs are only in the adolescent stage of their growth. We distinguish them from the other two types because they are based on a logical development from the basic premises of our primitive beliefs. That is, they not only are based on sense data but also are developed from this data through our use of accepted arguments derived from recognized authorities. This being the case, we have full confidence that the positions we take on these subjects are right, and we feel a certain amount of confidence in taking these stands.

One of the major tools for arriving at decisions is statistics. We allow statistics to dictate many of the positions we take on various issues. Sometimes these are justifiable stands, e.g., those against smoking and those for seat belts, but just as often they are not. Statistics usually illuminate what the researcher feels is the common ingredient in the cases he is studying. Yet, if he has been misled by his own reasoning process, he may come to an erroneous conclusion. For example, whisky and water make you drunk, bourbon and water make you drunk, rum and water make you drunk, as do scotch and water, gin and water, and vodka and water. Therefore water makes you drunk because it is the only apparently common element in these drinks. It is easy to see the fallacy in this argument, but such fallacies are not so easily found in many of the arguments we use to develop our positions on many topics.

The above example leads directly into the next category, superstitious beliefs. The major difference between enlightened and superstitious beliefs is that of "cause." If we put the cause of an action on something that is only superficially related to the action itself, we have a belief that is based on superstition. Athletes are notorious for having this belief system. A basketball player may wear a particular pair of socks because he happened to score 30 points in the first game in which he wore them. Most athletes realize that they are being superstitious but would rather not "break the spell." A prime example of a superstitious belief is that of the African natives who were being taught the rhythm method of birth control. They were given an abacus containing green and red beads and were instructed to move one bead each day. As long as a green bead was on top they could have sexual relations. However, many times a man became impatient with the red beads and moved them in mass so that a green bead appeared. He thought that this was all that was necessary to keep his wife from becoming pregnant. Civilized man acts as irrationally at times.

The final category of beliefs, emotional, differs from the others in that the person who takes a stand on a topic because of emotional beliefs realizes this when he considers it logically but cannot change his position because of his emotional involvement in the situation. We find this belief system quite often in college students who have never been allowed to think for themselves before coming to college. When they arrive there and are forced to make their own decisions, they continue to take the same stands they did at home, though they do not know why. The fault does not lie in taking these stands for perhaps they are the correct ones to take. The difficulty lies in what the students ascribe as the reason for their stands. The fact that a student's parents are atheists and it would break their hearts to see him acquire some religion does not mean that he has to close his mind to all information dealing with religion.

If one hopes to be a mature individual, he must consider the evidence and make up his own mind. Until you have acquired enough experience to take a positive position on a particular belief however, there is nothing wrong in admitting that you plan to follow the position of whomever you are emotionally tied to. By admitting this to yourself and to those who are interested, you make the communication process much more effective, for both you and your friends know why you are interpreting certain information as you are. This knowledge causes far fewer misunderstandings on everyone's part. Realizing that you are committed to a certain belief for intellectual or emotional or superstitious reasons helps you to properly interpret the information you receive.

Because it is subject to all situational variables plus our own physical condition at the time, our attitudinal frame of reference is very changeable. Couple with this the fact that no two people can ever have the same conditions existing in their entire beings at the same time, and you realize the impossibility of having perfect communication. In fact, the communication process has so many built-in difficulties that it is a wonder we ever communicate effectively. The field of general semantics has been concerned with determining how our communication can be made more effective, and, though it has developed a number of theories dealing with this subject, the basic idea it has given us is that a person must be aware of as many of the variables as possible in any communication

situation. Two of the variables we so often forget are those of the values
of the two communicants and of how these interact with the interpretation phase of the communication process. In general, we should realize
that our listener may not have the same attitudinal frame of reference
as we do and thus may take an entirely different view of the information
we are supplying him. Given this awareness we can strive to present
our information in a way that will fit into his cognitive processes more
constructively.

Any number of examples illustrate the role of our attitudinal frame
of reference in controlling our behavior in the communication process.
We accept or reject statements made by various politicians on the basis
of our political beliefs, the statements of various theologians on the basis
of our religious beliefs, and the statements of our friends and neighbors
on the basis of our social beliefs. Nearly all arguments and disagreements stem from a difference in the basic frames of reference of the people involved. As we shall see later, communication functions to change
the mental states which compose these attitudinal frames of reference.

THE THINKING PROCESS

Now that we have, in our mechanistic way, posited that the human
mind is composed of both a cybernetic, its governing force, and the
many mental states among which the cybernetic tries to maintain some
equilibrium, we must press on to see what happens when a new piece
of information is admitted into our consciousness.

We have already mentioned that we extend our knowledge of any
given topic by abstraction and extrapolation. In essence this is the
process we commonly call *thinking*. Any time our sense organs send information to our brain or our brain recalls some information from
memory, something must be done with it. We know when we are consciously in thought, but we should also realize that the processes of storing
information or associating information or both are usually unconscious. Once we have information stored in the brain, it begins to
process this information and never stops until death halts the neurological processes. If we equate thinking with neurological activity in
the brain, we have to say that a man is constantly in thought. We may
even go further and ask, "Can you not be thinking?"

As our sense organs feed information into our brain, the brain filters
out that which is useful to it and discards the rest. Regardless of
whether we accept this theory or the theory that the brain soaks up all
the information sent to it by the sense organs, we still realize that something must be done with the information other than simply storing it. In

our RIPT schema of the human-communication process (see the introduction to Part I) we have one phase called *information-processing*. This includes *decoding*, in which the incoming code is translated into meaning for the receiver. In much the same way a telegraph operator decodes a message by translating the Morse Code of the original message into English. The human being does this during the process of communication by associating the neurological impulses received by his brain with impulses he received previously.

Although the interpretation process is not this mechanical, it does follow similar lines. In decoding, or interpretation, whichever you prefer, the incoming signals evoke meaning in the mind of the listener. Decoding takes place when these impulses trigger off memory traces of past impulses; thus we associate the present experiences with those we have perceived before. Depending on whether the situation calls for immediate reply as in conversation or delayed responses as in class lectures, the stimulus calls up similar memory traces or is stored in memory to be recalled later and allowed to interact then with other memory traces. In either case, the process of interaction which takes place is called *thinking*.

It is during this process that we continue to develop our attitudinal frame of reference by associating and interrelating the three memory areas. (See the second section of Part I.) As every new piece of information fits into the mental states of the individual, his attitudinal frame of reference continues to change. He calls up previous information, compares it with the new, and makes the appropriate decision. If we take this approach to the thinking process, we may compare the process with the electronic computer in the way it processes information. The major difference is that the electronic computer has a fixed program which tells it what to do with the data it processes, whereas the human mind rewrites its program as many times as necessary to make it agree with reality. Each new piece of information may cause the next piece to be handled differently.

The question always arises as to what precipitates the thinking process. Why do we as human beings have the capacity to review our past, correlate our present, and project into our future without ever leaving our easy chair? We are able to carry out these functions because we have memories and are able to abstract, correlate, and extrapolate the information stored there. If we accept this answer, our next question may be, why do we carry on this activity we have called *thinking?* Several answers may occur to you. Now ask yourself, "How did they get there?" and "Why did I think of these answers?" One answer may be that any question to answer or problem to solve activates the data-processing activity of our mind, which then considers all of its past knowledge and chooses the most feasible answer it can find or manufacture.

Most psychologists have tended to think of a goal-directed behavior sequence in three stages. First, they postulate that the agent experiences a particular state of inner disturbance; he is in a state of tension, unrest, or disequilibrium which must be brought to quiescence. Secondly, he is in this condition in virtue of a particular stimulus impinging upon him from his physical and social environment; this is either a perception directed towards a goal object or a sign pointing towards the existence of a goal situation yet to be realized. The goal may be the attainment of some physical object, the achievement of social recognition, or the solution of a problem. Finally, through a series of actions the agent either attains the goal situation, and in so doing terminates his condition of unrest, or fails to do so, and withdraws from the environmental situation which imposed this complex activity upon him.[5]

If, then, thinking takes place only when the mind is shaken out of its orbit, we must also postulate that the mind has a relatively stable position from which to be jarred. This does not mean that the mind or our state of knowledge is necessarily a static thing (although we all know people for whom it is). It merely means that the dynamics of the mind are such that in its ongoing processes it tends to move in a smooth curve unless jolted out of its track. Each time our brain receives new information, it assimilates it into its present view of reality, and, because it is new information, it thereby changes our view of reality. Our present mental state then is not only our attitudinal frame of reference, by which we evaluate all incoming data, but also the balance which activates our cybernetic, which in turn activates the thinking process. The goal of the thinking process is to weigh and associate information in such a way as to maintain our mental balance within certain limits.

If we assume that the primary purpose of our cybernetic is to minimize the internal pressures of our mental structure, we may develop a model by which we can get a clear understanding of the mental process called *interpretation*. To give our model some tangible constructs, we shall use numbers to distinguish the different positions one may take in relation to any given concept. Suppose we have been reading favorable reports about Dr. Benjamin Spock and have developed a feeling in our mind about him that places him at a position of + 2 on some arbitrary scale. In the course of our daily activity a friend says, "Did you know that the hippies have nominated Dr. Spock as their presidential candi-

5 Robert Thomson, *The Psychology of Thinking* (Baltimore: Penguin Books, Inc., 1959), p. 149.

date?" If our general opinion of the hippies is negative, our overall evaluation of Dr. Spock will go through a period of modification. The extent to which our opinion changes will depend on what we think of the hippies, on the person who told us the news, on the situational variables involved, and on any added information we may obtain. Several possible modifications are evident.

At this point we must make it clear that our mental equilibrium is not necessarily the zero point on some evaluative scale. In fact, more often than not it is not the zero point. We always have an opinion about almost everything. Thus, when we are confronted with new information, we must assimilate it into our memory, and in doing so we alter our opinion in some way. If we agree with the news, it reinforces our present position (pushes us on in the same direction we are going mentally). If we disagree with it, it may cause a temporary or permanent change in the direction of our thinking, or we may distort the message or the source of the message until we discount it entirely. Whether a conscious dismissal of a message means that our subconscious self no longer considers the message may be debated. The important factor for the process of interpretation is whether the new information agrees or disagrees with our present values.

Osgood and Tannenbaum[6] indicate that a principle called *congruity* is active in our opinion-forming process. Others have shown how this theory works in various situations and have shown the necessity of adding more factors to the modifying process. A person's original opinion on the topic, the position the speaker takes on the topic, and the person's opinion of the speaker can be combined to give a very good prediction of the resulting opinion of this person toward the topic. We shall not delve into the equation for this combination at this time. The important point is that the content of the message received is often completely neglected. Thus, factors extraneous to the message itself can account for most of the opinion change taking place within the individual. The interested student may want to press further into this research to see just what factors have been considered important to opinion change.[7]

Of course the underlying hypothesis of the congruity principle is that our minds tend to remain on a steady keel, always striving for equilib-

[6] Charles Osgood and Percey Tannenbaum, "The Principle of Congruity in the Prediction of Attitude Change," *Psychological Review*, 62, No. 1 (1955), 42–55.

[7] George A. Borden, "Cognitive Dissonance: A Theory of Persuasion," *The Pennsylvania Speech Annual*, 22 (September 1965), 43–50; Robert Harper, Charles Anderson, Clifford Christensen, and Steven Hunka, eds., *The Cognitive Processes—Readings* (Englewood Cliffs, New Jersey: Prentice-Hall, Inc., 1964); Eckhard H. Hess, "Attitude and Pupil Size," *Scientific American*, 212 (April 1965), 46–54; and, Osgood and Tannenbaum, "The Principles of Congruity in the Prediction of Attitude Change."

rium. Thus, they may tend to go in a favorable or an unfavorable direction, but seldom do they take a giant step in any one direction. The magnitude of the change that occurs in our opinions due to any one message or series of messages may be an index of our mental stability. Of course, so many factors are active in opinion change that it is almost impossible to say exactly what it is that influences opinion change the most. We may be interested in the relationship of factors to opinion change and may become frustrated trying to keep track of all the factors acting in any given situation, but we should not forget that our opinions are constantly in a state of flux. The mind revises and modifies its positions on various topics to keep them in harmony with each other and thus to maintain internal consistency.

We have been using such terms as *internal conflict* and *pressures* in constrast to such terms as *coherence* and *internal consistency*. We shall now equate the first set of terms with dissonance and the last set with consonance. Two beliefs or opinions are dissonant if for some reason they do not fit together. For example, if we stepped out into a rainstorm and did not get wet, we would suffer cognitive dissonance, i.e., our mind would be unable to conceive of our body's being subjected to rain and not getting wet. A more realistic situation occurs when we hear a negative report about a person we have positive feelings about. This new information does not harmonize with the opinion we have created from all the previous information we have received about this person. On a piano two notes which do not harmonize are dissonant, and we can tell this by the vibration they cause on our eardrums when we play them together. In the same way, cognitive dissonance causes a vibration in our mental stability.

It is safe to conclude that cognitive dissonance exists. Though it may be impossible to measure this phenomenon, we can all recall examples of times when we felt dissonance. The first time a girl friend or boyfriend turned down our request for a date, he probably had to do some fast explaining to make us believe that he still loved us. The amount of dissonance we felt depended on the strength of our belief that love and control go together. Festinger says this of cognitive dissonance:

1. If two cognitive elements are relevant, the relation between them is either dissonant or consonant.

2. The magnitude of the dissonance (or consonance) increases as the importance or value of the elements increases.

3. The total amount of dissonance that exists between two clusters of cognitive elements is a function of the weighted proportion of all relevant relations between the two clusters that are dissonant. The term "weighted proportion" is used because each relevant relation

would be weighted according to the importance of the elements involved in that relation.[8]

Thus all the factors that have contributed to our present position on any given topic also contribute to the strength of the dissonance we feel when a conflicting piece of information is being processed.

The question that should be in your mind at this point is, "What happens when dissonance occurs?" Perhaps you have already jumped beyond this point. Nevertheless, we should consider what others have said about this question. Festinger states:

> The presence of dissonance gives rise to pressures to reduce or eliminate the dissonance. The strength of the pressures to reduce the dissonance is a function of the magnitude of the dissonance.[9]
>
> The maximum dissonance that can possibly exist between any two elements is equal to the total resistance to change of the less resistant element. The magnitude of dissonance cannot exceed this amount because, at this point of maximum possible dissonance, the less resistant element would change, thus eliminating the dissonance.[10]

Thus, cognitive dissonance builds up psychological pressures within the individual to alleviate it, and the maximum pressure that it can build up is that equal to the resistance to change offered by the less resistant of the two ideas that are in dissonance.

The magnitude of dissonance which a person allows within his mental makeup depends on the stability of the individual's mental balance. Thus, some people are able to accept with no anxiety at all a dissonant condition that would drive other people mad. Many people have the ability to overlook or to completely refuse to acknowledge the fact that dissonant conditions exist in their belief systems. One of the prime differences between an inquisitive mind and one that is not seems to be a refined sense of dissonance detection. A person is driven by the dissonance he feels in his understanding of a subject to find out more about the subject and thus to alleviate the dissonance. Another person may resort to drink or may have a mental breakdown because he is unable to alleviate a dissonance that has come to control his every thought. His cybernetic strives in vain to harmonize the dissonant elements, so he tries to alleviate the dissonant feeling by other means.

The individual may alleviate cognitive dissonance in any number of ways. He may raise his allowable dissonance level, push the dissonant

---

[8] Leon Festinger, A Theory of Cognitive Dissonance (Stanford, California: Stanford University Press, 1957), p. 18.

[9] Festinger, A Theory of Cognitive Dissonance, p. 18.

[10] Festinger, A Theory of Cognitive Dissonance, p. 28.

elements into the background of his conscious, ignore the consequences of such dissonance, shift his beliefs to coincide with the evidence he has received, or reject one of the elements that effected the dissonance. The reader may be able to think of other ways to alleviate cognitive dissonance. We must never underestimate the role this phenomenon plays in one's ongoing view of reality.

We learn to expect certain behavior in certain situations. If this behavior is not forthcoming, we are confronted with cognitive dissonance. Thus expectancies play an important role in our communicative behavior. Our cybernetic develops expectancies so that we can prepare ourselves to meet new situations. Probably, we are most easily persuaded to modify our position on a given topic through the manipulation of the dissonance that occurs because of our expectancies.[11] If we were able to determine whether dissonance had been formed in our listener, we could probably be a better persuader than we are. However, it is nearly impossible to determine when someone else is going through a period of dissonance by the feedback we receive in a communicative situation.[12]

SUMMARY

We shall stop here to summarize the information presented so far and to recapitulate the theory advanced. We have seen that one is born with a cybernetic—an internal steering and organizing system—and that this cybernetic is the basic control mechanism for the interpretation of incoming information. It associates verbal and nonverbal stimuli with the knowledge we have stored in our memory from past experience. As the mind correlates the experiences, concepts, and words we have stored in our memory, we develop mental states which collectively make up our attitudinal frame of reference, or view of reality. Against this view we evaluate all incoming information. One aspect of our cybernetic is its tendency to strive for equilibrium (to keep dissonance below a certain level with which we are content to live).

We may summarize the steps in the interpretation process:

1. Information from an external or internal source is fed into the brain during the communication process.
2. The attention mechanism filters this information to determine whether the brain should consider it at this time. If not, it is stored for future use in the ongoing development of our world view. If it is to be

---

[11] Borden, "Cognitive Dissonance: A Theory of Persuasion," 43–50.
[12] Natalia Chapanis and Alphonse Chapanis, "Cognitive Dissonance," *Psychological Bulletin,* 61 (1964), 1–22.

considered immediately, it is sent through the information-processing routine peculiar to our mind.

3. The information is evaluated against our attitudinal frame of reference to determine whether it conflicts with our present position on the topic. If it does not, it is assimilated into our belief system. If it does, our mind begins to debate the two dissonant ideas and continues this debate until it decides what to do with the dissonant condition.

The interpretation process may take no longer than a split second or it may go on for days, weeks, or years. Regardless of how long it takes, it is one of the major factors in determining how we accept a given message and what messages we send in return.

The Recall of
Information

We have talked for some time about the activities of the mind and have briefly mentioned the role of recall in our communication process. We shall now consider recall in more detail. During the data-processing phase of the human-communication process, one is continuously recalling, evaluating, and re-storing data. The ability to think depends on the ability to recall bits of information from our memory system. The ability to communicate depends on the ability to recall thoughts and to transform them into some overt behavior. Much of this activity is at the subconscious level. In fact, one distinguishing characteristic between speaking and writing is that in the former this transformation from thought to behavior is predominantly subconscious while in the latter it is predominantly conscious.

According to one well documented concept of memory, the memory system records all impressions whether conscious or not. Intent, then, is not necessary to ensure this recording of data. And, when one investigates the recall of information from our memory system, he finds that intent again is not necessary—in fact, it may be a hindrance. All of us have had to recall a name or an experience or an answer on an examination and have found that we were unable to do so. This breakdown in our communication apparatus is often embarrassing and costly. Yet, when we cease to try to recall this information, often it pops into our mind. Thus, the forgetting of an item of information does not necessarily mean that this item has ceased to be in our memory.

In temporal memory the memory traces include all the sensations necessary for the whole experience. Recalling these memories is much like showing a reel of film; whole episodes flash into our consciousness at one time. If we are sufficiently adept at recall, we are able to remember all the sensations that were present at the time of the experience. This is also true of categorical memory; i.e., all the sensations associated with a concept are included in the memory trace. For this reason one may bring any memory trace to mind either by reperception of the stimulus or by willful recall. Further, any one of the various

49

sensations associated with a concept may bring it to mind. For example, sight, smell, taste, or feel may bring the picture of an orange to mind. And, if any of these avenues of recognition is destroyed, stimulation of the others continues to bring the orange to mind.

Why does one forget? Have you ever attended a party and been introduced to someone, then, when you had to introduce this same person to someone else a few seconds later, found you could not remember his name? Even while talking to this individual you may have suddenly found yourself searching your memory for his name. We usually ascribe this loss of memory to misperception for we usually say, "I'm sorry. I didn't quite catch that name." However, most of the time we did catch the name at the time it was first given, but, between that time and the time we wished to recall it, it slipped our mind. The ability of some people to remember better than others has probably been made agonizingly clear to you at one time or another. Can you *remember* when that was?

We may explain differences in recall ability in a number of ways. Much of this ability is a learned behavior which can be substantially increased with practice and motivation. However, one still must have the required neurological capabilities in order to facilitate this phenomenon. A brain lesion may make it neurologically impossible to remember for any length of time. Psychological factors may also bear directly on one's ability to remember. We have seen that the psychological set of the receiver influences his ability to receive information; in the same way it may influence his ability to remember, or to recall, this information. In addition the selectivity with which our brain operates may cause us to remember selected items and to forget others that are closely related spacially or temporally. You should be able to give examples of selectivity operating in both storage and recall.

Researchers have hypothesized that long-term forgetting is due to interference. Experiments show that organized or essential material is remembered just as well after a period of waking or sleeping, while nonessential and nonsense material is remembered better after sleeping than waking. Thus it would seem that, while the brain is actively collecting data, it is relegating unimportant information to a lesser place in the memory system. The importance of the information, of course, depends on the circumstances under which the data are gathered. When one finds that what he previously thought was unimportant has now become important, he may try in vain to recall these data. The exasperating fact is that conscious attempts to remember any information may prove futile.

Having looked at various aspects of memory, perhaps we should now ask about reliability. How reliable is our memory. Of course the reliability of what we recall is closely related to the reliability of our reception of information. But, assuming that one's receptions are accurate, can he really rely on his recall of the information received? Has anyone not had his recollection of an incident challenged by someone else? Petty disagreements most often result from differences in recalling various events. Perhaps our ability to remember words is our best developed memory. We usually even remember concepts much more precisely than events. The worst thing about false memories is that there is no indication that they are false. We put as much faith in one memory as we do in another. This inability to tell a true from a false memory should make one very conscious of the fact that in any situation in which he has to rely on his memory he may be relying on a false recollection. Thus, when we communicate information, we should be consciously aware of its source.

Another difficulty is inherent in the human memory system. We have talked about faulty reception and faulty memory contributing to faulty human communication. What about the well established fact that humans sometimes believe that memories of their own warped thinking are memories of external events? In this case, regardless of how accurate their memories are, the fact remains that they are basing their future behavior on memories of something different from reality. This instance is much like that of misperception. You should be able to draw the conclusion that it is not only our perceptions that are remembered but also our thoughts—at least the conclusions of our thoughts. Thus, these memories play an important role in our communication with other individuals.

It would be beneficial if we knew exactly how our recall mechanism works. Perhaps then we could train it to function more effectively and could increase our intelligence level to that of a genius. You realize, of course, that all tests merely indicate your recall ability and not what is in your memory. We find it easier to recall those things that have been rehearsed, that have come to mean something to us, or that made a deep impression on us when they were perceived. Evidently these processes enhance some neurological activity. We put much emphasis on having a quick mind. Perhaps some day we will know how to acquire one.

As we have stated, the recalling and processing of our memory traces add information to our memory bank. This extrapolation, abstraction, and creation of information are continuing activities of the brain and are governed by the constant push of our cybernetic for mental equilibrium. Somehow our cybernetic maintains an index of what is real, what is imaginary, what is desired, and what is possible. Given this information it seeks to direct our mind to control our overt and covert behavior in such a way that we obtain those things we desire most.

The Transmission of Information

One of the major ways of obtaining what we want is by the behavior we put on display for others to criticize. This transmission phase of human communication is overt, though it may be intended or unintended, conscious or unconscious. The overt acts become messages by which others decide who and what we are. Many times our unconscious, unintended messages communicate more than do our conscious, intended messages. Perhaps an example will make this point clear.

Clad in a brief bikini, her body with every movement whispered softly, "Come take me. I'm yours." The warm breeze, the full moon, and the sound of the waves lapping the beach all combined to enhance the romantic aura of the moment. As she came closer, Bill caught the faint odor of cologne, and it sent his mind spinning. Here he was, his first night on the beach, and already he was being approached by the most beautiful creature he ever hoped to see. The emotion of the moment so overpowered him that as she approached he leaped to his feet, took her in his arms, and kissed her passionately. The warmth and smoothness of her body only increased his desire. Taking his mouth from hers, he whispered breathlessly in her ear, "I love you! I love you! I love you!"

Freeing one of her hands, she slapped him soundly on the face and, taking advantage of his stunned reaction, gave him a violent push backwards. This proved too much for his balance, and he found himself lying on his back in almost the same place he had been before. Standing over him, now with her eyes flaming, she began to lecture him on the common courtesies due a woman. Dazed and startled, he was finally able to tune in on these words: "What do you take me for, a common tramp? Can't a decent woman walk along the beach at night without being attacked by some young punk?" And, with this, she wheeled and strode off in the direction from which she had come. Bill stared after her in disbelief, for how could someone who looked so sensuous refer to herself as a decent woman?

What messages were sent and received in the above example? Do you see the difference between an intended message and one that is extraneous or unintended? Appearance and bodily actions tell us something about an individual. However, as in the example, we may interpret these messages incorrectly. Both the girl's actions and Bill's actions were misinterpreted. The messages they transmitted would probably have been innocent under other conditions, but, because of the interpretation placed on them by the receivers in this situation, they led to unexpected conclusions. The fact that the verbal and nonverbal messages were contradictory only confused Bill.

The above example, though exaggerated in places, reminds us of a fact depicted by many clichés—e.g., you can't tell a book by its cover; looks are only skin deep. That is, in human communication the verbal and nonverbal messages we receive in any given situation are sometimes dissonant. When we are confronted with this situation, we usually act much the same as Bill did, though often we are able to conceal our mistakes so that we are not publicly rebuffed for them.

The fact that all Bill's senses (including taste when he kissed her) told him the same story shows that none of our senses are immune to this phenomenon of dissonance. It should be clear to you by now why this is so. Since the senses merely transmit signals to the brain, it is immaterial which sense the brain gets the message from. The important thing is how it interprets the message. In the example, Bill was evidently laboring under the false assumption that the dress makes the woman. He interpreted the messages his brain received from his senses against this value system and acted accordingly. Had she had the same value system, the story would have been censored from the point of the kiss on.

You should be able to imagine yourself in the place of either of the characters of the example, and, by changing your value system, devise all kinds of variations for the episode given here. In technical language this is called *role playing*, and it is an effective method of gaining insight into the way people with various value systems react to specific communication situations. Although this technique usually depends to a great extent on the manifestation of stereotypes, it is easily and frequently used in classroom teaching. You might try it with the examples given in this book.

EXPRESSION

In the remainder of this part of the book we shall consider the methods we use to express ourselves and the reasons for the expressions we make. We must begin by making clear what we mean by the concept *expression*. We shall take the term to mean any overt, i.e., externally manifested, behavior. In other words, any behavior that one is able to perceive in another is an expression. Thus, a wink, a nod of the head, a frown, a clenched fist, a loving pat, or a spoken word, phrase, sigh, laughter, scream, or other audible symbol is a form of expression. Although we usually think of expression as a stimulus received by our sense of sight or hearing or both, it should be apparent that the stimuli which we call *expression* may be received by any of the five senses.

In the introduction to Part I we mentioned that the messages received by our five senses are in the form of codes. That is, the person who is attempting to communicate with us has some piece of meaning in his mind which he would like to evoke in our mind. To do this he uses the only means available to him—he formulates (encodes) a signal which he feels will evoke the desired meaning in our minds when we decode this signal (compare it with our past experiences with similar signals).

If we define a signal as any overt behavior which may be detected by another human being, we recognize two basic codes in which a signal can be formulated—verbal and nonverbal. A verbal code consists of words and their syntactical relationships. It may be transmitted either vocally (by speech) or nonvocally (in writing). A nonverbal code does not depend upon words to carry the message. This code may also be transmitted both vocally (by screams, vocal inflections) and nonvocally (with gestures, bodily movements, pictures, music). We should not confuse the codes of a signal with the internal code by which we consciously relate the incoming signal to past experiences with similar signals. This internal code is almost always verbal. Thus, the verbal-nonverbal dichotomy concerns only the vehicle which conveys the information from source to receiver.

Before discussing verbal and nonverbal expression further, we shall concern ourselves with the reasons for expression. As we have already indicated, our expression patterns develop from our past experiences and are thus intimately connected with our attitudinal frame of reference. However, it is not enough to say this. We must examine our communicative behavior and try to ascertain why we behave as we do. What motivates us to say the things we do, to react to communicative situations as we do, or to express ourselves as we do? Perhaps we are motivated by the way our mind adjusts to or alleviates cognitive dissonance. Since we were committing ourselves to this conclusion earlier, we shall continue with this line of reasoning.

If dissonance reduction is the motivating force for our communicative behavior, then one should be able to look at his mental makeup and predetermine how he will act in any given situation. As a matter of fact, this is precisely what most of us do. When we are given enough time to think about a particular situation in which we expect to find ourselves, we usually transport ourselves to that situation in our mind and rehearse how we will react when certain events occur. Thus, we set up an expectancy of how things will go for us and what we will do if this or that occurs. If we were honest with ourselves and could probe deeply enough into our subconscious, we would find that this expectancy principle is active in most if not all of our interactions. Carrying this expectancy principle to the cognitive level, we see that it is precisely our attitudinal frame of reference. It is a psychological set which binds us to a certain communicative behavior pattern for each situation we are in. We then speak or write or react nonverbally as we have been pro- gramed by our past experience, our cybernetic controlling both the de- coding of signals received and the encoding of signals to be transmitted.

We may divide the signals we transmit verbally or nonverbally into two purpose categories—internal tension reduction and external control. In other words, we use forms of expression to relieve our own tensions or to control the behavior of those around us. Although this is a sensible way to look at the signals we transmit, clearly these two categories are not always mutually exclusive. In fact, both purposes may be present in any given communication. We often find that we say something or do something to release our own mental tensions but that in the process we transmit a signal by which we seek to control others. We probably all know people whose internal mental balance becomes disrupted to the point where they do not function coherently unless they are in control of external situations.

As examples of expressions which relieve internal tensions, we may start with crying, singing in the shower, or laughing while reading a story to ourselves. Most of the time these expressions are not meant to con- vey a message to someone else, although you should be able to give instances in which even these forms of expression are used by a person to control someone else. Such expressions probably come under suspi- cion more than they should. Since we seem to think that the person who is communicating with us is completely aware of what he is doing or say- ing, we often misjudge his intentions. Thus, we may think that he means to influence when in reality he is only letting off steam or speaking his mind to relieve internal tensions.

We may analyze the example given previously in this manner. Per- haps the girl had a slight exhibitionist instinct, and in the moonlight she felt perfectly safe wearing scanty clothing and walking sensuously. When she was caught in the act and her attentions were brought to it so violently, she reverted back to her dominant value system and rebuked her assailant forcibly. In other words, she did not intend to have anyone see her in this state of behavior; she was only transmitting this message to relieve her own tensions, which resulted from the dissonance between the two value systems existing at the same time in her mind.[1]

Perhaps you have already grasped the one factor which determines whether an expression reduces tension or controls a listener. The essential difference is the intent of the source. When expressions reduce tension, the communicator has no intention of communicating with anyone other than himself and perhaps God. He is prompted only by the need to express the feeling welling up inside him. An important fact to remember is that the need for such expression is as essential as the need for the other kind. Physicians and psychologists increasingly recommend to people with tension-producing jobs that they relieve this tension before it leads to heart trouble. Much of it can be relieved through physical exertion, playing an instrument, or painting; however, much of it can be relieved by vocal expression as well. When one hurts one's self, he often yells or swears to relieve the tension, and it seems to help. Women are notorious for crying to reduce their tensions. We must conclude then that there is some therapeutic value in expressions for tension reduction.

However, our main concern in this book is the second type of expression—expression to control an external listener. Thus, we are interested primarily in expressions that are purposeful or intentional. To be more precise, we are interested in signals encoded from the experience of the communicator as a result of his desire to evoke a particular meaning in the mind of the listener. Many times, of course, the resulting signal does not evoke the correct meaning, and then we have a breakdown in communication. When this happens, one may be able to trace the cause to differences in the backgrounds of the two communicants. If one misjudges the previous experience of his listener, whether he be a friend or an enemy, the probability that he will communicate effectively with this individual is very low.

If you think for a moment, you will see how important it is for a speaker or communicator to analyze his audience—whether it be a single friend, a group, or a huge crowd in an amphitheater—before delivering a message. And, even if the audience receives his message correctly, each individual must still decode the signals according to his own experience and evaluate them against his value systems; in the process, he may generate a different meaning from that of the communicator. Thus, in purposeful communication, when the communicator intends to evoke a specific meaning in the minds of his listeners, he must take into careful

[1] *The Three Faces of Eve,* by Corbett H. Thigpen, M.D., and Hervey M. Cleckley, M.D. (New York: McGraw-Hill Book Company, 1957), gives a good example of the outward manifestation of extreme inner dissonance.

consideration the mental makeup (past experiences, value systems, commitments, etc.) of his audience.

What are some of the implications of this theory? Is it easier to speak to one person than it is to a dozen? What about the difference between a dozen and 5000? Given a particular idea to get across, how would you change the message for these three types of audiences? How does explaining something to one person differ from trying to explain the same thing to various sizes of groups? When speaking to one person, the communicator may refer to many experiences and beliefs in trying to make his meaning clear. However, as the size of the audience increases, the number of common experiences and beliefs which may be used to effect meaningful communication decreases. We shall discuss this idea in more detail in later parts of this book.

In the context here, that of the individual communicator, you should be aware that a variety of signals are being sent at any given time. We have seen that, from the receiver's point of view, communication takes place whenever he attaches meaning to a signal he has received. However, from a transmitter's point of view, we have now seen that two entirely different messages may be sent—one purposeful, the other unintentional. If these two messages are contradictory, what will the resulting meaning in the mind of the receiver be? The communicator is concerned only with the intended message, and, from his point of view, communication takes place when the receiver decodes the signals to mean what he had encoded. However, many signals fail to evoke the desired meaning—not because the intended message is not clear, but because the unintended messages being decoded by the receiver nullify the meaning encoded into the intended message.

For example, if a teacher walks into a classroom on the hottest day of the summer dressed in a suit (just because this is a university regulation), the class may miss most of his lecture because they either are sympathizing with him in his discomfort or are ridiculing him for adhering to such absurd regulations. Thus, a completely extraneous message colors or obliterates the proposed message. You have probably been in situations in which an unintended message clouded the effectiveness of the communicator. In any communication situation, then, it behooves the communicator to be sure that all the signals he is sending at any given time complement each other and add to the meaning of the proposed message. Of course this is much easier to say than to do. We usually do not know enough about receivers' backgrounds to know how they will decode many of the signals we send.

Previously we asked, Which sense gives the most reliable messages to the brain? Now we may ask, Which channel is the best transmitter of purposeful messages? Of course the answers to both these questions are completely individualistic. What is best for one person may be bad for another. One's ability to express himself may be highly cultivated in the verbal medium and exceedingly poor in the nonverbal. At the same time one may put more reliance on what he sees than on what he hears. Since we humans have developed such an elaborate symbol system, we tend to believe that most meaningful messages are transmitted through the verbal medium. If this were true, the study of the human-communication process would be relatively simple. However, short reflection on the fact that our linguistic abilities develop much later than our senses do—for an infant gains much more knowledge through observance of human behavior than through linguistic manipulation—leads us to see the importance of the nonverbal mode of communication in human interaction.

Do actions speak louder than words? This question was tested in a public-speaking situation, and the results were surprising. We often hear someone say, "I have never heard anyone speak so fluently. He seems to be able to speak fluently on any topic." Here *fluent* usually means the opposite of stumbling, hesitant, and incoherent. Supposedly, then, we pick out fluent speakers by the way they sound. However, evidence shows that this is not the case. Although more testing must be done to confirm the results, "as of now it would seem justified to say that fluency may have more visual phenomenal attributes than voice and diction attributes."[2] Perhaps then, we should become aware of what we do nonverbally that communicates to our receivers.

THE NONVERBAL CODE

We have defined nonverbal communication as any overt behavior which cannot be symbolized in linguistic terms. Though we may describe this behavior using language, we cannot reproduce it by any linguistic symbol. This being the case, one should be able to identify many types of nonverbal communication. We shall see that a specific discipline usually studies each type of nonverbal communication. Let's begin by looking at the type farthest removed from the individual and then move to the individual himself.

Cultural variables are visible to most people as they travel from one country to another. These variables affect the way a person communicates since they affect the experiences he has and thus the structure of his attitudinal frame of reference. If we think about these environ-

---

[2] Milton Horowitz, "Fluency: An Appraisal and a Research Approach," *The Journal of Communication,* 15 (March 1965), 12.

mental factors and ask how they affect human beings, we soon begin to wonder how our environment affects us. Since most of us have grown up in a gradually changing environment, we have assimilated this change into our experiences so steadily that we fail to see how it influences our communicative behavior. In fact most of us are unaware that our environment plays a role at all in our communicative behavior. Only recently have researchers begun to step outside the stream of culture and to study the effects of various environmental changes on society.

Probably 99 per cent of the students who read this text cannot imagine a world without television for they have known it all their lives. Yet the authors have had the experience of seeing this new medium emerge as an influence in the lives of man, and at least one of them has experienced normal existence without radio, telephone, or electricity. What is the effect of these phenomena (nonverbal signs and symbols) on our communicative behavior? What has been the effect of the various communication media on our thinking? If we could go back to the time of the Greeks, when communication depended entirely on being in the presence of the communicator so you could hear his voice, we would realize how differently we think today. Much has been written on the effects of the printing press, radio, and television, yet most of this material neglects to inquire into changes the assimilation of this means of communication brings to our attitudinal frame of reference. Marshall McLuhan points out that, with the advent and assimilation of each new medium into our everyday life, a new environment enters and with it a restructuring of our whole world view.[3] New media give us new psychic experiences, and these must be assimilated into our overall attitudinal frame of reference.

Today we are affected not only by many different communication media but also by the need for more and better media. This feeling of urgency is everywhere and is part of our cultural heritage. It is difficult for us to imagine anyone not wanting to "better" himself by acquiring the way of life we have. Yet many people want no better way of life than the one they are now experiencing. And, indeed, it would be a terrible shock for them to experience some of the behaviorisms we have grown accustomed to, e.g., for an African Bushman to ride on a subway in New York City or to see television or to see any number of other nonverbal signs of our everyday life. All these environmental factors—the various media, the desire for change, and the feeling of urgency—are nonverbal forms of communication and as such are usually not considered by the communicator. Yet they all affect the way he expresses himself.

Man has developed numerous ways to communicate certain kinds

3 McLuhan, *Understanding Media: The Extensions of Man*, pp. 3–21.

of feeling. Many would say that these forms are really intended not to convey a message but rather to reduce tension. However, many of these forms are designed to elicit a response from one who either views or uses them, and therefore they are meant to communicate feelings that cannot be communicated by using language. Thus, the architect designs buildings for both usefulness and aesthetic value. The sculptor copies reality but for a purpose. The artist, in whichever school he paints, tries to convey some message to the viewer. These are not only signs of our culture but also symbols by which we communicate.

Just as art is a medium for expression, so music conveys thoughts and ideas that can be evoked in no other way. Anyone with musical ability recalls times when he could "say" what he wanted to only through this form of expression. The subtle interactions of pitch, rhythm, harmonics, and quality of sound have a way of communicating that can be duplicated in no other medium. Both the communicator and the receiver find this true. Virtuosos of any instrument play as though the instrument were a part of them. And in one sense this is the case. On the other end, people who enjoy music may empathize with a performance to such an extent that they seem to become part of it. When these two conditions exist at the same time, one may say that the soul of the musician and the soul of the receiver are speaking to each other through the medium of music.

We have seen that architecture, sculpture, art, and music are all nonverbal languages by which one may express emotions or feelings; they convey messages that can be transmitted in no other way. Each of these media is time-binding, i.e., it can be put in such a form that many generations may learn from its messages. Other nonverbal communication could, perhaps, be put in a form that would last for a certain time, but it seldom if ever is. This nonverbal communication includes all those nuances of behavior that go to make us what we are—the way we look and the things we do that communicate so much about us. These nuances divide into three categories—how we deal with time, space, and our own personal self.

We are probably so accustomed to our observances of time that we are unaware that other cultures do not have the five-day workweek and, in fact, may not even have what we call a *week*. Our division of time into years, months, days, hours, and minutes makes it convenient for us to show the little idiosyncrasies that tell people so much about us. Had we no concept of a minute it would make slight difference when we showed up for an appointment. If hours were nonexistent, we would probably not have a sense of urgency when we received a telephone call at 2:00 A.M. Although the natural division of day and night would keep our body functions going, our society has nevertheless become time dependent, and our watches are symbols of this dependency. Our notion of time enters into almost everything, and we feel that those with whom we communicate should be mindful of it. How many of your worries and frustrations are due to this abominable thing called *time?*

You probably cannot remember when you had no concept of time, but when you begin to raise children you will see that the communication of time to one who has no way to perceive it other than through bodily functions is very difficult indeed. A child says, "When are we going to Grandma's?" And, if you say, "At ten o'clock," it will mean nothing to him. If you say, "In a little while," you may get the response, "How long is a little while?" And so it goes. Yet, everything we do is based upon some time schedule. The procrastinator is constantly in trouble, and the word soon spreads that he cannot be depended upon. If you are late to class or late with a term paper, the professor may hold it against you when he gives out the final grades. We have become slaves to time.

Of course, some societies and some individuals are more time conscious than others. In the hotter climates people tend to move more slowly, and they look upon time more generously than those in cooler climates do. In some societies the time of day seems to make no difference to the activities being carried on. A college student who is used to studying until two and three in the morning may think nothing of calling a classmate at one in the morning to ask a question about the next day's lesson, but he has to remember the difference in time observances when he goes home for vacation. And, when he gets the urge to call a professor at 1:00 A.M., it may also be advisable for him to remember that professors are usually not operating on his time schedule. The way we handle time soon stereotypes us and colors all our attempts to communicate.

The same results come from the way we handle space. Our attitudes toward this concept soon become apparent to those around us, and we have thus communicated something about ourselves through this non-verbal form of expression. Do you always sit in the same chair in a classroom or at the dinner table or at home in your living room? What happens if someone takes your parking space or parks too closely to you? "I need elbow room" is an apt description of our desire for territorial rights. A young business executive who stands too close to his boss's wife at a party may find that his friendliness has lost him his promotion. His proximity might not have been noticed had it been anyone else's wife, but the ideas of rank and honor are very often communicated through the nonverbal medium of space. The seat of honor as well as that of dishonor are still very much in evidence.

Though our concept of distance is changing each day because of the newer modes of travel, some distances never seem to change. You still like to keep a comfortable distance between yourself and the person you are talking to even if you have to keep backing up to do so. This talking distance varies from society to society and is often the cause of communication difficulties. You stop at a specific distance and present yourself to an officer in the Army, to a member of the opposite sex, or to a business acquaintance. Being closer than the accepted distance in any of these situations communicates the idea of intimacy or secrecy. Our own personal habits relative to space communicate many things about us to those who observe.

When one presents himself in any communicative situation, he should be aware that he may be saying more nonverbally than he is saying verbally. As a receiver, we invariably receive more than just the verbal signals. Though we seem to be programed to overlook some bodily actions, others make definite impressions upon us and so influence the meaning decoded from the signals we have received. Though it has been found that our auditory sense dominates our visual sense in most communicative situations, a sufficiently strong stimulus in the visual field reverses this situation. Thus our bodily action is also speaking nonverbally while we are delivering a verbal message—whether we are in a bull session, in a formal discussion group, or the speaker at a public rally.

If we return to the definition of communication given earlier and look now at the two types of messages proceeding from the communicator at any given time, we understand why the extraneous messages must either be kept to a minimum or be forced to complement the meaning of the intended message. Our appearance, gestures, movements, body odor, etc. all may play an important role in the message our listener interprets. If some of these messages are in opposition to the verbal message we are delivering, then our listener must choose which meaning he will accept as being the true intent of our communication. The need to choose is evident from the example at the beginning of this section. Erving Goffman gives the following example of this phenomenon:

> For example, in Shetland Isle one crofter's wife, in serving native dishes to a visitor from the mainland of Britain, would listen with a polite smile to his polite claims of liking what he was eating; at the same time she would take note of the rapidity with which the visitor lifted his fork or spoon to his mouth, the eagerness with which he passed food into his mouth, and the gusto expressed in chewing the food, using these signs as a check on the stated feelings of the eater.[4]

---

[4] Goffman, *The Presentation of Self in Everyday Life*, p. 7.

We do not need to say much about physical attractiveness and body hygiene.   Our T.V.s are filled with ads for hair preparations, mouth washes, hygienic soaps, and deodorants.   Still, we should think what nonverbal cues our appearance communicates to our audience.   We may be the homeliest person in the world, but our appearance is overlooked if we make it inconspicuous by using the other signals we are transmitting to cover it up.   Or we may have a perfect physique and yet fail to communicate effectively because other signals are coming through too strongly or because we fail to subdue this message sufficiently to allow the important message through.   The nonverbal cues which accent or cloud an intended message are as important to the overall communication situation as the main message we want to transmit.   Failure to realize the importance of nonverbal cues may very well cause us to fail in our communicative effort.

THE VERBAL CODE

We have seen how both verbal and nonverbal behavior may either reduce tension or control others, and we have tried to show some of the aspects of nonverbal behavior.   Now we must turn our attention to man's verbal behavior for, after all, this is really what makes him man.   For some time, members of the discipline called *linguistics* have been studying the history, interrelationships, and structure of languages.   Their theories indicate that, when we speak, a set of rules called a *grammar* structures the words we use.   Of course we learn to speak a language mostly by imitation.   But, at the same time, we develop the structural grammar that allows us to use this language in an appropriate way.

In terms of the concepts we have discussed so far, language results from an interassociation of word, concept, and experience memory traces. Our cybernetic tends to develop symbols from these associations and then to use these symbols to structure reality.   And, as a child develops this symbol system, he also internalizes the rules for using it.   Then, when he has an idea to express, his mind uses the rules to develop the style in which to express it.   Because there is more than one way to react to any stimulus, we create a new verbal expression every time we speak or write.   Our ability to generate such expressions is infinite. Their caliber is a result of our cybernetic and our linguistic learning.

Thus, one of our distinguishing characteristics is that verbally we do not make a one-to-one relationship between stimulus and response.   At times we come close to such a relationship, e.g., in greetings, salutations, and exclamations, but even then we can change the response pattern when we desire.   The verbal responses we make to social stimuli depend to a great extent on the society we grow up in. Thus, New Englanders and Texans talk differently not only in their pronunciation but also in their word usage. Evidence of less distinct social climates than these two is found in the languages their members use. You have probably already noticed that your friends and classmates have different meanings for words like *soda*, *evening*, the quantity *couple*, and many others.

Our verbal responses depend on the words we have stored in our memory. We encode the meaning we want to express into the words that we feel will best evoke that meaning in the minds of our listeners. Thus, we are cognizant not only of what we want to say but also of how our listeners will decode (get meaning out of) what we say. Because this process entails a great amount of guesswork on our part, we can never be sure what meanings our listeners obtain from our discourse. Think of the added difficulty of obtaining the correct meaning from a message when two different languages are native to speaker and listener. The translator's problems are monumental.

Many times we hear people say, "Why did I say that?" after they have hurt someone by a remark they made, or we find ourselves wondering why we let a particular secret out after confiding in a friend. We should realize that the language we use and the ideas we express all help to tell others who we are. Weighted most heavily in our attitudinal frame of reference are those things we talk about the most. The language that we have become accustomed to using is the language we use when least conscious of it. Regardless of how hard we try to keep up a front, when our guard is down, the true self shows through the verbal medium. Many of us go through life linguistically acting like the person we think we should be or the one others think we should be. In conversing with a person who is attempting to do this we find that his linguistic cues are so mixed up and oscillate from one role to another so much that we have a difficult time understanding him; e.g., is she really the sophisticate from the big city or just the girl from the farm down the road?

At other times we speak to someone or he speaks to us, and we find no understanding between us. Somehow we completely bypass each other. There are many reasons for the misunderstandings associated with language.[5] We shall mention only a few of the chief causes of linguistic ambiguity. Most of these will be self-evident once they are mentioned. Our primary goal is to make you aware of language and the many difficulties involved in using it.

One of the difficulties in our language is its tendency to stereotype,

[5] J. Samuel Bois, *The Art of Awareness* (Dubuque, Iowa: Wm. C. Brown & Co., 1966); and, John C. Condon, Jr., *Semantics and Communication* (New York: The Macmillan Company, 1966).

e.g., communist, lazy, dumb, and criminal. Children learn the language of bias very early in their lives. They hear about the "wrong side of the track," "niggers," "Jews," and "rich kids" before they have any way to evaluate these terms. Thus, they are likely to use the terms in the wrong context quite innocently at a later time and suffer the consequences. And the bias that these terms carry with them colors all of the rest of their language and thinking about the groups of people referred to by these labels. Thus, we tend to misinterpret the information we receive about these groups and consciously or unconsciously spread the prejudice by our own communicative behavior.

Some language also carries with it the connotation of saying all there is to say about a subject: "He is a communist." "She always acts that way." "This is the only way it can be done." These statements set the speaker up as the authority and allow for no alternatives. But, in reality, we know that the only thing that is constant is change. What appeared one way yesterday may appear completely different tomorrow. The very fact that our nervous system is in a constant state of change and produces a dynamic rather than a static attitudinal frame of reference means that, if we are honest with ourselves and do not let our language get in our way, we will change our attitudes toward people and concepts from day to day. We should let our language help rather than hinder this process. We can do this mainly by placing an "as far as I can see" before each of the above statements to make us realize that our statements are very subjective and really reflect only our attitudinal frame of reference.

Another vice of language is its ability to get such a hold on its user that he uses it just to hear it. We all know people who talk incessantly, thereby controlling all those around them. This condition is bad enough, but occasionally they listen to themselves, begin to believe what they hear, and are pulled by their linguistic exercises into untenable positions. They then must defend these positions or admit defeat, and either of these alternatives may be devastating to their egos. One must be aware then of the almost magical power language may have on its user.

We have defined *verbal* as that which may be put into linguistic symbols. Thus the true test of whether a message is verbal or nonverbal is not whether it can be uttered vocally but whether it can be written. It remains, however, that these are the only two means of delivering a verbal message. For example, a verbose person may speak or may write more than what we feel is the average for an individual. Although one cannot say which of these means of expressing verbal messages is the more important as far as information transmission is concerned, most of us rely more on the spoken than on the written message in our everyday socializing. The similarities between speaking and writing should be evident, so we shall take a brief look at the differences.

As a child begins to learn to talk, he finds a certain magic in speaking. If he makes the right sounds, all kinds of things begin to happen. No wonder he learns to lie nearly as soon as he learns to speak, for why need there be a positive correlation between what he says and what he does? To the child, words and actions are two completely separate worlds, until he finds that those around him seem to put a strange belief in the message of the words he utters. Even then he may try to continue to develop these two separate worlds until he is convinced in some way that language and behavior must be in agreement. The extent to which he learns this lesson is the extent to which his word can be trusted.

At one time, if a man gave you his word, you knew that he would do whatever he said he would. However, with spoken language, you may easily forget just exactly what you said. And, when the time comes to fulfill your vow, you can conveniently say, "I don't remember that," or in some way try to modify your original statement. The ease with which spoken language may be modified is one of its chief attributes. If we are not understood or if our declaration is too strong, we can always modify our statement to fit the occasion. However, for precisely this reason we tend not to pay attention to what we say unless we are in a very tight situation, and then we usually write out our message first. Spoken language becomes such second nature to us that we often reveal as much through it as we do through our other behaviorisms. Because we seldom put much active thought into our social conversations, what we say on these occasions often more nearly represents what we are than it does at any other time. However, speech has a decided disadvantage in that it must be instantaneously understood; once it is spoken it is gone and cannot be recalled without fear of misquoting. Until the age of electricity, it had another disadvantage in that one had to be within earshot to use it.[6]

Writing, on the other hand, does not have many of the disadvantages of speech. Though great civilizations existed before modern writing techniques, one can easily see that they have probably been the chief reasons for man's fantastic technological developments. Writing, in the simplest sense, is an almost permanent memory of what we say. Because of this permanence and because of the material that has been developed to write upon, we can send our messages through limitless distances in space and time. Thus, generation can learn from generation, and we can build and modify our theories based on the findings of all

[6] For a thorough analysis of speech, the interested reader should see Giles W. Gray and Claude M. Wise, *The Basis of Speech*, 3rd ed. (New York: Harper & Row, Publishers, 1959).

who have gone before. This phenomenon occurs not only because writing serves as a memory but also because it tends to be a more precise utterance of what we actually want to say. We think more about what we write than about what we say for two reasons: Writing cannot be easily modified, and we usually have more time to formulate the exact language in which we couch our message. Because of this precision and because written language is usually more formal than spoken language, the messages committed to writing seem to be more objective.

We have looked briefly at the two ways of using language to communicate. Now we shall look at the main characteristic speech and writing have in common—language. Human existence is welded to language. Most of our thinking is done using language. And, if we did not have a common language with our neighbor, we would find it very hard to communicate anything but the very basic essentials. Yet the commonality of language which we all feel with those who speak the same one is so often misjudged that it is precisely this point that must be examined and understood if we are to communicate effectively. We shall not go into a detailed study of any one language for that is beyond the scope of this book, but we shall attempt to bring out some of the more obvious difficulties in the uses of language.

Linguistics, psycholinguistics, and general semantics have added much to our basic understanding of the language we speak. Strangely, we are adept at using language long before we begin to study what it is. For this reason we have difficulty understanding the various intricacies that make up a language. We cannot see the forest for the trees. Yet we are all sure that we do not know enough about language itself to understand why it works so well sometimes and so poorly at other times. Why can two people be talking about the same thing and never understand it? Of course most of this misunderstanding has to do with the way in which each person interprets the message. Here we are concerned only with the language itself.

To begin, we must understand that language, whether it be French, German, Chinese, or Bantu, is a man made, arbitrarily designed set of symbols. All languages are redundant—a source of both concern and delight. Because we may always say something in more than one way, our listeners may not always understand the way it was said. But for this same reason we enjoy Hemingway, Tolstoi, and Shakespeare. Since language is an arbitrary set of symbols, one must know what these symbols stand for or refer to before he can understand what a speaker is saying or a writer is writing. Because language is an artificial means by which to understand reality, as soon as we realize what a certain symbol refers to, we can use it to enlarge our own comprehension of the world about us. But, unless we have had some experience with the thing signified by that symbol, it can evoke no meaning in us other than that it is a word we do not understand.

Language undoubtedly developed so that we could communicate with others. The first language was a set of vocal symbols by which one person could evoke meaning in the mind of another. As man increased his knowledge of language and decided to write it down, he again made symbols of the sounds he had just uttered. Thus, writing is a symbolization of a symbolization. The symbolization process has become so precise and regular that one can cut out every fourth word of a text and nearly everyone will be able to fill in the missing words. Once we have begun a sentence, we have definite restrictions on how we must end it and what words we may use in it. A shrewd listener very seldom listens to an entire sentence. His brain immediately sets up the probable conclusions after receiving the first few words. This is why it is so difficult for us to understand a foreign language. We think that the speakers are going too fast, but in reality our mind does not have the necessary familiarity with the language to guess at what is going to be said. Therefore, we must listen to every word that the foreigner is saying in order to make sense out of his message.

Although language obviously transmits information, we often lose sight of how it does this. We often feel that each word we use has only one definite meaning and that everyone who hears us knows what this meaning is. This is not true, of course, and herein lies our greatest difficulty. Words evoke more than one meaning, and the meaning they do evoke may be so abstract that we have no way of knowing what was actually meant. Abstract concepts, such as beauty, love, liberty, and religion, may never be defined well enough for everyone involved to agree to their meanings. This fact alone should make us aware of the necessity of being as sure as possible of the meaning a speaker has for a word before we jump to conclusions as to what he meant when he said, "You're a real beauty."

Naming things is an essential part of learning, and, although many names may apply to the same thing, one has the assurance that he knows something about this thing if he knows what to call it. If we look deeply enough into any language, we see that words exist for everything that is essential to the people who use it. We also see that the degree of specificity in a certain area may be greater in one language than in another. The elaborate distinctions that have developed in a language may very well indicate the importance to that society of what is being distinguished. As cultures using different languages grow closer in communicative distance and interests, they tend to use much the same language, some words borrowed from one culture and some from another.

Many books discuss language and its use in our everyday life. Some of these are listed in the bibliography at the end of this part of the book. We do not have room to give a thorough analysis of language, though much of the rest of this book will be based on the way we use language in different situations. The reader is reminded here that, though language (both written and spoken) is usually looked upon as our chief means of communication, it is not always the one we rely upon or the one we trust the most. All our overt behavior at any given time is a form of communication to those around us. If we are aware of this, then perhaps we can make all these messages complement the intended message and thus give greater probability of effective communication.

CONCLUSION

We shall now conclude this part of the book with a brief review of the individual's communication system. As we have stated, this view is rather mechanistic and therefore you should use it only as a guide to some of the important points for study. It is, at most, a superstructure from which we may view the ongoing human-communication process. We chose a simple model consisting of reception, information-processing, and transmission phases. If we begin with the reception phase and pass through information-processing to transmission, we may describe the human-communication process in the following way.

We receive a message through one or a combination of our senses. Our sense receptors transform this message into neural impulses and send it toward the brain. As it passes from neuron to neuron, our nervous system may block or modify it. Thus we have no guarantee that the message our senses received is the one our brain receives. If the reticular formation arouses our brain to receive the incoming signals, it receives, decodes, and stores them in a randomly accessible memory system of words, concepts, and experiences. Our cybernetic, which is innate, governs the storage and subsequent processing of this information.

Over the years our cybernetic directs our brain in the development of many mental states, e.g., fears, desires, beliefs. The total effect of these mental states is to form a basic attitudinal frame of reference. Then, as the cybernetic directs the processing of information, it is evaluated against the present state of our attitudinal frame of reference with the constant goal of obtaining and maintaining mental balance. As this new information is processed, associations are established between its memory traces and those of previous information that has some substantive connection with it. The addition of this new information to our mental states changes them to some degree. Thus, our attitudinal frame of reference is a dynamic system, and we should take this fact into consideration when communicating. The conscious processing of information we call thinking; it involves the recall of previously stored data, their extrapolation, and correlation. How one recalls information is still a mystery, but we know that one's ability to do this is directly proportional to his ability to communicate.

If, after the data has been processed, we decide to transmit a response to the received message, our cybernetic directs the encoding of the desired message into both verbal and nonverbal codes, taking into consideration how the listener will decode this message. The proper muscles are then stimulated, and a message is transmitted using the appropriate signals.

At any point along this pathway the intended meaning of the message may be distorted and thus interfere with the resultant communication. We pointed out that, although language is only one of our means of communication, it may cause the most ambiguity in the communication process. We know that we are language bound and that it is this symbol system which has made us what we are. However, you should be aware that language is only a part of the communication process. Please keep this in mind as you study the following parts of this book.

ADORNO, T. W., ELSE FRENKEL-BRUNSWIK, DANIEL J. LEVENSON, and R. NEVITT SANFORD, *The Authoritarian Personality*. New York: Harper & Row, Publishers, 1950.

ANDERSON, RICHARD, and DAVID AUSUBEL, eds., *Readings in the Psychology of Cognition*. New York: Holt, Rinehart & Winston, Inc., 1965.

BENNIS, WARREN G., *et al.*, *Interpersonal Dynamics*. Homewood, Illinois: Dorsey Press, 1964.

BERELSON, BERNARD, and GARY A. STEINER, *Human Behavior*. New York: Harcourt, Brace & World, Inc., 1964.

BERLO, DAVID, *The Process of Communication*. New York: Holt, Rinehart & Winston, Inc., 1960.

BOIS, J. SAMUEL, *The Art of Awareness*. Dubuque, Iowa: Wm. C. Brown & Co., 1966.

BORDEN, GEORGE A., "Cognitive Dissonance: A Theory of Persuasion," *The Pennsylvania Speech Annual*, 22 (September 1965), 43–50.

BREHM, JACK, and ARTHUR COHEN, *Explorations in Cognitive Dissonance*. New York: John Wiley & Sons, Inc., 1962.

BROADBENT, D. E., "Flow of Information Within the Organism," *Journal of Verbal Learning and Verbal Behavior*, 2 (1963), 34–39.

————, *Perception and Communication*. New York: Pergamon Press, Inc., 1958.

BROWN, ROGER, *Social Psychology*. New York: The Macmillan Company, 1965.

————, *Words and Things*. New York: The Macmillan Company, 1958.

BRYSON, LYMAN, ed., *The Communication of Ideas: A Series of Addresses*. New York: Harper & Row, Publishers, 1948.

CHAPANIS, NATALIA, and ALPHONSE CHAPANIS, "Cognitive Dissonance," *Psychological Bulletin*, 61 (1964), 1–22.

CHARDIN, PIERRE THIELHARD DE, *The Phenomenon of Man*. New York: Harper & Row, Publishers, 1961.

CHERRY, COLIN, *On Human Communication*. New York: John Wiley & Sons, Inc., 1957.

CONDON, JOHN C., JR., *Semantics and Communication*. New York: The Macmillan Company, 1966.

DEMBER, WILLIAM N., *The Psychology of Perception*. New York: Holt, Rinehart & Winston, Inc., 1960.

DEUTSCH, KARL, *The Nerves of Government*. New York: The Macmillan Company, 1963.

————, "On Communication Models in the Social Sciences," *Public Opinion Quarterly*, 16 (1952), 356–80.

ECCLES, SIR JOHN, "The Synapse," *Scientific American*, 212 (January 1965), 56–66.

EISENSON, JON, J. JEFFERY AUER, and JOHN IRWIN, *The Psychology of Communication*. New York: Appleton-Century-Crofts, 1963.

FANO, ROBERT M., *Transmission of Information*. Cambridge, Massachusetts: M.I.T. Press, 1961.

FANTZ, ROBERT L., "The Origin of Form Perception," *Scientific American*, 204 (May 1961), 66–72.

FESTINGER, LEON, *Conflict, Decision and Dissonance*. Stanford, California: Stanford University Press, 1964.

————, *A Theory of Cognitive Dissonance*. Stanford, California: Stanford University Press, 1957.

FRENCH, J. D., "The Reticular Formation," *Scientific American*, 196 (May 1957), 54–60.

FREUD, SIGMUND, *Psychopathology of Everyday Life*, trans. A. A. Brill. London: Ernest Benn, Ltd., 1960.

GERARD, R. W., "The Material Basis of Memory," *Journal of Verbal Learning and Verbal Behavior*, 2 (1963), 22–23.

GOFFMAN, ERVING, *The Presentation of Self in Everyday Life*. Garden City, New York: Doubleday & Company, Inc., 1959.

GRAY, GILES, and CLAUDE WISE, *The Bases of Speech* (3rd ed.).   New York: Harper & Row, Publishers, 1959.

GRINKER, R. R., *Toward a Unified Theory of Communication.*   New York: Basic Books, Inc., 1956.

HALL, EDWARD, *The Silent Language.*   Garden City, New York: Doubleday & Company, Inc., 1959.

HARPER, ROBERT, CHARLES ANDERSON, CLIFFORD CHRISTENSEN, and STEVEN HUNKA, eds., *The Cognitive Processes—Readings.*   Englewood Cliffs, New Jersey: Prentice-Hall, Inc., 1964.

HAYAKAWA, S. I., *Language in Thought and Action.*   New York: Harcourt, Brace & World, Inc., 1964.

HERTZLER, JOYCE, *A Sociology of Language.*   New York: Random House, 1965.

HESS, ECKHARD H., "Attitude and Pupil Size," *Scientific American*, 212 (April 1965), 46–54.

HILLS, CAROLE P., and R. G. SPECTOR, "The Nerve Cell," *Developmental Medicine and Child Neurology*, Supplement #8, London, 1964.

HOLLANDER, E. P., and RAMOND HUNT, eds., *Current Perspectives in Social Psychology.*   New York: Oxford University Press, Inc., 1963.

HOROWITZ, MILTON, "Fluency: An Appraisal and a Research Approach," *The Journal of Communication*, 15 (March 1965), 4–13.

JACKSON, WILLIE, ed., *Communication Theory.*   New York: Academic Press Inc., 1953.

KATZ, BERNHARD, "How Cells Communicate," *Scientific American*, 205 (September 1961), 209–20.

KNAPP, PETER, ed., *Expression of the Emotions in Man.*   New York: International Universities Press, Inc., 1963.

KOCH, SIGMUND, ed., *Psychology: A Study of a Science*, Vol. 4.   New York: McGraw-Hill Book Company, 1962.

LANGER, SUSANNE, *Philosophy in a New Key.*   New York: New American Library, Inc., 1961.

MCLUHAN, MARSHALL, *Understanding Media: The Extensions of Man.*   New York: McGraw-Hill Book Company, 1965.   Paperback.

MELTON, A. W., "Implications of Short-Term Memory for a General Theory of Memory," *Journal of Verbal Learning and Verbal Behavior*, 2 (1963), 1–21.

MELZACK, RONALD, "The Perception of Pain," *Scientific American*, 204 (February 1961), 41–49.

MEREDITH, PATRICK, *Learning, Remembering and Knowing.*   New York: Association Press, 1961.

MILLER, GEORGE A., *Language and Communication*. New York: McGraw-Hill Book Company, 1963.

———, "The Magical Number Seven Plus or Minus Two: Some Limits on Our Capacity for Processing Information," *Psychological Review*, 63 (1956), 81–97.

MILLER, WILLIAM H., *et al.*, "How Cells Receive Stimuli," *Scientific American*, 205 (September 1961), 222–38.

MONTAGNA, WILLIAM, "The Skin," *Scientific American*, 212 (February 1965), 56–66.

MORGAN, CLIFFORD T., *Physiological Psychology* (3rd ed.). New York: McGraw-Hill Book Company, 1965.

MORTON, J., "A Preliminary Functional Model for Language Behavior," *International Audiology*, 3 (1964), 216–25.

NEUMEYER, ALFRED, *The Search for Meaning in Modern Art*. Englewood Cliffs, New Jersey: Prentice-Hall, Inc., 1965.

NEWCOMB, THEODORE, RALPH TURNER, and PHILIP CONVERSE, *Social Psychology*. New York: Holt, Rinehart & Winston, Inc., 1965.

NIELSEN, J. M., *Memory and Amnesia*. Los Angeles: San Incas Press, 1958.

OSGOOD, CHARLES, and PERCEY TANNENBAUM, "The Principle of Congruity in the Prediction of Attitude Change," *Psychological Review*, 62, No. 1 (1955), 42–55.

PENFIELD, WILDER, and LAMAR ROBERTS, *Speech and Brain-Mechanisms*. Princeton, New Jersey: Princeton University Press, 1959.

PIERCE, JOHN R., *Symbols, Signals and Noise*. New York: Harper & Row, Publishers, 1961.

PRITCHARD, ROY M., "Stabilized Images on the Retina," *Scientific American*, 204 (June 1961), 72–78.

PROSHANSKY, HAROLD, and BERNARD SEIDENBERG, eds., *Basic Studies in Social Psychology*. New York: Holt, Rinehart & Winston, Inc., 1965.

ROKEACH, MILTON, *The Open and Closed Mind*. New York: Basic Books, Inc., 1960.

ROSENBLATT, FRANK, *Principles of Neurodynamics*. Washington, D.C.: Spartan Books, 1962.

ROSENBLITH, WALTER A., ed., *Sensory Communication*. Cambridge, Massachusetts: M.I.T. Press, 1961.

RUSSELL, W. RITCHIE, *Brain, Memory Learning*. Oxford: Clarendon Press, 1959.

RYCENGA, JOHN, and JOSEPH SCHWARTZ, *Perspectives on Language*. New York: The Ronald Press Company, 1963.

SAPORTA, SOL, ed., *Psycholinguistics: A Book of Readings*. New York: Holt, Rinehart & Winston, Inc., 1961.

74 The Individual's Communication System

SECORD, PAUL, and CARL BACKMAN, Social Psychology. New York: McGraw-Hill Book Company, 1964.

SHANNON, CLAUDE, and WARREN WEAVER, The Mathematical Theory of Communication. Urbana, Illinois: University of Illinois Press, 1962.

SHERIF, MUZAFER, In Common Predicament. Boston: Houghton Mifflin Company, 1966.

SOLLEY, CHARLES M., and GARDNER MURPHY, Development of the Perceptual World. New York: Basic Books, Inc., 1960.

SPERLING, G., "The Information Available in Brief Visual Presentations," Psychology Monographs, 74, No. 498 (1960).

STEINER, IVAN, and MARTIN FISHBEIN, eds., Current Studies in Social Psychology. New York: Holt, Rinehart & Winston, Inc., 1965.

STRAUS, ERWIN, The Primary World of Senses: A Vindication of Sensory Experience, trans. Jacob Needleman. New York: The Macmillan Company, 1963.

SWETS, JOHN A., Signal Detection and Recognition by Human Observers. New York: John Wiley & Sons, Inc., 1964.

THOMSON, ROBERT, The Psychology of Thinking. Baltimore: Penguin Books, Inc., 1959.

VON BÉKÉSY, GEORG, "The Ear," Scientific American, 197 (August 1957), 66–78.

VON BUDDENBROCK, WOLFGANG, The Senses. Ann Arbor, Michigan: The University of Michigan Press, 1958.

WALD, GEORGE, "Eye and Camera," Scientific American, 183 (August 1950), 32–41.

WEAVER, RICHARD, The Ethics of Rhetoric. Chicago: Henry Regnery Co., 1953.

WEAVER, WARREN, "The Mathematics of Communication," Scientific American, 181 (July 1949), 11–15.

WHITESIDE, T. C. D., A. GRAYBIEL, and J. I. NIVEN, "Visual Illusions of Movement," Brain, 88 (1965), 193–211.

WIENER, NORBERT, Cybernetics. New York: John Wiley & Sons, Inc., 1948.

———, The Human Use of Human Beings. Garden City, New York: Doubleday & Company, Inc., 1954.

WITKIN, HERMAN A., "The Perception of the Upright," Scientific American, 200 (February 1959), 50–56.

ZIPF, GEORGE, The Psycho-Biology of Language. Cambridge, Massachusetts: M.I.T. Press, 1965.

II

Interpersonal
Communication

The first part of this book described the mechanisms of the human
communicator and how man uses those mechanisms as he collects,
stores, processes, remembers, and expresses information. It also
discussed certain implications which these five processes, because of
their natures, have for man's behavior. Part II of this book will attend
primarily to the settings in which face-to-face communication events
take place, including where they occur, with whom they occur, why they
occur, and some of the behavior which results when the communication
mechanisms of one human being collide with those of another. In the
first section of this part of the book the importance of the several
processes discussed in Part I will be before us as we begin to consider the
whole man and what his communication potential means for his thinking
and his behavior. The focus of our comments will stray away from the
topic of the individual communicator in the next section, on dyadic
communication, where relationships between pairs of individuals will be
the central issue, and still farther away in the last section, on group
communication, where sets of relationships among group members will

be considered. We shall find ample occasion in all sections to refer to both the equipment and the processes which have been our subject matter to this point.

Social Bases of
Interpersonal Communication

It is fundamental for an understanding of interpersonal communication to know (1) how communication plays a role in interpersonal relationships among humans, (2) that man gets to know what he is through the information he receives from those around him, (3) that his ability (perhaps, because he has no choice, we should say his fate) to think symbolically gives him an identity and a self-concept which in turn are likely to affect his communication behavior in important ways, and, finally, (4) that his predisposition to evaluate information plays a key role in determining what he is and what he cannot be to himself and to others around him. A brief description of some of the processes contained in these topics is a necessary antecedent to a consideration of dyadic and group communication. The next five subsections will provide that preparation.

INTERPERSONAL COMMUNICATION IN
INTERPERSONAL RELATIONSHIPS

Although this section is concerned exclusively with face-to-face interpersonal communication, the writers recognize that enduring interpersonal relationships have formed and are still being formed without face-to-face confrontation ever having taken place among the parties to the relationship. Pen pals, lonely-hearts correspondents, and the international sponsors of underprivileged children are examples. Many of these interpersonal relationships can be as dear and essential or as hateful and repugnant to the parties involved as many face-to-face interpersonal relationships, in which speech communication plays a major role among the several available channels for information flow among the relating persons. The latter is the immediate subject however, even though speech is not necessary for the formation of strong and complex relationships, as teachers of the speechless can attest. We have already seen how speech helps convey the intricacies and subtleties of one's self when and to whom one chooses to reveal portions of that self, in addition to occasions when the self does not prefer its revelation. Our subject for the rest of this book will be that of persons talking, moving, listening, and looking together as they coact to carry on their everyday affairs.

We shall begin by limiting our definition of interpersonal communication and our definition of interpersonal relationships more than we have so far. Interpersonal communication is necessary for the formation and maintenance of an interpersonal relationship, but mere attempts at communication or expression do not ensure that interpersonal communication will result. In addition to individual expression, all the processes of reception and interpretation discussed earlier must be operative at the same level in two people for the communicative process to function. Attempted communication with a sleeping person, a psychotic, or one under heavy influence of alcohol or narcotics is ample evidence of the validity of this proposition. Other ingredients too must accompany the expression. A certain cognition is necessary on the part of both persons. And various perceptual activities must also occur during the attempted communication for appropriate cognition to take place.

On the other hand, just as expression alone does not lead to interpersonal communication, perception alone does not either—for instance, as through the mechanisms of nonverbal communication discussed earlier. One can perceive many things: budding trees, a dogfight, a man coughing violently. One may also infer from his perceptions, make judgments on his inferences, and take action on both. So spring brings buds, a contended bone causes the dogfight, and maybe the man has an infected throat. One may enjoy the spring, remove the bone, and offer the coughing man a throat lozenge. Sentient man obtains new meaning complexes from his perceptions, complexes which add a constellation of inferential and evaluative knowing to his store of information. Both the inferences and the resulting overt behaviors contain meaning. Our point is that the budding trees, the fighting dogs, and the coughing man do not communicate their condition in any sense; the observer perceived some data through his sensory end-organs, acted, and, in acting, possibly communicated certain meanings to those who were acted upon. We shall not take A's perception of B's behavior to be interpersonal communication unless B's behavior somehow is influenced by or consummated with an awareness of A's presence. In this way we should exclude the frustrated scramblings of ant packs, the phototropic gropings of Virginia creepers, and the incidentally perceived, "ouch-damn-it" behaviors of human beings from the realm of interpersonal communication relevant to the foci of this book.

Having delimited the notion of interpersonal communication somewhat, we may consider in more detail the role that this phenomenon plays in the broader interpersonal-relationship phenomenon. The fact that communication occurs among persons in a face-to-face setting does not necessarily signal the existence of an interpersonal relationship at the level we wish to consider it here. For example, one may say "hi" or make some other traditional greeting to a recognized face or to a stranger one passes in the corridor or street. Although this speech act may qualify as communication, it does not reflect an interpersonal relationship, and it does not necessarily help to build one. "Hi" and many other speech behaviors are like go lights among human beings. "Okay fellow, I recognize your presence," one says; and, through the resultant head nod or returned greeting, the other says, "I see you too and acknowledge you as one of the human race." Now, depending on the intonation and other nonverbal and verbal data that are perceived—depending on the way one says "hi"—more meaning may be intended. A "hi," a smile, and a hesitation with eyes fixed on the other may invite a longer conversation or lead to a luncheon date, a marriage, a fight, or a business partnership. That is, an interpersonal relationship may begin to form if the two parties do not already enjoy or deplore one.

From another perspective, when the way I relate to Joe B. is fuzzy or indistinguishable from the way I relate to many, many others, no interpersonal relationship exists. The fuzziness occurs because Joe B. and I share little information. I do not have much data for a relationship. In this situation I base my evaluations of Joe B. on categorical thinking as opposed to sensory information. If I must evaluate or think about him, I can only apply broad stroke labels: "He's a Jew . . . WASP . . . Negro . . . history major . . . frat man . . . bright." However, when circumstance or design throws Joe B. and me together for an evening or a year to work on a problem or to socialize or the like, then the beginnings of an interpersonal relationship may emerge. I find myself thinking about Joe B. more than about many others that I know. He stands out more clearly in the sea of faces I can recall when alone. I can hear the sound of his voice. I remember increasingly more of his specific attributes and behaviors, which I like or dislike. I come to think about and evaluate Joe B. on the basis of specific behaviors—statements which he has made and the various ways that he has acted while around me and toward me. That is, I have more personal information about Joe B., largely from our shared communication. I can think about him in characteristically personal terms because shared information has established a fund of knowledge at the unique personal level about Joe B. Likewise Joe B. begins to relate to me differently because of his increasingly more refined information about me. Joe and I are no longer likely to rely on broad categorical strokes in thinking about and describing one another to a third party. As an illustration of this phenomenon, consider the geographical interpretations of three native Americans, one having lived all his life on the East Coast, one in the Middle West, and one on the West Coast. The first man places Denver in the Far West; the third man knows that Chicago is back East; and the Midwesterner makes finer distinctions east of the Mississippi than the Westerner does and finer distinctions west of the Mississippi than the Easterner does. A fourth man who has lived at one time or another in all three regions probably is not even very impressed with the cartography of the Midwesterner. Personal information makes broad categorical statements (or maps) inappropriate—not descriptive enough to satisfy partners in an interpersonal relationship. An interpersonal relationship then is a function of information shared through interpersonal communication.

The Joe B./me relationship sketched above implies that the frequency or the amount of information-sharing is directly related to developed interpersonal relationships (to deep mutual knowing)—that the sheer magnitude of "bits" of information shared makes a relationship. This is not always the case. We think of people with whom job or daily routine throws us together all the time—people with whom we do not really have an interpersonal relationship in the above sense. A useful concept for explaining this phenomenon is that of level of interpersonal communication. It is true that, in some cases for a very definite reason, in other cases for no reason we can think of, many of our associations never go beyond the "hi there" level. On the other hand an infrequent contact between two people may be on such a deep level that in fact a lasting interpersonal relationship does form. Successful marriage preceded by a whirlwind romance and friendship between people who on first meeting sense that they hit it off and correspond faithfully thereafter are two extreme examples of interpersonal relationships formed not because of the amount of information traded over many encounters but because of the information shared at an intensely personal level in a single or a few encounters. What is communicated is as important a determinant of the existence or the level of an interpersonal relationship as the frequency and amount of shared information.

Consider two hypothetical conversations between you and Suzy in which Suzy shared one of two different sets of information with you. As a result of one of these conversations you know that: Suzy has an uncle; the uncle is lazy; Suzy has a dog. As a result of the other conversation you know that: Suzy has an uncle; the uncle tried to rape Suzy when she was a child; Suzy is afraid of boys. The amount of information in terms of thought units is equivalent in the two sets, yet the degree of meaning imparted to you is extremely different—quite shallow in the former set of information and quite deep in the latter.

Shared information at deeper levels carries additional meaning not contained in or necessarily related to the intended content of the communication itself. In this example, for instance, Suzy is communicating, perhaps unintentionally, that she trusts you enough to share this deep level or somewhat privileged information with you. Jurgen Ruesch and Gregory Bateson refer to this aspect of language communication as a command function as opposed to the reporting function present in all language communication.[1] Meaning may be found in the content of the message itself or in the command function, where the content of the message may be just a carrier wave for information that defines and elaborates the characteristics of the interpersonal relationship, or in both the reporting and the command functions. Of course, command functions do not always increase the intimacy of an interpersonal relationship. Had the content of Suzy's remarks, while remaining on a shallow level, implied that there was a great deal that she was reluctant to say concerning the subject, the effect of this command might have been to freeze the level of intimacy in its present state.

So it is not just the frequency but also the content that defines the degree of the relationship. Redundant "good mornings" may be strung out over 50 years with little information-sharing and no relationship expected or forthcoming. On the other hand many friends for whom circumstances permit only a chance annual meeting find this meeting rewarding enough in its level of information-sharing to last the whole year with no essential change in the intimacy level.

Before leaving this topic, we must emphasize the importance of individual differences in interpersonal communication. For example, the process of interpersonal communication involves revealing one's self to the accompaniment of the same revelations on the part of the other person. This process may take considerable time because the layers of information must be peeled back with much attention to balance between the two rates of disclosure. Some persons peel back their layers more rapidly than others.[2] Others hardly reveal themselves at a deep level to anyone at all. Sidney Jourard soundly argues that the willingness or reluctance to reveal one's self in interpersonal communication is an extremely important difference among individuals—a difference which reflects the personal adjustment and mental health of those individuals.[3] That normal human beings do have a need to share or disclose themselves to others to some extent was supported by a study of experimentally isolated pairs of men. Isolates revealed more intimate information about

---

[1] *Communication: The Social Matrix of Psychiatry* (New York: W. W. Norton & Company, Inc., 1951), pp. 79–81.

[2] Bruce W. Tuckman, "Interpersonal Probing and Revealing and Systems of Integrative Complexity," *Journal of Personality and Social Psychology*, 3 (1966), 655–64.

[3] *The Transparent Self* (Princeton, New Jersey: D. Van Nostrand Co., Inc., 1964), pp. 19–39.

themselves to partners than nonisolated controls revealed to their partners.[4]

This individual difference in rate of disclosure can influence our immediate interpersonal-communication behavior in other ways. Too rapid self-disclosure may be labeled immaturity or egocentricity, and too slow disclosure may be labeled standoffishness or snobbery or frigidity. Yet, we all have our different styles of communicating, and, since they may not be the same in a particular relationship, we often encounter difficulties. Some of us actively look for others to share ourselves with, and others of us find it difficult to offer a hand when another extends his whole life to us. Many problems arise if such seemingly trivial but important individual differences are overlooked when human beings share information.

What is unfolded in interpersonal communication—what becomes known—is increasingly more personal information about the way the other thinks, the way he acts, his values, his beliefs, his interests, his idiosyncratic habits—good and bad. In short, to communicate with another is to be known, to be partly exposed, or, in Jourard's language, to be "transparent."[5] No wonder some so carefully guard the secret which is the self and so grudgingly enter with all defenses down into mutual co-relation with another. Abraham Maslow, in citing some of the problems of social science research, indicates that human scientists often forget that much of human communication is skillfully executed subterfuge, practiced with a finesse acquired from a lifetime of learning—that we spend much time trying to avoid becoming known.[6] This one aspect of individual differences suffices here; we shall discuss additional aspects later on.

In summary, both the sheer amount of shared information among persons and the level of that information operate together to determine the existence or the intensity of an interpersonal relationship. Without some minimal amount of sharing it is misleading to speak of an interpersonal relationship, but the attainment of that minimum by two persons does not in itself set the intimacy level of the relationship or even assure that a relationship exists. Once that minimum is reached the nature of the information shared from that point on furnishes the material out of which an interpersonal relationship is created or deferred, and, as well, it determines the eventual level of intimacy of that relationship. At base the whole matrix of links and bonds that bind or alienate two humans in a deep interpersonal knowing of one another

---

[4] Irwin Altman and William Haythorn, "Interpersonal Exchange in Isolation," *Sociometry*, 28 (1965), 411–26.
[5] Jourard, *The Transparent Self*, pp. 101–3.
[6] Address at Northwestern University, Spring 1963.

consists solely of information-sharing of many kinds.   The tiny related
and unrelated units of meaning that combine into the picture that the
one comes to have of the other are the results of interpersonal communication.

FORMS OF INFORMATION

We sketched the role of interpersonal communication in interpersonal
relationships at the level of sets of interpersonal relations among persons
since it is misleading to speak of relationships from the standpoint of a
single, individual communicator.   In the next four subsections we shall
rely on these concepts as we regress to focus on the individual.   In this
way we shall consider several important variables that affect the speech
behavior of all individuals in social interaction before we return to the
larger relationship-as-a-whole focus, which dominates the subsequent
section on dyads, or two-person groups.   We shall explicate the several
topics considered below from the point of view of the individual communicator, though we assume that the reader will not forget the social
context in which our individual communicates—that the processes discussed occur, often simultaneously, within several interacting persons.

Shared information was the central theme in the discussion above,
and information also constitutes the core idea in the present subsection,
where we further consider verbal and nonverbal codes and other characteristics of the origins of information pertaining to interpersonal communication.   Information gained by reading about, observing, and listening
to others influences and molds a particular instance of interpersonal
communication among persons.   Information about other persons, about
their expectations, and so forth influences these face-to-face encounters in
various ways.   As just one example, John Darley and Ellen Berscheid
found that persons tended to like those with whom they anticipated future interaction significantly more than those with identical descriptions
with whom they did not anticipate future contact.[7]   So, information as
seemingly trivial as foreknowledge of a meeting with a stranger ultimately affects the subsequent encounter with that stranger.   Other
kinds of information—information about the past behavior of the other
and the like—also influence the speech behavior of one in his social interactions.

For a brief time let us focus once again on the verbal- and nonverbal-
communication codes for the purpose of making some distinctions in
addition to several already made in Part I.   For the most part interper-

---

[7] "Increased Liking as a Result of the Anticipation of Personal Contact," *Human
Relations*, 20 (February 1967), 29–40.

sonal communication proceeds quite fully with the aid of only the sight and hearing of the participants. One sees and hears the verbal and nonverbal messages directed at one and encodes his own messages so that the other may either see or hear in turn. Verbal messages in the majority of interpersonal-communication settings are only heard, while the various nonverbal forms are both heard and seen. Without attempting to exhaust the possibilities, we suggest in the following list the range of nonverbal forms typically observed in interpersonal communication: vocal intonation, selectively exaggerated articulation, throat-clearing, yawning, laughing, crying, decreasing and increasing volume, gesturing with arms and hands, facial expressions and changes of expressions, bodily posture, speed of movement, and movement pattern.

In interpersonal communication the receiver hears or sees something and interprets it. The separation of visual information from auditory information rarely occurs because meaning is unitary to human communicators in all speech-communication situations. In other words, the immediate sense impressions perceived simultaneously by ears and eyes (and sometimes by other organs as well) are, in fact, inseparable. The incoming combinations of sight and sound information are mixed in some unknown way to produce the meanings elicited in the receiver; although one may attempt to associate a certain meaning with a certain information source in a given instance, we do not know much about how sight and sound information, or even verbal and nonverbal information for that matter, intertwine to produce their effects. For example, one may have observed at one time or another that an utterance such as "I love you" was accompanied by various other sight and sound information which indicated that the speaker actually meant the opposite. Close scrutiny of the way some persons say, "I couldn't care less," often reveals the speaker's strongly felt emotion and indicates that he cares rather more than he wishes to reveal. Try an experiment sometime when you are watching a familiar television program. Turn off the sound, watch the picture, and try to notice the different impressions and meanings conveyed to you. You can often turn disgustingly trite commercials into wild experimental art films in this way. Then turn the sound back on, black out the picture, and try the same comparison with the auditory form. You have done something mechanically which you rarely, if ever, do in interpersonal communication. You have separated the effects of sight information and sound information. The program did not elicit the meaning and impressions in you that it usually did, unless you supplied certain meanings from memory.

Naturally, it is possible to make sense out of a single communication code. Radio programing must work around this very separation since its sole communicative vehicle consists of sound waves. Sometimes radio dramas like Jack Armstrong, Captain Midnight, and I Love a Mystery created striking illusions and works of art by the very absence of the visual aspect of interpersonal communication. The listener was forced to use his imagination to make sense out of the spoken words and the noises emitted from the sound man, and the result was often far more communicative than the reality of sight or the electronic vision provided by television. In other cases too people are capable of making sense out of this separation—the blind and the deaf being two such classes. But, in normal interpersonal-communication situations, not only what you are but also how you say something, whether you have said it before, and what you look like when you say it have a vital and often unanalyzable effect on the reactions of others to what you say. For example, vocal aspects of communication are at least as strong as language content in affecting the cognitions of listeners, according to a number of investigators.[8] Unless the storm is a long way off, we human communicators simply do not separate the lightning from the thunder; meaning is bound up with both.

A large number of books and published studies report the results of extensive research on all aspects of the verbal code; for these we refer you to Part I. On the other hand the aspects of the nonverbal code have been neglected until rather recently. Ruesch and Kees provide a thorough survey of many aspects of nonverbal communication.[9] At the time of writing it is certain only that nonverbal communication is capable of transmitting nuances of meaning yet unknown. We shall say more about nonverbal communication in subsequent sections. Having considered several of the forms in which information is presented to communicators, we shall now consider the users of these forms themselves and the role that information plays in making these communicators what they are when they interact together.

SELF AND SYMBOL

Who is me? Basic to all interpersonal communication is the question, "Who is me?" It is not a silly question to ask from time to time, and one should not be surprised to find that he answers it in dramatically different ways at different times and in different places. There are

[8] See, for example, Paul Ekman, "Differential Communication of Affect by Head and Body Cues," *Journal of Personality and Social Psychology*, 2 (November 1965), 726–35; and, B. G. Rosenberg and Jonas Langer, "A Study of Postural-Gestural Communication," *Journal of Personality and Social Psychology*, 2 (October 1965), 593–97.

[9] Jurgen Ruesch and Weldon Kees, *Nonverbal Communication* (Berkeley, California: University of California Press, 1961).

several reasons for these differences. Me is not a homogeneous block of wood carved from the same tree but a complex of remembered perceptions, cognitions, and bodily sensations from within, and recalled utterances and other sensory impressions from without—in short, a variety of nervous activity. Me is a morass of information filed away for future recall or eventual repression. Me is a million things at once and none of them separately, even though one's data-processing system generously permits one, on occasion, to select his best me from among the many existing combinations of data. The different me's one can detect are just partial selves called to any situation that demands a certain part of me be dominant or brought into focus more than the other parts, according to one investigator.[10] Clusters of information which we call "qualities" and "behaviors" are selected from the combination that is me. The me who studies for and begins to take a test is not the same me who is paralyzed by the "D" on the graded test. Reasonable me gives way to emotional, irrational me; concerned me is always being replaced by indifferent me and vice versa; winner me all too frequently is replaced by loser me, and smart me by average or even dumb me.

A real me is nonexistent then, except as represented by several millions of bits of information encased in a remarkable structure which we call a *body*. This informational me changes from second to second as well as from year to year, as new information pertaining to me is acquired, and old information is temporarily or permanently forgotten. Is there anything that is stable about me—anything that seemingly never changes or changes so imperceptibly as to appear constant at my level of perception? Information about my physical person—the sound of my voice, the visual data of my external body, and the feeling data of my internal body—includes many apparent constants at my level of perception. External objects and persons, even though they may change somewhat over time, may, by their constant presence or proximity to me, comprise relatively stable bundles of information—information that is always dependably available to be identified with the self. These constants of information from body, objects, and other persons in my external environment form a common core of self that endures across the periods of my self-consciousness. We will term the organized entities contained within this common core of information our "self-symbols." These symbols, when present or remembered, are just so much information. But, without the sister me has known since birth, the dandruff me has had since the sixth grade, the coat me has worn for several years, the remembered vocal quality of me; without a family, a job, a name, a

[10] See Erving Goffman, *Interaction Ritual* (Garden City, New York: Doubleday & Company, Inc., 1967), pp. 5–46; and, Goffman, *The Presentation of Self in Everyday Life*, pp. 16–76.

memory, who or what am I? People with amnesia tell us that having no identity is like death. But even amnesia cases can perceive new information which develops a new memory and thereby a new identity. Me is a cybernetic memory, and a developed identity based on that memory is equivalent to what we refer to when we think about or talk about self.

Me is the product of a million triangulations. Like premodern ships' navigators and contemporary surveyors, we keep shooting the sun and plotting our markers to locate ourselves in the chaos of perceptions and information we take in. We look in the mirror in the morning and say to ourselves, "Yup, he's still there." Identifying scars and moles are helpful not only to the FBI but also to millions of me's around the world. All the phenomena discussed above are symbols of ourselves, reminding us of different aspects of ourselves.

The majority of me-reminders are words or verbal symbols. The importance of these verbal symbols to our notion of self is clearly indicated from research studies which show that the kind of symbols one employs in describing himself has a direct relationship to his important life decisions, such as vocational choice.[11] Storage space is less costly for these portable, ethereal properties than for bracelets, automobiles, sisters, and other physical objects. Of course, physical self-symbols— clothes, cars, sundry possessions including houses, wives, things mine and of me in general that have corporeal being—are very important in helping various me's to separate the self from the nonself attributes of the world. But portable self-symbols are probably the most important just because we can and do use them more than any other property. Words are always with us. One's name is the most completely economical, portable self-symbol of all the verbal symbols. Just saying it aloud to one's self or hearing it said by another at a role call or in a distant group of friends (or enemies) fosters immediate self-awareness. "There's Scruddly"; and one thinks to himself, "Yeah, by golly, here I am."

Language plays an important part in our individual mental lives in still another way. We label a complex of phenomena with a verbal symbol and then express the thoughts and feelings we have concerning where we fit, if at all, in relation to these entities. We thereby manage to employ impersonal fictions in the service of our self-description. These entities may be institutions, companies, socioeconomic classes, vocational groups, governments, and even nations and races. Through language we can symbolically contain these entities in a way that we could not if we were to attempt to observe physically all of the actual workings and parts of these phenomena.[12] The institutions and the like

[11] J. Super, "Self and Other Semantic Concepts in Relation to Choice of a Vocation," *Journal of Applied Psychology*, 51 (June 1967), 242–46.
[12] Bois, *The Art of Awareness*, pp. 62–68, 70.

that are so labeled or thought of by a person are, of course, nonexistent in the sense that too many aspects of these entities are not included in the denotations and connotations of the verbal symbol used to describe them. These symbols are reifications, or phenomena that have existence only at the symbolic level. Although it frequently causes communicators difficulty, use of reifications in thought and speech becomes absolutely essential at times when the complexity of such entities demands oversimplification for people to think about, talk about, and deal with them. Personification is one kind of reification. Examples of reifications or personifications familiar to us are Big Business, Government, and Labor. According to a well known psychotherapist, a person may have an interpersonal relationship with a personified entity, with literary characters that represent people, with governments, with churches, and with schools.[13] In all these relationships the personified thing presents a constellation of characteristics, real or imagined, against which the relater gauges and evaluates his own self.

A self-symbol that did not make it easier for us to identify ourselves from others would not be of much value. We all have similarities with and differences from other human beings. Yet, when it is necessary for our self-image, we forget the similarities; when it is convenient in our interpersonal communications, we ignore the differences. Me does have uniquenesses, although it would take more than a million-page self-reference book to keep them all available for handy recall and use. The sources from which our self-defining information comes are just too many and too diverse. Most of us have had a grandmother or an aunt who through her retelling of incidents involving our younger selves has contributed material that we convert into a self-symbol; it then becomes incorporated into the me that we believe. "So that's what I did! I must have been (or maybe still am) a strange bird" (or whatever role characteristics grandma casts us in). Short of hauling around an up-to-date, computerized information system, a million-page personal biography with stenographer attached on a string, or a wonderful grandmother, one must fix on other forms of identity. Verbal abstractions fit the task nicely for, as mentioned before, they are less bulky and easier to maintain, even though they exclude most important and all really personal information concerning one's past and present self.

Communist, Democrat, Republican, hippy, criminal, do-gooder—each of these labels and many more purport to represent important similarities possessed by the members of the class so named. Thus, mass nouns and group labels lend themselves to evaluative statement and thought—both derogatory and complimentary in nature. The information-distortion

---

[13] Patrick Mullahy, "Some Aspects of Sullivan's Theory of Interpersonal Relations," in *Readings in the Psychology of Adjustment*, eds. Leon Gorlow and Walter Katkovsky (New York: McGraw-Hill Book Company, 1959), pp. 180–81.

processes discussed in Part I also support the ease with which self and others may be made to fit into such shallow and unwieldy symbolic slots. The age-old, important epistemological questions like "What is Johnny Carson (or Jimminy) really like?" cannot be answered by us or by the objects of the query despite the claims of the nosey magazines. In the end the only answers that we can rely on are those portable symbols like "performer" (or "cricket"). Beyond that and the rest of the thin symbolic film of self-labels, we are confronted by "randomness"—a mélange of data out of which we must sort the self. It is our memory, with its composite of information, that acts to give an impression of "me-ness" and provides us with the sense of mental and physical continuity that we call *self*.

In discussing the several kinds of symbols that aid one in locating what he is, we stressed the importance of verbal symbols because of two characteristics: (1) as mentioned above, the verbal symbols are exceedingly handy; and (2) they lend themselves quite well to the evaluation of human experience. The all-important process of evaluation will be the focus of the next subsection, where we consider the informational constitution of the human communicator from a perspective different from that of the present discussion.

EVALUATIVE INFORMATION AND EVALUATION

Two writers suggest that human beings have certain important characteristics in greater degree than any other "thing" in the world does.[14] And thus, for one human the most outstanding or dramatic object in his field of perception during his entire life is other humans. Some characteristics which humans have more of according to these writers are mobility, capriciousness, unpredictability, power, sensitivity, and reciprocal reactivity. They point out that other objects in our environment also have some of these characteristics: animals, a vicious stone that falls on us, lightning. But human beings are more powerful, changeable, unpredictable, and capable of threatening or supporting us than anything else which we experience in our world. We must give special attention to other people during every waking moment of our existence for they have the power to affect our bodies, feelings, and our very lives. Other humans are the most significant agents of causality for us.[15] One need not suffer an intimate interpersonal relationship to understand these

[14] David Kretch and Richard Crutchfield, *Theory and Problems of Social Psychology* (New York: McGraw-Hill Book Company, 1948), pp. 9–11.
[15] Fritz Heider, "Consciousness, the Perceptual World, and Communications with Others," in *Person Perception and Interpersonal Behavior*, eds. Renato Tagiuri and Luigi Petrullo (Stanford, California: Stanford University Press, 1958), pp. 27–31.

peculiarly human qualities; observe only the changes in one's behavior—embarrassment or self-consciousness—when after believing he has been alone for some time he is surprised by the presence of a human friend or stranger. One's perceptual and cognitive center of gravity tips wildly in these circumstances and of course in the direction of the human being, even if it is only a child.

The point is that, because of these special traits or attributes that only other human beings possess, we function as concentrated packages of information or loci of meaning that stand out from the other meanings contained in the environment surrounding us. Each human is a potential information center concentrated in a rather small amount of space. Also, persons are spilling over with their information in contrast with the relative reticence of all the other objects and phenomena in the world, whose information scientists have characterized as "secrets" which one must work tediously and luckily to discover. In short, we know what we are largely because of the information we derive from other men and women around us and especially information obtained through interpersonal communication.

A recent investigation added to the growing body of evidence which indicates that those with whom we interact shape the self that we come to recognize.[16] After a strong manipulation designed to persuade the subjects of the undesirability of certain elements which they had ranked as very important to their self-concepts, the subjects continued to place high importance on those elements which five significant others attributed to them. However, they markedly reduced the importance placed on elements for which the five others' opinions were incongruous.[17]

The various *others* in our interpersonal communications are the instruments that can remind us what we are like. The other is the person whom we bounce ourselves off of. How do we look? taste? feel? smell? move? think? act? Are we good or bad? loved or despised? or even unnoticed? We need to be evaluated and to know some things that we can believe about ourselves. The other in our interpersonal communications fulfills this need with no urging. This other is the backboard of our personalities. How can we come to know ourselves except through gauging the reactions of others toward us? What am I? Data pours in. And the question is answered, whether to our satisfaction or not, largely by other persons—persons who are also asking, "What am I?" One noted psychiatrist builds a theory of interpersonal behavior on his conviction that an

[16] Carl Backman, Paul Secord, and Jerry Peirce, "Resistance to Change in the Self Concept as a Function of Consensus Among Significant Others," in *Problems in Social Psychology*, eds. Carl Backman and Paul Secord (New York: McGraw-Hill Book Company, 1966), pp. 462–67.
[17] Backman, Secord, and Peirce, "Resistance to Change in the Self Concept as a Function of Consensus Among Significant Others," pp. 462–67.

individual's sense of self is a direct result of how significant others have treated him.[18]   In two experiments on self-concept Harold Hass and Martin Maehr managed to change the subjects' self-ratings by inducing varying strengths of approval and disapproval for several characteristics. Changes in self-ratings indicated a sensitivity to the different dosages of disapproval and approval used and were durable over the six-week period prior to the delayed posttest.[19]   Man, whether he attends tea parties or not, is indeed a social animal—which is to say, a communicator.

We should not be surprised that a significantly large portion of the self-defining information we take in comes from our interpersonal communication with other people.[20]   We are surrounded by people almost every waking minute of our lives.   Even some of our physiological needs are fulfilled in a manner that accommodates interpersonal communication.   If you doubt this, reflect on your self-consciousness the next time you patronize the campus restaurant alone, if you ever do.   Our deeds, ideas, and our very selves are constantly being evaluated for us through speech communication in many very direct and indirect ways.   If we did not wish to be evaluated by others, we would have a difficult time living in this world.

The child sees himself largely through his parents' eyes; he reacts to parental labels and reactions.   He sees himself as his parents evaluate him, good or bad.[21]   He always prefers to be evaluated as "good," but, like adults, he usually finds that even "bad" is better than no evaluation at all.   In the child, awareness of self begins only after two or three years. Ross Stagner gives three factors that delay this self-awareness process: (1) the child has a very poor memory; (2) an inadequate amount of experience is contained in that memory; (3) the language of the child is not well enough developed to assist his making differentiated responses between experiences that do and those that do not refer to him.[22]

As we grow older we learn to be sensitive to the way others see us. If we do not like what they tell us by what they say and by the way they do not say anything, the magic of our nervous system may desensitize us to some of our potential experience.   Our data-processing mechanism may rearrange information so that some will be lost to our awareness. Then, we may further modify our natures by careful selection of what we

[18] Harry Stack Sullivan, *The Interpersonal Theory of Psychiatry* (New York: W. W. Norton & Company, Inc., 1953).

[19] "Two Experiments on the Concept of Self and the Reaction of Others," *Journal of Personality and Social Psychology*, 1 (January 1965), 100–105.

[20] John J. Sherwood, "Self Identity and Referent Others," *Sociometry*, 28 (1965), 66–81.

[21] For example, see Sidney Jourard and Richard Remy, "Perceived Parental Attitudes, the Self, and Security," *Journal of Consulting Psychology*, 19 (1955), 364–66.

[22] *Psychology of Personality* (New York: McGraw-Hill Book Company, 1961), pp. 184–85.

express about ourselves to others. To complete the cycle, we may so position ourselves that we are less likely to perceive what is objectionable about ourselves and more likely to perceive the data gratifying to ourselves. Much of the despised experience that we cannot avoid is again lost to our awareness, and further selection modifies and omits data which we allow to pass from our awareness to others through oral expression. The selection processes in data reception, interpretation, and expression discussed earlier are thereby intimately tied to what we are to ourselves, to others, and to each interpersonal-communication setting in which we move. Later we shall present a specific formulation of the operation of the above processes in the development of our self-knowledge.

One's self is most evident in a changing environment because such an environment contrasts with the supposedly nonchanging self—with those somewhat consistent traits each of us seems to possess. If you move to a new locale or are a stranger at a party, you notice qualities in you that you never noticed before or had forgotten. Perhaps, just as we learn about ourselves from the social ripples that we make and that wash back over us, so also, in communicating to new others, the depths we are sounding come in different levels and contours than those we have experienced before. We see portions of our self that the behavior of these others toward us permits us to see. Because we relate to a new person with few interpersonal rules to guide us, we are uniquely aware of some self-consistency or selfness and often have happy or unhappy surprises because of these self-disclosures.

Considerable evidence shows that how we evaluate ourselves is in part a function of how we are evaluated by *reference groups*—groups in which we are members and groups that we would like to join. To the extent that these groups approve some values, attitudes, and behaviors and disapprove of others, they provide a reference point with which our own values, attitudes, and behaviors may or may not match up.[23] The way these groups evaluate us can be extremely important for our self-assurance and well-being in addition to adding other dimensions to our self-symbol list. We sift slaps on the back, disapproving glances, being ignored, comments like "that's just perfect" and "*you* again" and selectively retain them all through our communicative lives.

We are so used to being evaluated and are so anxious about the outcomes that often we believe we are being evaluated even when this is

[23] For example, see Herbert Thelen, *The Dynamics of Groups at Work* (Chicago: University of Chicago Press, 1954), pp. 223–42; Muzafer Sherif and Carolyn Sherif, *Reference Groups* (New York: Harper & Row, Publishers, 1964); Alberta Siegel and Sidney Siegel, "Reference Groups, Membership Groups, and Attitude Change," in *Group Dynamics* (2nd ed.), eds. Dorwin Cartwright and Alvin Zander (New York: Harper & Row, Publishers, 1960), pp. 232–40.

not the case. Grim stares have frequently been taken as a negative evaluation of something one has done or said when they derived only from a headache. A letter not received does not mean that a far-off friend has forgotten us, though it has been interpreted in this way. Evaluation from those around us permeates our conversations. From comments about a tot to funeral eulogy—from "what a cute baby" to "he was a fine man"— our lives are one long series of evaluations, both of and from others. Scholastic anxiety is not the only reason students are so very interested in their grades on examinations to the delight of high school teachers and the dismay of college professors. Having the verbal abstractions one has written in a blue book graded is simply an extremely global evaluation of one's person; it is almost like being graded for what you are. In this way we find out or think we find out and sometimes wish we had not found out a great deal concerning the evaluations of a significant other.

Perhaps the demands for clarity and consistency in our attempts to make sense of experience explain the frustrations and anxieties humans suffer in being made to take in many experiences without any accompanying evaluative data with which to sort and order those experiences. We are disturbed, some more than others, until we can evaluate the new man on the job or in the office. Man the evaluator is synonymous with man the communicator. Interpretation is served by the evaluative information derived from social experience. One's self is interpretable only in relation to something outside the self. Objects, events, and people puzzle us when we have no way to relate them to ourselves—they lay unclaimed in a box with a blank address card building up pressure to be priced and moved out to make room for more data. Thus, we witness the drive for snap judgments, the urge to measure people on first impressions, and the tendency to feel uneasy until the uncommitted deliver themselves up for easy interpretation and self-use.

All the forms of evaluative experience and the sources of that experience, when taken together, indicate that an important part of the mechanism through which man interprets experience is devoted to value relations —the ought's and oughtn't's—in his experience. With this as background the following discussion offers one possible explanation of how the process of evaluation develops and proceeds within individual communicators. Among the information that slides past the individual's reception warp are certain data that define value relations in his experience, including data pertaining to what others do and to societal and group norms in thinking, acting, and speaking. These value components of experience indicate the thinking, acting, and speaking which elicit rewards and punishments under certain conditions; indicate sanctions abroad in the environment; indicate rules and conditions under which sanctions are used to the benefit or detriment of others and one's self.

All these single items of information, such as the first time a child witnesses the spanking of another child, combine to form a pattern of locally and societally determined evaluations as they are implicitly and explicitly communicated to the receiving party, in whom they accumulate. The patterns introduced by these accumulated data form the *social grid* of that particular individual.

Experience per se does not necessarily contain any means by which the receiving individual can evaluate or interpret its meaning for his own behavior. No evaluation occurs when a small child knocks over a vase for the first time; he has the same unsuspecting and cheerful mien with which he kisses mama goodnight. In a similar case, a foreign high school student enters the locker room of a football team which has lost its first game of the season and violates the culturally defined sorrow penance being played out by the team members when he suggests a night on the town to live it up. He has not yet learned certain rules of conduct and the trappings of competitively oriented high school athletic programs in the United States. Indeed, as with the child who broke the vase, this incident rapidly adds an evaluative datum to his store of information.

The complex of accumulated evaluative information builds the social grid. Important parts of this evaluative data are the portable verbal symbols, which, as we have seen, fit the requirements of evaluation so well through the formation of abstracted entities and high-order concepts pertaining to classes of people, classes of behaviors, and even classes of acceptable and unacceptable thoughts and ideas. Examples of data that form a social grid are "breaking vases assures pain," "report card 'A's make Daddy smile," and "answering the door without clothes on makes Daddy shout." The social grid is a verbal grid composed of linguistic representations of clusters of experiences which are associated with negative and positive values for the perceiving individual. The particular grid that a person has organized depends on his own collections of experiences and is unique because of that. However, many similarities exist among different social grids, especially among those of persons in the same society, because the evaluative data which order the construction of the grid are drawn from the data of everyday social experience and are conveyed in a common language to the recipient. The social grid is both a result of and, once formed, the source of evaluative experience because it is formed from incoming value experience, and, once formed, it evaluates future incoming experience, thereby producing evaluations of other persons, events, and objects, many of which are manifested in speech and action.

In summary, data with value meanings attached—data that carry information about good/bad, rejected/accepted, and rewarded/punished relations—accumulate to form consistent patterns which become principles of evaluation and which affect future incoming data of all kinds. These principles are in accord with the current socially defined norms and conventions operating in the environment from which the information derives. The accumulating bundle of principles tells the receiver what others prefer and what he will be punished or rewarded for in his acts, thoughts, and communication behavior. Very young children do not have social grids because they do not have the linguistic capacity through which the social grid is organized.[24] In adults and even in adolescents the social grid is the *sine qua non* of evaluation, as the example below and the accompanying discussion of self-concept and self-image describe.

SELF-CONCEPT, SELF-IMAGE, AND SELF-CONSCIOUSNESS

Before we pursue the topics of self-concept, self-image, and self-consciousness, we must implore the reader to look afresh at the complexities of human consciousness within interpersonal communication, even from our recent limited perspective of one human actor. The subtleties of which human thought is capable need no elaboration beyond this pointed, if humorous, example from a novel by John Barth entitled *The Sot-Weed Factor*.[25] Ebenezer Cooke, self-proclaimed poet and virgin, held captive on a pirate ship bound for the colonies in the New World, has just in turn (1) witnessed the rape of the "Cyprian," a whore-bearing ship transporting its product to the colonies; (2) observed with particular fascination while the giant Moorish first mate, Boabdil, climbed the ship's rigging to ravish a member of the ship's cargo who was helplessly entangled high above the deck, where she had taken what Ebenezer believed to be her innocence on first noting the intentions of the boarding pirates; (3) crossed to the captive vessel himself some minutes later, passing by the several willing and indifferent professionals who lined the ship's rail; (4) climbed the ship's rigging with a singularly glandular purpose to a few feet below the ensnared girl; and (5) been summoned back aboard the pirate ship, which was preparing to get under way, thereby frustrating his purpose in the rigging. Some weeks later Ebenezer learned that Boabdil was suffering from the "French pox" or some painful social disease, and the poet, sitting in the hold of the pirate ship, reflected upon what this news along with the above-described events meant for him.

[24] Stagner, *Psychology of Personality*, pp. 184–85.
[25] *The Sot-Weed Factor* (Garden City, New York: Doubleday & Company, Inc., 1960), p. 284.

Ebenezer readily assumed that it was the girl in the mizzen-rigging who had been infected for, though Boabdil had assuredly not confined his exercise to her, none of the other pirates showed signs of the malady. The disclosure gave him a complexly qualified pleasure: In the first place he was glad to see the Moor thus repaid for the rape, yet he quite understood the oddity of this emotion in the light of his own intentions. Second, the relief he felt at so narrowly escaping contagion himself, like the relief at having his chastity preserved for him, failed to temper his disappointment as he thought it should. And, third, the presence of infection suggested that the girl had not been virginal, and this likelihood occasioned in him the following additional and not altogether harmonious feelings: *chagrin* at having somewhat less cause to loathe the Moor and relish his affliction; *disappointment* at what he felt to be a depreciation of his own near conquest; *alarm* at the implication of this disappointment, which seemed to be that his motives for assaulting the girl were more cruel than even the Moor's, who would not have assumed her to be virginal in the first place; *awe* at the double perversity that, though his lust had been engendered at least partially by pity for what he took to be a deflowered maiden, yet he felt in his heart that the pity was nonetheless authentic and would have been heightened, not diminished, during his own attack on her, whereas the revelation that she had not lost her maidenhead to Boabdil materially diminished it; and finally, a sort of overarching *joy* commingled with *relief* at a suspicion that seemed more probable every time he reviewed it—the suspicion that his otherwise not easily accountable possession by desire, contingent as it had been on the assumption of her late deflowering and his consequent pity, was by the very perverseness of that contingency rendered almost innocent, an affair as it were between virgins. This mystic yearning of the pure to join his ravished sister in impurity: Was it not, in fact, self-ravishment and hence a variety of love?

"Very likely," he concluded, and chewed his index fingernail for joy.[26]

The interwoven self-analyses, motivations, feelings, imputed feelings, self-justifications, and condemnations exhibited by Ebenezer may seem farfetched until the reader quickly searches his own experience and inevitably finds ample occasions that vie with this illustration in complexity of thought if not in sameness of circumstance. The example furnishes ample material for aiding exposition of several topics, including that of self-concept.

The pieces of information that pass through the data-warping attributes of reception in a particular individual are facets of his experience of which he is aware or which he apprehends. Depending on the individual, a relatively large or small part of this data has relevance

[26] Barth, *The Sot-Weed Factor*, p. 284.

for his self. Stagner distinguishes between experiences which have self-reference and those which do not.[27] Consider the statements "I love her" and "He loves her." The first expresses an experience or feeling that has self-reference; the latter does not. The experiences connected with the former, or self-referring, statement are self-relevant and form part of the self-concept. All the physical self-symbols discussed in a previous sub-section, to the extent that they belong to one person, have self-relevance for that person. In addition some data that are not self-referring—data that we obtain by reading about others' experiences or data acquired in other ways—may indeed have self-relevance in a particular case. For example, Ebenezer's reflection, "Boabdil has the pox," while lacking self-reference, certainly has self-relevance in Ebenezer's state of affairs. If a datum is lodged in one's attitudes toward other objects in the world in a basic and important way, if it is a part of one's philosophy of life, then this datum has self-relevance even though the verbalized statement gives no outward sign of self-reference. The self-concept is a rather poorly organized mass of information about, around, concerning, and somehow connected with one's self.

All information of experience filters through the above-described social grid, which acts like a censor. Most of these data are evaluated and forgotten or remembered; they are manifest in the pronouncements and actions of the communicator. ("Boabdil is a rat.") Some of the information in the self-concept flows through the social grid to form the self-image of the individual. Thus, the self-image is an abstraction from the self-concept. Only those consistent and well-organized data in the self-concept which meet the test of the social grid participate in the self-image. For example, Ebenezer reflected that, out of pity, he would have given over his highly treasured purity. Of all of the data in his self-concept at that time, only that one abstraction was sufficiently congruent with his social grid to pass into his self-image for future preservation. The lust that he experienced, the suspected cruelty of his attitude, and all the other information violated the socially derived principles of his social grid —his value relations. He resolved these contradictions neatly and in characteristically human fashion without doing damage to his maintenance of a desirable self-image. As Fig. 5 illustrates, the self-image is a product of the editing performed by the socially determined, linguistically structured values in the social grid on the raw material of self-relevant experience in the self-concept.

Once formed, one's self-image provides an easier way for one to conceive of himself than does the unstructured, almost random data batch that constitutes one's self-concept. The individual communicator draws on his self-image for cues to his communicative behavior. The self-image,

[27] Stagner, *Psychology of Personality*, p. 183.

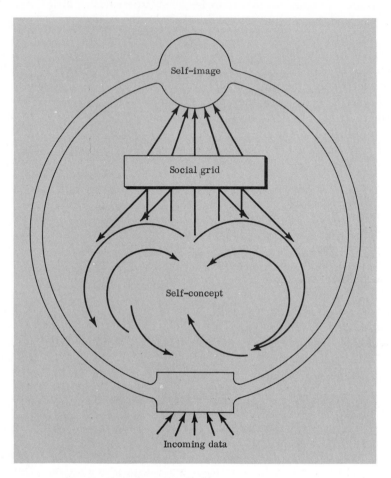

Fig. 5. The informational self.

through its congruent elements and neat verbal packaging of self, comes full circle to modify the way in which original data, including self-relevant data, are received and interpreted. Because it is reinforced selectively by the mediating influence of the social grid, the self-image is naturally more enduring and less subject to sudden change than the self-concept, whose particular combination of data at any one time is likely to possess many inconsistencies. The self-image may set limits on what can be brought to awareness or received at all by a person and thus come to affect the very data-processing mechanisms through which it came into being.

Arthur Combs and Donald Snygg state that the self-construct changes with changing needs.[28]   The self-concept and the self-image, then, are not static mechanisms but vast processes that are constantly changing, the former more rapidly than the latter since order and control characterize self-images to a much greater degree than they do self-concepts. Man's linguistic distinction-making capabilities make this order possible. We have seen how Ebenezer's self-image worked back on his self-concept to effect changes in incoming self-relevant information in a way that was congruent with the unifying elements in his social grid, even eliminating from memory some information that was incongruent with his developed self-image.   It is consistent with the processes described above that repression of too much information may lead to hysteria, too little, to schizophrenia.[29]

Finally, the self-image may be connected to the world of other people, places, and events, and these data are also fair game for orderly distortion, repression, and restructuring—all processes which bring available information into line with the existing self-image.   Note how Ebenezer used the purity factor of his self-image to ally himself with the girl in the mizzen, whose former purity he had mistakenly assumed.   The somewhat edited pool of incoming data is likely to reinforce the demands of the self-image since the editing is accomplished through components of that self-image.   The self-image and the less manageable self-concept together with the world of self-irrelevant information are thus brought into a more orderly and less random state than that which they are actually in.   Carl Rogers describes this problem as an unceasing attempt on the part of persons to maximize the congruence among their awareness, experience, and behavior.[30]   One can better understand infinite complexity when it is simplified.   If we can obtain a perspective on our world and ourself, we can proceed to communicate and act with some degree of confidence and purpose—assets which our fictionalized world of self and nonself makes possible.   Having much mutually incongruous data from which to derive meaning, Ebenezer went through a very complicated chain of reasoning to achieve his simplistic interpretation—faced, as he was, with the unacceptable alternative of radically changing his self-image.   That this alternative did occur to him indicates a measure of sophistication and introspection that few of us possess.   Ebenezer is almost sure to forget some of the more threatening aspects of his experience.   He will remember his near sacrifice at least until the end of the novel.   Similarly one remembers an important trophy or honor bestowed

---

[28] *Individual Behavior* (rev. ed.) (New York: Harper & Row, Publishers, 1959), pp. 157–64.
[29] Jurgen Ruesch, "The Role of Communication in Therapeutic Transactions," *Journal of Communication*, 13 (September 1963), 138.
[30] *On Becoming a Person* (Boston: Houghton Mifflin Company, 1961), pp. 338–46.

on him as an integral part of his self until death, while his perennial cheating on income tax returns may be lost to memory immediately.

Self-relevant data accumulates to form our existential self, the "thing" that we are never able to explain or describe to others or even to ourselves. The self-concept may best be described as the disorganized I/me/mine feelings that the continuity of our cybernetic memory makes possible. The self-image on the other hand is organized and multi-faceted, and later we shall see how we draw on different parts of it in different interpersonal-communication situations.

Consciousness of self was prerequisite to Ebenezer's relational self/ other thoughts and indeed is necessary to the development of any self-image at all. Edward Gross and Gregory Stone write that children are embarrassed by loss of identity, poise, and confidence, and that this loss of self-equilibrium when tripped, shamed, or caught in an awkward position serves a valuable socializing function.[31] Self-consciousness in one form at least reaches its zenith in adolescence, according to these two investigators. In studying over 1000 cases of embarrassing incidents from almost as many people, they conclude that people recall suffering the largest incidence of embarrassing moments during adolescence. Certainly, consciousness of mannerisms in speech and bodily movement, and sensitivity about how one looks, acts, and speaks are parts of adolescence which we all remember. What adults often refer to as giddiness, growing pains, excessive shyness, and the awkward age are actually preparation for the demands of the social roles that adolescents will have to perform throughout their lives—roles in which interpersonal communication does not always go smoothly.

Many of the processes discussed above in connection with self and symbol, evaluation, and self-image seem to be closest to the surface or most visibly manifested during adolescence.[32] This age period is permeated with a search for social support through the quest to be like others. Support is gained largely through verbal abstractions like popular and smart and differentiating down to more easily achieved and more specific subgroup values such as wild, sexy, attractive, cool, and fashionable. One writer even recalls how he developed pride, strong interpersonal relationships, and a sense of self-identity when he dubbed his group of five socially outcast high school boys "the rejects," thereby

[31] "Embarrassment and the Analysis of Role Requirements," in Backman and Secord, pp. 383–94. Erving Goffman's essay on "Embarrassment and Social Organization" argues that the functions of embarrassment impose heavily on face-to-face communication among adults as well. Goffman, *Interaction Ritual* (Garden City, New York: Doubleday & Company, Inc., 1967), pp. 97–112.

[32] Elizabeth Hurlock, *Adolescent Development* (New York: McGraw-Hill Book Company, 1955), pp. 102–85, 463–500. For excellent case studies of these processes in adolescents, see Sherif and Sherif, *Reference Groups*.

redefining many potentially embarrassing and self-testing events as humorous and nonthreatening irrelevancies for members of his group. These problems of coping—of learning how to react—present a challenge to the adolescent. His response may (1) further define and establish his self-image and (2) embody valuable training through adjustment to threats to his interpersonal-communication behavior at a time when the stakes are not very high because the demands of his developing self-image are not so exacting—not so fully elaborated—as they will be later in his adult life. This flexibility allows the unbalanced adolescent to apply a broader range of acceptable solutions in his attempt to come out of an evaluatively loaded situation "smelling like a rose" . . . or at least a geranium. Communication responses thus learned help fix his self in social space.

Keeping the self-image intact during interpersonal communication is basic to the ability of an individual to communicate effectively in a given situation. The self-image is the starting point or base line from which the communicator must adjust. To communicate at all, one must have information and an acceptable or at least tolerable self-image. The information contained in the self-image on what one is or thinks one is organizes what one says and does. Unfortunately for many would-be communicators no one knows the precise rules through which one's self-image may be changed in a controlled way and in a facilitative direction. Hopefully, it will encourage some to know that changes can be brought about, as indicated by the earlier references to experimental and psychiatric manipulations of self-image.[33] We speculate that a rapidly changing self-image or a truncated self-image, as in adolescents, probably produces less effective interpersonal communication than a fully developed self-image does.

C. G. Jung defines *self* as the product of intrapersonal communication, or the behavioral result of the dialogue between unconscious values and conscious experience that is going on within every person.[34] Presumably, intrapersonal communication may occur independently from as well as in relation to interpersonal communication.[35] That is, in a world without other humans, Adam could still perceive, interpret, and express information; we discussed these processes in some detail in the first part of this book. Here in Part II we have taken liberties with the intra- and interpersonal distinction in order to discuss important tendencies of human information processors which cannot be confined to either realm but which are important bases of interpersonal communication. The

[33] See Sullivan, *The Interpersonal Theory of Psychiatry;* and, Hass and Maehr, "Two Experiments on the Concept of Self and the Reaction of Others."
[34] Donald Washburn, "Intrapersonal Communication in a Jungian Perspective," *Journal of Communication,* 14 (September 1964), 131–35.
[35] Washburn, "Intrapersonal Communication in a Jungian Perspective," pp. 132–33.

previous subsections dealt with some of the important aspects of information-processing in the human being as those processes affect and are
affected by social interaction. These discussions provide the groundwork
for the analysis of dyadic communication systems and small-group communication systems in the two subsequent sections.

Dyadic
Communication

It should now be clearer why intrapersonal- and interpersonal-communication processes are best viewed as interacting processes, for some purposes at least. The information which humans process that is most important for their conscious lives is that information which comes through interpersonal communication. The widely held view that "the core of all psychiatric therapies is the improvement of the communication behavior of the patient"[1] provides additional evidence of the interconnectedness of self and interpersonal communication.

Thus far we have been discussing self and other in a separate fashion, but the reader knows that in interpersonal communication at least two "selves" are involved—two mutually initiating and responding persons. The processes discussed so far are occurring at the same time in both parties. They do not occur as two separate processes but as one interinfluential set of behaviors and consciousnesses which reshape one another from moment to moment as information flows. Face-to-face communication between two persons, or *dyadic* communication, is mutually influential to the parties involved. It is best viewed as an ongoing process rather than as a static happening with a beginning, causal speaker/listener relations, and an ending. For example, while one person is receiving information, he may also be transmitting information, as with the person who, intent on listening to the remarks of another, reacts visibly and meaningfully throughout the time the other is talking. In this sense communication in dyads is truly an information-sharing process at a particular stage of development and not just an encounter between two separate entities. An integration occurs in which both sources of information are influenced and changed by the other. The static relationship is nonexistent; relationships are always growing or

---

[1] Jurgen Ruesch, "The Role of Communication in Therapeutic Transactions," *The Journal of Communication*, 13 (September 1963), 138. Although this view is by no means shared throughout psychiatry and psychotherapy, it has gained substantial support from influential psychiatrists and clinical psychologists. But, see O. Hobart Mowrer, *The New Group Therapy* (Princeton, New Jersey: D. Van Nostrand Co., Inc., 1964); and, Jourard, *The Transparent Self*.

diminishing, narrowing or broadening, exploding or disappearing. Yet we still feel and talk as though our person is complete, unified, and constant. We continue to think of ourself and the other as intact little packages which have never been opened. But, in fact, the very process of sharing information or of relating demands that we dump out old contents, add new material, and reshape and repack ourselves constantly as we move from one dyad to another.

DYADIC COMMUNICATION IN SOCIAL ROLES

Processes which facilitate man's capacity to interpret his experience are present throughout all human communication. Some of these facilitative processes which we have already discussed include self-concept, self-image, linguistic oversimplification, evaluation, and reification. Whether one wants to say that these processes facilitate communication because they build a phoney world for us by lying to distort "reality" or because they make things simpler than they really are, the fact is that, because these processes all help in some way to prune the glut of information around us into interpretable patterns, we are able to interpret experience and to communicate that interpretation to other people who, using the same pruning equipment, are usually able to make sense out of the experience. Facilitative processes pervade all levels of human functioning, including that perceptual process we place so much faith in called *vision*. The reader knows that his vision has a limited range and that he finds it convenient to aid it by both micro- and telescopic apparatus. Psychology textbooks present scores of line drawings and figures for which our visual perception is fallible or ambiguous. After studying the effects of cultural and regional settings on visual perception, several investigators conclude that individuals draw *visual inferences* according to the visual learning experiences presented by their particular visual environments.[2] Further evidence of the faultiness, or distortion character, of our vision, so physicists tell us, is that many things which appear to be rather solid, immobile, and impenetrable, like chairs, tables, and mountains, are, at the atomic level of reality, just whirling and fantastically complex energy concentrations in some sort of balance. They tell us that all matter may be construed as energy and that there is no solid matter, as we understand that concept, anywhere in our world. Seeing may be believing—but only at the truncated human level of perception, where we find people sitting on chairs and writing on tables. If

[2] Marshal H. Segal, Donald T. Campbell, and Melville J. Herskovits, *The Influence of Culture on Visual Perception* (New York: Bobbs-Merrill Company, Inc., 1966), pp. 213–14.

one does not agree that the imperfection of vision is facilitative, think of writing on a desk or sitting on a chair while your eyesight performs at the level of the powerful electron microscope. Consider the assaults on your heart that the possession of X-ray and telescopic vision would produce in a world of continual earthquakes and exploding suns.

The communication-facilitation processes whether they be at the level of receiving, interpreting, or expressing experience all have one feature very much in common—that of *abstraction;* that is, they leave out, distort, and rearrange information. Omitting information gives a degree of consistency to some of these processes. It gives complete consistency, for example, to visual data at the subatomic level. We never see the smallest subatomic energy patterns with the eye, aided or unaided. At other levels of visual data—color, shape, amount of detail, and emphasis—there is less consistency since perceived properties of a single object vary with individuals and within the same individual from one occasion to the next. The hungry man spots the small sandwich in a complicated picture before anything else; the otherwise satisfied man, the nude pin-up.

In the realm of social interaction as well, linguistic abstraction and the incomplete perception of persons facilitate individual interpretation, although, as one might suspect, interpersonal communication is most threatened when abstraction processes proceed according to different rules in two different persons who are attempting to communicate. The abstraction process works like this. For experience to be interpreted by a human, it must be refined, blocked out, rearranged, sorted, and labeled by his limited data-processing equipment. But, since the same abstraction processes occur in other human beings with somewhat different results, information-sharing encounters many difficulties from the resultant incongruous data sets and interpretations. Just as one man employs a number of physiological, nervous, and linguistic facilitators through whose abstraction function he is able to find some meaning in his experience, so in dyadic communication facilitative processes exist which serve interpersonal communication; they serve both the two persons and the space that separates them. We may best view *role sets* as one of these communication-facilitation processes.[3] Like its cousins, it performs an abstracting function for human communicators. The other processes discussed thus far serve communication at the atomistic level by facilitating individual interpretation of experience.

[3] The concept of *role set* used throughout this section on dyads is *not* similar to Thibaut and Kelley's concept of *set* as used in their work on dyads. And our role set is not to be confused with Goode's conceptual use of that term. See John W. Thibaut and Harold H. Kelley, *The Social Psychology of Groups* (New York: John Wiley & Sons, Inc., 1959), pp. 11–12; and, William J. Goode, "A Theory of Role Strain," in *Problems in Social Psychology,* eds. Carl Backman and Paul Secord (New York: McGraw-Hill Book Company, 1966), p. 373.

Role set is the first process we shall discuss that serves communication at the molecular level by facilitating an interindividual, or social, phenomenon. In the next several sections we shall elaborate the concept of role set—a concept which we feel is valuable in understanding and inquiring into communication in dyads.

ROLE SET

A role set is a cluster of expectations regarding a number, large or small, of norms of speech and of other communication behavior pertaining to communication between a pair of positions. A role set, furthermore, exists exclusively to facilitate communication in that particular dyad from which it has evolved. These expectations pertain to such matters in a dyad as how to proceed in general, whether deference is demanded or expected, which forms of address and style of language are to be used, and what the climate of verbal interaction (including degree of spontaneity and pace) is. Each of the two positions in the set is filled by a person whose conduct is influenced to a certain degree by the aforementioned expectations regarding norms of communication behavior while in that dyad.

A particular role set influences the two persons occupying the positions in a dyad and the interpersonal relationship between those persons. A role set does not prescribe all the behavior in its dyad. The behavior finally produced in the dyad is a product of the interaction between the two selves occupying the positions and the role set pertaining to that dyad. We shall say more about this interaction in subsequent sections.

Role-set expectations always apply to the relationship in the dyad and never to only one position since a norm of interpersonal communication may not affect one position in dyadic communication without affecting the other. Because norms evolve from the communicative demands of the task or social activity of the dyad and from the needs of the persons in the dyad, the norms facilitate the relationship and thereby are facilitative to both positions as well.

We shall compare several facets of role set to conventional role theory to clarify the above points. In conventional role theory a single position is the unit which generates a role. The role carries rights and obligations that are attached to the position around which the role has evolved. In role theory one position with its role may be related to many other positions and their associated roles at once, as in a small group. The behavior emanating from the person filling a particular role is a product of (1) situational factors, (2) the role characteristics of that position, and (3) the unique properties of the person filling that position at that time. The latter includes the extent to which the person is aware of, is willing to, and is capable of performing the role.[4] Role set contrasts with role (see Fig. 6) in that expectations in the former have evolved from the communication activity of specific pairs of positions, and therefore norms specifically germane to a particular pair relationship, like doctor/patient and employee/employer, have selectively endured to facilitate and automate the relationship in that dyad. While role is a position-centered concept and is applicable to many human communication situations, role set is relationship centered and is applicable only to dyadic communication.

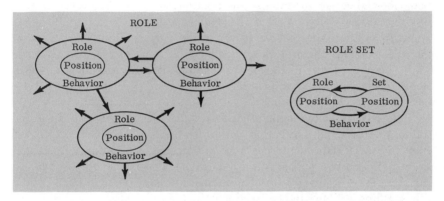

Fig. 6. Structural comparison of role set theory and role theory.

Another contrast between role and role set derives from the fact that communication norms by definition do not necessarily need to be interpreted as being advantageous to or in the possession of a single person or position because they pertain to an interpersonal phenomenon—one which subsumes both positions in the dyad. A norm of communication, when adhered to or recognized or expected, simultaneously influences the behavior of both positions in the dyad and is as much an obligation or right for one position as it is for the other. For example, expectation in a particular role set may provide that position A never will be permitted to interrupt position B. In the language of conventional role theory this norm may be called the right of position B and the obligation of position A toward position B. It thereby confers some power on position B. But, in a role-set formulation of the dyad, the norm is neither the right nor the obligation of one position or the other because a posi-

[4] Theodore Sarbin, "Role Theory," in *Handbook of Social Psychology,* ed. Gardner Lindzey (Reading, Massachusetts: Addison-Wesley Publishing Co., Inc., 1954), pp. 223–58.

tion by itself is just a fraction of the dyad from which that norm evolved. For example, Gergen and Wishnov studied the effect of the perceived self-evaluation of a partner on the self-concept one communicates to that partner in a dyad.[5] Self-centered self-evaluations from partners cause a person to communicate more positive evaluations of his own self, and self-deprecating self-evaluations from partners cause one to communicate a more negative evaluation of his own self than that which he communicates with partners who communicate an evaluatively mixed or average self-concept. This emerging norm governing communicated self-evaluations to one another is equally binding on both positions in the dyad. The norm influences the overall character of the communication behavior and serves to stabilize the relationship—to maintain the dyadic task or social activity. Within the dyad, one norm, as in the above example, may affect the relative power of the persons filling the positions, but the positions themselves are defined by and locked into the role set. Therefore, many of the power relationships are defined in advance by the communicative norms in the role set. Power relationships will be considered in a later section.

Role sets are of two general kinds—*traditional* and *unique*. In a traditional role set the norms that constitute the set have been abstracted from the social data of the past and are located within an interpersonal event in which two persons occupy positions associated with the task or social activity of the dyad. Traditional role sets include such dyadic relationships as husband/wife, doctor/patient, lawyer/client, and employee/employer. Because of their prevalence and importance to society, expectations have evolved pertaining to communication in those dyads. These communication norms have derived from the nature of the task activity and have a task-maintenance function. For example, in a doctor/patient dyad occupants of both positions assume that direct orders from the doctor will be followed by the patient. These role sets, once established, exist regardless of the persons who fill the positions in the dyad and are passed down through generations in the society in which these particular dyads are found. They are ready made for the persons who come to those positions.

A position within a traditional role set is *stylized* to some degree. Two positions in a set may be *balanced* or *unbalanced* depending on the relative stylization of the two positions. Power differences are defined in an unbalanced traditional set when positions within the set differ in stylization because of the time each person spends in his position in that dyad. For example, in the unbalanced sets priest/parishioner and

---

[5] Kenneth Gergen and Barbara Wishnov, "Others' Self-Evaluations and Interaction Participation as Determinants of Self Presentation," *Journal of Personality and Social Psychology*, 2 (1965), 348–58.

dogcatcher/dogowner, the latter position in each case is the less stylized because the occupants of the former positions spend more time in that dyad.

The second major category of role set is the unique role set. These sets are not ready made like the traditional sets but form during the lifetime of persons filling the positions and cease to exist when the particular relationship ends. A traditional role set is structured by the demands of the principle activity of its dyad; a unique role set is structured by the individuals who fill the positions and who communicate together in many activities. For some traditional dyads like husband/wife and neighbor/neighbor, it may not be possible to identify a primary activity. As two persons spend much time in a dyad in different settings performing different activities, a unique role set replaces, wholly or in part, the traditional set. A traditional role set is characterized by its task-maintenance functions; a unique role set may be characterized by its person-maintenance functions.

A unique role set emerges when a particular dyadic relationship between persons forms and grows in complexity. Friendship and acquaintance dyads may form a unique role set, consisting of some norms of expected behavior pertaining only to that particular dyad. Any dyadic communication between the same partners, if recurrent, forms a unique role set from observed, successful communication behaviors. An acquaintance is formed. The two people meet and share information. As they interact together speech and other communication norms develop which later come to govern corners of their relationship in future meetings. Normative behaviors of the past generate expectations for the future. An increasing number of expectations which are fulfilled in the dyad define the developing unique role set for the two persons. In a unique role set one person occupies the same position all the time; therefore stylization of the positions is always in balance in unique sets.

Traditional and unique role sets are not always separate processes. In some dyads they merge. In one dyad a traditional role set may be replaced by a unique set. A doctor/patient traditional role set may change to a unique role set when the doctor moves next door. It is also possible for one traditional set to supplant another traditional set within the same dyad. For example, when the doctor in the doctor/patient set moves next door, another traditional set like neighbor/neighbor, one with more balance, may supplant the former set. In these cases it is not unusual to observe traces of the old set still active in the dyad, as in the case of the person who, communicating within a neighbor/neighbor set, becomes embarrassed when he realizes he has been discussing, in a neighborly fashion, a recent illness and his own best remedy for it with his neighbor-doctor. Overlapping and merging role sets are more common to dyads than the single role set is; we shall discuss such sets in another section.

The extent to which dyadic communication is guided and governed by role sets is suggested by an analysis of what happens when role sets merge or change. Changes in the location of the dyad may often precipitate a merger. For example, when a friend or colleague becomes one's boss, a former unique set may change to a traditional employer/employee set. Adjustments must be made to alter the initial ambiguity and uncertainty of both positions while the changeover is being accomplished. Traces of the unique role set will likely remain or fall off gradually, while demands of the new set will modify, for better or worse, the old relationship. Protocols in speech and manner suddenly become matters of self-conscious concern and attention until the merger is consummated through additional communication.

A role set may be barren and contain only a few expectations, or it may be elaborate and contain many norms of communication for a dyad. If the dyad is too barren of norms and thereby barren of behavioral expectations, it does not contain a role set at all. We shall consider some barren sets in the section on balance in role sets.

ORIGINS AND FUNCTIONS OF A ROLE SET

Role sets are socially derived processes which owe their existence and natures to the communicating human performers who have established them during dyadic communication. To know that the floor will not drop out from under you, to know that the other will not hit you in the nose or embarrass you or ask you a question you cannot answer are all security-oriented desires, self-protection devices; they spawn the probing, searching behavior that individuals engage in during dyadic-communication events. To know what one can expect within limits is all one can ask in this unpredictable world. Role sets serve these very basic needs.

What can you expect or predict about a particular person? This question often occupies our minds before we enter into a communication dyad; we try to guess the other's mood and thoughts. Of course, we can predict personal behavior in some of our closer friends up to a point. The extreme case of interpersonal predictability is that of husband/wife dyads in which the participants know what the other is thinking and often say the same word or phrase at the same time. This predictability is not a supernatural event but the natural outcome of intense information-sharing over a long period of time. Those involved become tuned in to one another and react in the same way to an event presented to them in the same way at the same time. The friend who looks at you across the room and communicates that he is thinking what you are thinking by that glance is the friend with whom you have probably lived, worked, or spent a great deal of time sharing experiences and information. For your wife or husband and your friend, you are better able to forecast ideas, reactions to others, and feelings in general than you are for any others you know. In this way expectations build up over a period of time, following norms of behavior which we come to expect from that other.

Of course, often, just when we think we know someone, he violates our expectations in such a way that we wonder if we really know him at all. These surprises tell us that there is indeed more to this person than we shall ever know; with him as with all others the regularity of the familiar current hides less obvious eddies and occasional riptides. Even in these instances our unique role set with that person provides the base of expectations which smooths our communicative voyage.

Traditional role sets are no less helpful. Strangers violate our expectations more often than do those we feel we know; or probably we are less likely to venture a guess about an unknown person than about more familiar people. Familiar faces that are scant more than names or titles in our information store do not give us a sufficient basis for confidence or accuracy in our speculations concerning their behavior and feelings. Dyadic communication with these people rests very heavily on the appropriate traditional role set, the stereotyped bundle of expectations pertaining to that dyad. Our ability to predict what others think about events, institutions, and ourselves increases as the complexity and intensity of our dyadic communication increases through more frequent interpersonal communication.[6] Even before this familiarity point is reached however, a role set permits behavior to proceed according to the developed norms on which the participants have learned to rely.

Often we delude ourselves in our quest for stability of expectations, reading qualities into others that just are not present or are present in lesser amounts than those which we surmise. Evidence indicates that our feelings toward another and our perceptions of his feelings toward us are fairly congruent.[7] We usually feel that those we dislike also dislike us whether they do or not. This congruency may be modified when interpersonal cues from the other are unambiguous in revealing their feelings toward us. But we tend to change our feelings and attitudes

[6] Theodore Newcomb, "Aspects of the Acquaintance Process," in *Science and Human Affairs*, ed. Richard Farson (Palo Alto, California: Science and Behavior Books, 1965), pp. 89–91; Theodore Newcomb, *The Acquaintance Process* (New York: Holt, Rinehart & Winston, Inc., 1961), pp. 260–61.
[7] Renato Tagiuri, "Social Preference and Its Perception," in Tagiuri and Petrullo, pp. 316–36.

toward another to match our perception of the other's attitudes and feelings toward ourselves.

Liking plays a very important part in our dyadic communication with
others and is related to our attitude preferences and our perception of
others' attitudes in a very intricate way. Taylor studied attitudes toward
issues and sentiment for partner, using one confederate role player in
each dyad in an attempt to test aspects of the interpersonal balance
theories of Hieder and Newcomb.[8] He found that when one likes his
partner but is attitudinally incompatible with him or when one dislikes
his partner but is attitudinally compatible with him, one changes his
attitude toward the issue or his liking for the partner or both more than
he does in dyads in which his liking and attitude compatibility are in a
balanced state. However, when one's perception of how much the
partner likes him is manipulated in relation to attitude compatibility,
changes in attitude and sentiment are no greater in unbalanced than in
balanced conditions. We tend to like those with whom we feel we have
most in common. We migrate toward those whom we perceive are most
like ourselves in their attitudes and in other respects.[9] In general, the
more we communicate with another the more we probably like him;
and the more we like him the more we communicate with him. Yet, on
what little information do we make that initial decision about who is like
us and who is not! Many of the bonds we form might have been
formed as easily with another had we only moved in his direction.
After a time we perceive those we like as being better in almost everything—smarter, nicer, better looking—than those with whom we are not
on such a friendly basis. Our perceptions change with the relationship
in both positive and negative cases. Our friends shine brightly, and our
enemies are just plain rotten. Our evaluative mechanisms load all information pertaining to these relationships with a bias plus or a bias
minus. We are human. Not only is love blind, but so are hate and
friendship and repulsion.

We are more secure when we can define a situation—when we can
label it and when we can predict the limits of the other person's behavior. These sets of expectations facilitate interpersonal communication by simplifying matters which must pass between persons. Role sets
provide guidelines that, when followed, smooth information-sharing that
pertains to the task or social activity at hand.

We have here a special interest in the effect of role sets on speech

---

[8] Howard F. Taylor, "Balance and Change in the Two-Person Group," *Sociometry*,
30 (1967), 262–79. For Heider's theory see Fritz Heider, *The Psychology of
Interpersonal Relations* (New York: John Wiley & Sons, Inc., 1958), pp. 174–217.
For Newcomb's theory see *The Acquaintance Process*, pp. 4–23.

[9] See Donn Byrne and Ray Rhamey, "Attraction as a Linear Function of Positive
Reinforcements," *Journal of Personality and Social Psychology*, 2 (1965), 884–89;
and, Newcomb, *The Acquaintance Process*, pp. 195–220.

communication—the most important and elaborated mode of interpersonal communication. A role set is extremely valuable for dyadic communication as a linguistic economizing device. It demarcates what may go unsaid, yet understood. A role set instructs, "Don't bother about thus and so during the next X minutes, hours, or weeks because you both know our purpose here. Concentrate your entire attention and energy on the task at hand and forget the mass of interpersonal data that is defined as irrelevant in this situation." A role set serves the task demands and personal demands on a dyad by blocking out much communication and random stimulation as irrelevant to the immediate situation and by staking out the give and take aspects of balance and information-sharing in the dyad. Since interpersonal behavior is largely speech behavior, a role set modifies and structures speech communication more than it does any other dimension of information-sharing. A role set even defines a "grammar" and a "syntax" of interpersonal communication as it provides for appropriate language content and appropriate language combination for the dyadic event within which the communication occurs.

A role set facilitates communication in ways too numerous to mention. It focuses discussion on features relevant to the task, even if the task is social. It guides performers in what to do and say. It allows performers to communicate more efficiently on a narrow range of behavioral concern through what Sullivan terms *selective inattention*.[10]

Like many other facets of communication that we have studied, role sets are continually changing because social data are coming in all the time and expectations for a particular role set change over time. Old abstractions crumble around the edges and re-form to produce new sets of behavioral expectations. Even traditional sets change as the people filling those positions deviate in the same way and in great number over a long period of time. Subtle changes in the functions or the locations of the task activity of a dyad are other forces for change in the expectations of a traditional role set. One example is the changes that have gradually occurred over the last several decades within the United States in the professor/student role set. A unique role set changes when the circumstances demand a revised definition of the relationship for the best possible facilitation of that interpersonal event.

BALANCE IN TRADITIONAL ROLE SETS

The expectations constituting traditional role sets have been abstracted from the communication behavior in dyads in the past. These role sets—doctor/patient, for example—contain elements which have

---

[10] Harry Stack Sullivan, *Clinical Studies in Psychiatry* (New York: W. W. Norton & Company, Inc., 1956), pp. 38–76.

economically built up through usage—through the winnowing process that probably started a long time ago when the medicine man found it desirable for his income and status to keep a roomful of tribesmen waiting rather than to schedule visits too far apart, and when the tribesmen found it advisable to wait if they wanted attention. A dyad produces a role set when that dyad occurs sufficiently often to accumulate observable norms of behavior. These norms then become expectations which influence all the persons who on some occasion fill one of the positions in that dyad. If no norms are present to guide communication in a dyad, that dyad has no role set—it is barren. A man strolling by the beach hears someone in the water yelling for help, runs into the water, and pulls the nearly drowned victim ashore, thereby saving his life. This saver/saved dyad has not occurred with enough regularity in our society for any norms of communication to accrue to it. This dyad is completely barren; it lacks a traditional role set. No expectations guide the interaction as a peek at the embarrassed, uncertain communication of felt obligations and "never minds" following the rescue reveals. There is, of course, a likelihood that another kind of role set, a unique role set, will develop if, as a result of the fortunate rescue, the principals commit themselves to additional frequent encounters.

On the other hand, a husband/wife dyad is grounded in a major cultural institution, and, because marriage is so popular, it has a high incidence of occurrence. Therefore this dyad has spawned a veritable encyclopedia of expectations. It is, or can be, the most elaborated of all possible dyads. A dyad generates a role set only if it is deemed important in a society or if it occurs rather frequently. A role set varies in the number of communicative rules it contains, ranging from the highly elaborated husband/wife set down through the less elaborated but more than barren sets of doctor/patient, colleague/colleague, neighbor/neighbor, and the like. Husband/wife dyads are played by professionals, while saver/saved dyads are played by amateurs. This observation is not a reflection on the ability of the persons filling those dyads. It is only a natural result of the number of norms contained in each dyad.

In the examples of role sets cited so far, you may have noticed that the positions in some sets seem to be unbalanced while in others the positions seem to be equivalent. We attribute this balance phenomenon to the amount of time each person spends in his position relative to the amount of time the other spends in his position. People who spend roughly the same amount of time in their position within a dyad are peers; they are on equal footing in terms of their role set. Examples are husband/wife and neighbor/neighbor dyads. Norms in unbalanced sets establish dominant/submissive relations. We propose that the more time one spends in his position in a traditional role set the more stylized his behavior becomes in that dyad. A heavily stylized position confers a great deal of regularity in the behavior of the occupant of that position. In an unbalanced role set gross differences exist between the degree of stylization of the two persons filling those positions. These differences are a direct function of the time each spends in that dyad. An example of a position in an unbalanced role set is the doctor who sees 40 or 50 patients every week. His communication behavior in the doctor position in one of his numerous doctor/patient dyads is clearly more stylized than that of any of his many patients. Communication guidelines have structured or automated whole segments of his communication behavior compared to that of the uncertain patient.

The unbalanced nature of this role set stems from the specialist nature of medical activity. Garage mechanics, policemen, several brands of consultants, and many others share this specialist character. It has long been necessary, since there are more patients than doctors, for doctors to spend more time being doctors than for patients to spend being patients within the doctor/patient dyad. In these unbalanced role sets, the communicative initiative is on the side of the specialist, whose stylizations of communication from one dyad to the next economize energy that may then be directed to the task.

The highly stylized position is less subject to influence than is the less stylized one. We do not imply that a patient or a similar position in an unbalanced role set lacks stylization completely. But the relative inexperience of the patient or the car owner means that he is usually very susceptible to influence and somewhat uncertain and self-conscious in his communication behavior, unlike the other member of the dyad. There are occasional exceptions to our above generalization that dyads connected with a certain activity are always unbalanced. For example, differences in stylization within a mental patient/psychiatrist dyad may be very small if the patient has been undergoing therapy for a number of years. Patients, as well as other communicators, develop economy in expression, psychiatric knowledge and vocabularies, and all of the stylizations that sensitivity and time permit.

We shall draw on a barren dyad (a nonrole set) to further clarify the nature of stylization and the unbalanced role set. In a movie-goer/usher dyad the usher spends more time ushering than the movie goer spends being ushered. As in the case of the doctor/patient dyad the position for which the activity is more central (doctor and usher) is the more heavily stylized. A large portion of the communication behavior of persons occupying these positions is highly structured and is more nearly identical than that of their numerous, successive complements. However, we shall not continue to pretend that the usher/movie-goer dyad carries an attached role set. According to our definition it is barren of norms for communication behavior. In summary stylized positions produce stylized behavior on the part of a person while he is occupying that position. These stylizations are part of the expectations that go to form the role set and are used by both positions to ease the demands of interpersonal communication.

In a balanced role set, there are no a priori rules establishing a necessary or expected ascendancy of one position in the dyad over the other position. In other words either position in that set is no more central to the activity of that dyad (husband/wife, for example) than the other. Of course, everything is not equal in balanced role sets, and in some one performer has clear-cut control. Balance merely means that the positions are equal in stylization and that, unless we know the persons filling a particular set or have observed their interaction, we have no data that permit us to predict with any accuracy which performer will exert more influence on the emerging interaction pattern. We do not say "influence the other" because the reciprocal and contingent nature of human interaction, discussed in a previous section, sets a base line up to which each person necessarily influences the other, even in drastically unbalanced sets.

Remembering that dyadic communication is reciprocally influential— that each performer influences behavior to some degree even in unbalanced role sets—we may view balance as being on a continuum running from such unbalanced role sets as doctor/patient to such balanced sets as husband/wife. We must draw inferences about influence patterns in all dyads very carefully. What we see and hear in a dyad at any one time may not represent the overall pattern of that dyad. Examine, for example, a job interview—an unbalanced role set according to our definition (prospective employer/prospective employee). The prospective employee, the less stylized position in the set, may at one or several points so deviate from expected communication norms that he strongly directs the path taken by the interaction. An unexpected statement by the applicant might shake the composure of the prospective employer and momentarily throw the employer out of his position. In one instance an interviewer, after about one hour with an applicant in which nothing unusual had occurred, asked the applicant, "What else do you do well?" When the applicant thought a moment and responded, "I am pretty good with Malayan throwing knives," the interviewer first responded with an incredulous, "What!" Then he laughed for a moment, and, after some faltering, he inquired into the nature of that activity. Finally he reverted to his former behavior, manner, and line of questioning. Although for a short period the interaction pattern and content in the dyad were more dependent on the subordinate's behaviors than on the interviewer's, this was still an unbalanced role set, and the prospective employer was in the position of greater control considering the interpersonal event in its entirety.

Neither can one always tell who is dominant or more influential in the dyad by merely observing who is doing the most talking. The nature of the dyadic activity or task must be considered. For example, in most interviewing, it is desirable for the interviewer to produce a maximum number of responses with a minimum number of questions. This is an unbalanced role set since professional interviewers interview more than interviewees are interviewed (if one ignores certain national political figures and entertainers who are really professional interviewees). But, discounting these exceptions, it is likely that an interview dyad in which the oral dominance overwhelmingly favors the respondent position is one in which the interviewer is actually influencing the interaction most artistically and most thoroughly.

We may make some additional predictions about the effect of balanced and unbalanced role sets on communication and other facets of human experience in the dyad. For example, based on a study from student doctor/student nurse dyads, Turk concludes that equality of power leads to more communication, which in turn increases liking between the partners.[11] He also finds that communication between unequals involves some risk of losing self-esteem by the low-power partner and some risk of power loss by the high partner. But, the less partners in an unbalanced set communicate, the less they will probably like one another. Also, when a low-power person is dependent on a high-power person for help, the high-power person in the dyad communicates and helps the low-power person more if the high-power person thinks the other's dilemma is not his own fault.[12]

INDIVIDUAL VARIATION IN
TRADITIONAL ROLE SETS

Much variety is found in the communication behavior of different occupants of the same position. Role sets do not cover the whole range of behavioral possibilities for a given dyad; role sets are not 100 or perhaps even 50 per cent prescriptive in a given dyad. People fill dyads and embellish the position with all the idiosyncratic styles of communicating discussed earlier; they embellish them with their special views and purposes and with their abundance of acquired and unique

[11] Herman Turk and C. Robert Mills, "Authority and Interaction," *Sociometry*, 27 (1964), 1–18.
[12] John Schopler and Marjorie Mathews, "The Influence of the Perceived Causal Locus of Partner's Dependence on the Use of Interpersonal Power," *Journal of Personality and Social Psychology*, 2 (1965), 609–12.

information about the activity, the other, and the self. A role set provides only some limitations and some guidelines for dyadic communication. An individual performer however must go beyond the guide lines into areas which the role set does not reach, and he does this in a unique way. Each individual uses his store of information as he finds what he feels to be appropriate responses to his position; he performs it his own way. One employer maintains a distance—remains aloof—from his employees. Another employer tries to establish an informality in the work environment, perhaps by encouraging his employees to call him by his first name. The role is still there however, and the latter employer knows very well that the other trappings of his position maintain the respect that the functional aspects of his position as boss demand. Expectations in a role set serve communicative efficiency in a dyad.

The socially defined expectations of a particular role set may not be congruent with the expectations of an individual who comes to that role set. He may not have received the news. Of course, one can be aware of the nature of the role-set characteristics and still perform a position within the set incongruently. A segment of Theodore Sarbin's discussion of conventional role theory is pertinent here to our role set. He notes three prerequisites for congruent enactment of a role (position in a role set): (1) The performer must have correct knowledge of the valid role (position). (2) The performer must have appropriate motivation for that role (position). (3) The performer must have the repertoire of specific verbal and motor skills demanded by that role (position).[13] Various cues help to keep both parties in a role set communicating congruently with their position. Beyond language, cues abound in the form of various physical props, such as clothes, spacing, desks, conductors' sticks, and police badges, which function as role-set reminders.[14]

It is important to remember that different persons bring unique perceptions and styles to the role sets they fill. Even if one is aware of the nature of the role set and attempts to perform the functions of the position congruently, he communicates differently from another occupying that position because he performs functions and fulfills expectations in different ways. Self and role set combine to produce the communication in dyads. This is one reason why a shift from the doctor one has gone to for several years may require much adjustment on the part of the patient—as may a change of minister, school teacher, landlord, and so forth. Each one performs the position slightly differently.

In spite of individual variation within a role set, communication is so affected by the nature of a role set that one can often predict, just from a description of the dyadic event, the climate, style, and even communi-

13 Sarbin, "Role Theory," pp. 226–38.
14 Sarbin, "Role Theory," pp. 229–32.

cative content of that event. For example, the position of judge is more stylized in our definition than is that of the judged (unbalanced role set). Therefore more judges communicate in the same form and even with the same manner of expression than do any given number of defendants, whose position is sketchy indeed. The person in the less stylized position has more flexibility in communicating about the business at hand than does his highly stylized partner. But he also has fewer rules to guide his behavior and less influence on the dyadic-communication system in which he behaves if he behaves congruently with the set.

Role sets may be broken when they do not fit the communication demands of the task or the players' immediate high-priority needs. To completely break a role set is to cease using the expected communication behaviors to guide the interaction. We all know when this break occurs because the communicative rug is at least temporarily pulled out from under us. A tired lawyer who heretofore has maintained some degree of congruence in his conversations with a client may end a phone call that signals more work that night with an exasperated, "Oh God," and a sigh, thereby causing embarrassment for the client and ambiguity as to what degree he should adhere to the client position in solving the communication demands of the immediate future.

Another source of variation in the behavior of different performers of the same position in a role set is the self-image of the performer. Some persons communicate in a way that is dictated by the role set and that supports his self-image or at least neither conflicts with his self-image nor thwarts the goal of the dyad. An example of the effect of self-image on communication behavior in dyads, taken from role theory but equally applicable to dyadic communication and role sets, is that of role distance.[15] Above we indicated that performers in extremely stylized positions have less flexibility in communication than do those in less stylized ones because of the excessive demands embodied in what they must convey to others in a dyad and to the people within earshot. However, all set performers, but especially performers of the more demanding, stylized positions, may obtain more flexibility in their range of permissible behaviors without falling out of position like the lawyer in the example and while continuing to perform the functions of their positions. This flexibility is attained through role distance.

Goffman writes that when an individual has an attachment for a role, has the needed qualifications for performing that role, and actively and totally gives himself over to that role, he embraces that role.[16] Examples of performers embracing roles are the serious student during an examina-

---

[15] Erving Goffman, *Encounters* (Indianapolis: Bobbs-Merrill Company, Inc., 1961), pp. 85–162.
[16] Goffman, *Encounters*, pp. 106–7.

tion, the golf pro in deep concentration over his putter, and the child just learning to read. Goffman indicates that role distance is a mechanism for communicating, while you are in a role, that, although you are enacting the role adequately or perhaps even superbly, you are not embracing that role. Role distance communicates that the role does not tell all the person wishes to tell about himself; it by no means either contains his entire person or demands his complete and absolute concentration at all times while he is enacting it. We may communicate role distance in many ways; humorous remarks to others while performing the role frequently communicate this distance. When effectively expressed, role distance presents the individual performer as one who is capable of separating himself from his role requirements. This does not mean that the individual is denying the role. He is usually just letting onlookers or coworkers know that he does not need to take certain features of the role completely seriously to do an effective job in it. Showing role distance is a way of saying, "I am far more than this situation demands of me, so don't sell me short." Goffman's very good example is that of an 11-year-old boy riding a merry-go-round.[17] At this age he may go through all kinds of physical antics to show everyone that he does not need to give his complete attention to the activity; he is above the role of merry-go-round rider. A few years earlier the same boy would be embracing, figuratively and literally, the role and the horse. Role distance may even be used to set another at ease—to say, "Look how casual I am. Take it easy. I've got everything under control." Role-distance behavior in the form of kidding, horseplay, mock dramatics, and other strain-breaking interpersonal gambits also provides relief from intense concentration on a demanding task.

But, in our experience, the most frequent occasions for role-distance behavior are those that arise from a deep need of the performing individual to communicate an added dimension of his identity to the others in the dyad and perhaps by implication to suggest even further individual complexity and personal depth. We all know at least one chronic kidder, who, although we may see him only rarely, always manages to slip an annoying and distracting illustration of the fact that he is totally in command of things right into the middle of an important conversation. In contrast we also know the dynamo—the guy whom we characterize as humorless, or as having a one-track mind, or as the no-monkey-business, according-to-Hoyle communicator who never seems to take a look at himself in mid-stride and who embraces every position tightly and unremittingly.

The important and useful aspect of role distance is that it permits individuals to communicate their natures more fully to their coworkers

---

[17] Goffman, *Encounters*, pp. 107–9.

without endangering the information-sharing process or effective task work. The more stylized a position in a role set is, the more opportunity to display role distance. In role distance communicators have additional material out of which to fashion messages necessary for their work and in keeping with the demands of both self and other in the dyad.

Traditional role sets are also sensitive to the location of the dyadic activity. Many variations in behavior are produced by modifications of the role set when a student/professor dyad moves out of the classroom or when an employer/employee set meets at one of their homes or outside of the usual work environment. Uneasiness or ambiguity often prevail in these dyads while the performers grope for cues to stabilize their discussion in settings which are not fully appropriate for the old rules but in which new rules are not readily available.

The above discussion illustrates the point that the nature of the interpersonal event for which the dyad has formed is strongly instrumental in determining communication characteristics within that dyad. A particular event may define speech dominance as having negative, positive, or no relationship to the influence pattern in a balanced or unbalanced set. For those who have been interviewed through the window of an automobile by a policeman, it is not news that the burden for speech is on one's self. The policeman quite clearly interprets silence as an admission of guilt in this unbalanced set. To take another situation, silence on the part of a judge after one has just completed an explanation of an allegedly illegal act certainly communicates something. Although it is difficult to explain out of the context of the event and the role set in question just what silence means, it does have important and influential meaning in dyadic communication. Other dimensions of speech communication in dyads also are important. Brevity in speech may communicate succinctness or incompleteness depending on whether it follows lengthy comments by the same party or comes as a reply to an articulate and complexly formulated comment from the other, respectively, or whether it comes when time is limited or when time is not a factor.

We have said little concerning the manipulation or the direct defiance of specific norms in a role set and the effect of such manipulation on the communication in that dyad. Reverting to the patrolman/traffic violator set, we recall that the patrolman, who spends more time in his position than the traffic violator, is the dominant person in this unbalanced set. The next time you are stopped by a patrolman try this experiment. Pull to the curb, set your brake, jump out of your car, close the door, and wait for the officer by your car. If you have had previous experience in the violator position with which to compare this one, you will find that by the simple act of sitting rather than standing in this dyad you have been giving part of your communicative effectiveness away, in both speech and manner. If you try this experiment, you will not restore any balance to the role set, but you may find yourself effecting minor victories in the interaction. Although we fully expect the reader to eagerly anticipate his next opportunity to try such an experiment, we must go on record as discouraging such behavior as would ensure the opportunity. For most traditional role sets, important norms do exist and seem to be powerful only because they are not consciously credited with importance by unassuming communicators.

UNIQUE ROLE SETS

A traditional set contains sufficient norms to guide the relationship one has with the man in the office down the hall and other persons with whom our level of information-sharing is quite shallow or only moderately intense. But the more complex relationships, discussed in a previous section, demand more guidance—more specificity of expectations—than traditional sets provide. A particular traditional set is only a general model which we use over and over again with different persons filling the other position. One may escape more intimate communication in a dyad by reverting to or refusing to leave the boundaries of a traditional set.

In our intimate relationships we communicators go beyond the prescriptions of the traditional set and collect additional expectations for the other in the dyad. Communication would be very inefficient were it not for unique role sets. It is not likely that we would have time for even one intimate relationship if we did not form unique role sets. In other words, if one had to start afresh at each new meeting with his friends or enemies, no level of intimacy would develop because all energy would be used in groping for mutually satisfactory expression and common ground. If one were armed with no expectations, if he had to begin anew with no patterns to direct his behavior in communication with the other at each new encounter, he would have little incentive to communicate at all.

Fortunately, we do not cease to form expectations in our intimate relationships. A unique role set is formed with a unique other in our dyad—a role set based on old strategies and suitable patterns of relating that have worked to the mutual satisfaction of the parties in the dyad. One measure of the level of intimacy of a relationship is the ability of one to predict (expect) the present or future behavior of the other in that dyad on the basis of norms of communication formed in the past. In dyads governed only by traditional role sets the two persons occupying positions in the set vary their behavior within the limits defined by the norms of that set. In contrast, norms of a unique role set are a direct function of the past interaction of the same two persons in the dyad.

Once a unique role set is formed, the parties may rely on personal strategies for communication, may anticipate attitudes of the other, may stake out areas of acceptable and dangerous content for communication, and the like. A traditional set consists of norms established by many different persons communicating in a particular dyad for many years. A unique role set evolves from the immediate communication content of two specific individuals. The more intimate the relationship in terms of level of information shared, the more numerous the norms of the unique role set. Tested patterns of response, communication style and content, and accepted rules of conflict become automatically and unconsciously employed in a unique dyad. They thereby conserve our energy for task or social activity. In short, the problem of adjustment in these interpersonal relationships is alleviated because that problem does not have to be solved all over again once a workable pattern or norm has been established.

Traditional role sets correspond to dyads in which an interpersonal relationship has not developed, as is the case when one consults a person he will never see again in his life. Dyads in which we have developed moderately intense relationships are governed, alternatively, by unique role sets having relatively few norms and by the appropriate traditional role set. At one moment habits of communication with this unique other are clearly guiding the dyad; in the next, the traditional-set relationships are instrumental in producing or affecting communication in the dyad. In these moderately intense relationships one probably relies on remnants of the traditional set to fill in the holes in the relatively barren unique set. This merging of role sets is very common in many of our dyads. Reflect how, in your experience in dyads, your attention has flipped noticeably back and forth between (1) the demands of the positions occupied by one's self and the other and (2) the responses you made because of your knowledge of specific characteristics of the other gleaned from past dyadic communication with him. Most of our dyadic communication is characterized by this merging of role sets.

Relationships of this type may be static—may remain at that moderate level of intimacy. Here the relatively barren unique role set does not grow but is complemented by remnants of the appropriate traditional set. Or communication may regress in level of intimacy or information-sharing, resulting in a reduction in the number of reliable expectations for that dyad. Here the unique role set ceases to exist and a former traditional set, if any, is restored to handle what now is not a relationship but only an occasional dyad.

These middle-level relationships may take a third direction; an increase in contact and intimacy may foster numerous norms and thus produce a highly elaborated unique role set. Our friend and associate dyads provide many examples of merging role sets. This is the stage through which our new developing relationship and our old disappearing relationship must pass and in which many of our static relationships must remain.

Even in the purest of unique sets, traces of a traditional set may turn up momentarily and from time to time. It is not likely that the traditional set of husband/wife endures very long in a marriage before a unique role set emerges to supplant the former set and grows into the most highly elaborated unique set conceivable. Yet, we have seen how a change—in activity or location, for example—may affect a role set in a dyad. When man and wife take their dyad out for a walk in public or anywhere outside of the home location of that dyad, it is not unusual for each to employ remnants of the traditional set for the benefit of a third party or for other reasons. Some husbands are husbands only in public; some wives are wives only in public. In a particular dyad only the remnants of the traditional set may be visible, while the unique role set is reserved for privacy. Sometimes "that married couple that was so happy together last week" is even happier apart this week. In addition, when the persons in a dyad become momentarily or permanently incompatible but must continue their dyadic contact, they may purposely discard their unique set. We all have witnessed friends and close associates revert to communication forms that were appropriate for a traditional role set. "What do you think of that, *Mr.* Jones?" or "*Professor* Smart" or "*Doctor* Butcher."

In dyads endowed with a unique role set, one party brings a special self to the other; he is prepared in manner, speech, and thought for the other with whom he will communicate. Both parties have anticipated the other on the basis of past information and performance and thus already have been influenced by the other even as they walk toward one another in a room and before a word has been uttered. In this sense a unique self is brought to enter into a communication event with this particular other. We literally bring a new self to each dyadic encounter with a different person, and it is a very special self in those dyads with a unique role set.

As we begin to conclude our discussion of dyadic communication we must point out that all social behavior is not influenced by role sets. We do not maintain that persons are always filling one or another traditional or unique role set. Rather, our definition limits role set to those work and play activities in which some mutual enterprise—pulling a tooth, playing tennis, paying a bill, or just socializing—is engaged in by two people and demands some degree of cooperation between them. For these enterprises, norms of communication have evolved through generations or through personal relationships. Norms of traditional sets especially and unique sets only in part derive their natures from the characteristics and functions of the activity which furnishes the purpose and the setting for the dyad. The norms of a unique role set pertain to a dyad composed of the same two people who communicate in a variety of activities and locations. These norms are primarily a product of the characteristics of the occupants of the set. A somewhat oversimplified, but largely accurate, conception is that traditional role sets reflect the primary activity with which they are associated, and unique sets reflect the persons who fill them.

MULTIPLE ROLES AND ROLE PLAYING

Everybody fills a number of different traditional and unique role sets as he moves from dyad to dyad even in the course of one day. The boss who takes you to lunch moves to another position when he meets with his boss, another when he sees his wife at dinner, and still others with his son or his neighbor or his druggist. After a little careful or considerably more casual observation of this boss, we notice subtle and dramatic changes in his communication behavior from one dyad to another. This change in behavior is not a mask, although it can be used to mask things as in the case of the extremely other-directed man or the "marketing orientation" that David Riesman and Erich Fromm have described.[18] And this change is also not acting, although we may indeed feel the need to act often enough—a need to be other than ourselves. These behavior changes are as common or natural as are the differences between the self one brings to one's mother as compared to the self one brings to one's daughter, to a professor, to a bus driver, to the foreman of a road gang, to the President of the United States, to a Jack or a Jill. Mary Follett writes that "response is always to a relation."[19] We do not respond to the other or to pure things but to the relation of the thing or the other to ourself. So, as in calculus, we measure changing things by changing things. For this reason norms in a role set derive from and influence relationships primarily and people only indirectly and only because they are one part of the relationship.

Mutuality of influence and information-sharing in dyads does not

[18] Erich Fromm, "The Nonproductive Character Orientations," in *Readings in the Psychology of Adjustment*, eds. Leon Gorlow and Walter Katkovsky (New York: McGraw-Hill Book Company, 1959), pp. 352–55; David Riesman, Nathan Glazer, and Reuel Denney, *The Lonely Crowd* (New Haven, Connecticut: Yale University Press, 1961).

[19] *Creative Experience* (New York: David McKay Co., Inc., 1930), p. 63.

consist of two static entities each busy influencing the other, although we often flatter ourselves into believing that this is the case. Each of two persons presents a self that he feels is appropriate for the relation between self and other. This self-adjustment, as one moves from dyad to dyad, is so natural a process that one notices only a very small part of his change in behavior from dyad to dyad in comparison to what an observer is capable of noticing. In human communication we are all chameleons, automatically, spontaneously, and to an extent surpassing our awareness.

A communicator is able to shift from one dyad to another with facility because of his store of information pertaining to the different demands of the several dyads. He wears many hats. When he is confronted by several others at the same time, as, for example, in the small group, he must change hats rapidly and wear more than one at a time in order to satisfy the demands of the more complex communication situation. When more than two persons communicate in a small group, several traditional role sets and unique role sets affect communication behavior at the same time.

Groups of four, five, six, and seven members present the possibility of containing 6, 10, 15, and 21 role sets, respectively. The resultant complexity produces a number of strains on our role-set concept. Also, as we move from the dyad to the small group, we shall see how a quantitative change, an increase in the number of communicators, produces a qualitative change in almost all aspects of the communication activity. Appropriately, we shall exchange conceptual tools useful at the dyadic level of communication for ones most suitable to the new group level. However, we shall see many communication principles—principles regarding self-concept, evaluation of self and others, and norms and expectations in communication, to mention only a few—operating true to form in the new setting. Although we have only scratched the surface of dyadic communication, we hope our discussion has provided the reader with a basic framework from which to pursue his study of this sometimes exciting and ever complex level of human communication.

Small-Group
Communication

We define a small group as a face-to-face confrontation among from 4 to about 25 people who are interacting in some common work, play, or survival activity for which speech communication is the primary mode of interaction. We separate the small group from the human dyad, or two-person group, because of several important and consistent differences between the two, some of which have been discussed previously. We similarly separate our smallest small group (four members) from three-person groups, or triads, because of what mothers, William Gamson,[1] baby sitters, and others have observed about the overpowering effect of coalition formation in three-person groups. The upper limit on the small group reflects our interest in the group as a unit of interacting individuals; the individuals can get close enough to one another to communicate on the same matter to every person in the group through the media of unaided human sight and hearing.

The reader has spent and is now spending many of the most important minutes of his life communicating in small groups. Later, he will participate in several work groups in his job and in many more play groups and will experience countless events alone which he will later share with others in small groups. In small groups time and again he will acquire new information, change his attitudes toward other persons or social objects, and share in the creation of new ideas, objects, and maybe even institutions. He will inform others in small groups, change others' minds in small groups, and then go home to think about what has happened in small groups. When he is working or playing by himself, what he has done and what he anticipates doing in small groups will guide his thoughts and actions in part. He will return from a movie, an automobile accident, or a war and evaluate his experience in a small group. Later he will go to another small group and discuss the evaluations made in the first group. Always he will find himself talking in one small group about something that happened in another small group. If

---

[1] "Experimental Test of a Theory of Coalition Formation," *American Sociological Review*, 26 (1961), 565–73.

the reader lives in twentieth-century America or almost any other place in the world, much of his life will be spent in groups. He will have no choice. A small group will figure in an important way in his birth, or his marriage, or his death, or perhaps all three. His whole life will be influenced, even radically changed by ideas, goods, and institutions created by small groups. We shall first consider the nature of small groups by classifying them in several ways.

GROUP TYPE

Many groups, e.g., a city planning commission, are characterized by a purpose or goal which all the members share. In other groups no shared purpose can be observed beyond a vague agreement—"we are having fun; let's continue to meet." A routine coffee klatch among friends is an example of a group which does not have one primary goal or purpose. Members of all groups have unique personal reasons for being in a particular group. But a purposive group must have a fairly specific goal which is the main reason for maintaining the group and which is shared by most of the people in it. The goal of a purposive group is not necessarily static; it may change. For instance, a newcomers' club may have the purpose, or group goal, of acquainting new members in a community with other new members. After a time the newcomers become oldcomers and develop other friends and associations. If the activities of the newcomers' club are no longer relevant to the members' needs, the group may disband or re-form into a bridge group or book study club. So, goals shift according to the needs of the group members. However, a very basic criterion for the classification of a group is whether it has one overriding group goal. Purposive and nonpurposive group discussion divides the street-corner gab session from the planned group deliberation. Of course, a spontaneously formed group, e.g., the student classmates who started having a soda together and ended studying for an examination, can also be purposeful. Conversely, a planned, purposeful discussion group can devolve into subgroups of two and three people indulging in social conversation and, thereby, can deviate completely from its original purpose. If a group does not retain a widespread feeling for one identifiable common purpose, it moves into the nonpurposive category with the dormitory bull session and the street-corner chance meeting.

Decision-making is a descriptive term frequently used to classify groups. In all group discussions however, even those of the purposeless variety, individual members make decisions constantly; indeed, they cannot help but make them. Member X decides to challenge a remark made by member Y. Member Z decides to get an ashtray. Member W decides not to participate in the current argument. Individuals in groups are always making decisions. If decision-making refers to a decision made by the group as a whole, this term provides no distinctions since all groups make these group-level decisions, if only those of continuing meetings and where and when to meet. Any cooperative process such as group discussion implies that group decisions are being made all the time. Perhaps those who use this phrase are referring to groups whose group goal involves making a decision or decisions which will have some important consequences for the group members or someone in their society. If so, classifying groups according to their effects on the surrounding environment or on their members is a rather subtle and complex distinction. Better conceptual mileage will be obtained from this distinction in another connection in a later section.

A very useful classification system that Barnlund based on the nature of the group's goal generates five categories: the *casual* group, the *adjustment* group, the *learning* group, the *policy-making* group, and the *action* group.[2] In part, we may distinguish these groups from one another according to how member needs are satisfied. In the casual and adjustment groups, the interaction is very personal and group centered; in the policy and action groups, interaction tends toward the impersonal, centering, as it does, on the group task. Casual and adjustment groups exist for whatever values the members derive from them. In these groups the task is somewhat identical with the relationships that develop and with the activities that occur. Many casual and adjustment groups are nonpurposive or lack an overall, group-level goal. Examples of casual groups are tea parties, campus "jammies," and other groups whose primary activities are confined to socializing. Adjustment groups, like casual groups, usually form to satisfy various needs of individual members, but they have a special function of alleviating problems or tensions of individual members. Spontaneous adjustment groups frequently form in the halls outside university lecture rooms after particularly arduous examinations. In these groups students often find themselves talking with veritable strangers in a very animated and intimate manner about such matters as, "What did you answer for number 16?" "Do you think he will curve the exam?" "How do you think you did?" These tension-release, or cathartic, functions are characteristic of adjustment groups whether they be students on a college campus, inmates in a prison, professional groups at a convention, or psychoneurotics in a psychiatric hospital. All groups however, even

[2] Dean Barnlund, "Our Concept of Discussion: Static or Dynamic," *The Speech Teacher*, 3 (January 1954), 8–14.

those which are not primarily adjustment groups, engage in some form of tension-release occasionally.

Policy and action groups serve a purpose embedded in a social situation; they implement certain work in the society or in the organization in which they are contained. In this sense these groups always have a group goal; they are purposive in nature. A policy group deliberates on a problem and uses resources at its disposal to produce output to the external environment—recommendations, solutions or several alternative solutions, advice, and other guidelines. An action group has executive powers to initiate and carry out programs and activities within its purview. A meeting of officers of a corporation might stipulate how much money will be given to a foundation, when to start a new plant-expansion program, or where to invest new earnings.

Learning groups fall in the middle of this five-category classification system. College classes, business conferences, and short courses of various kinds are examples of learning groups. These groups are task-oriented in their attempt to master some subject matter which will be used outside the classroom. However, a great deal of interpersonal stimulation also occurs in these groups and, as some writers suggest, is even necessary to fulfillment of the task goals.[3]

In a casual-adjustment-learning-policy-action category system, groups near the action end of the scale need and usually employ a more controlled agenda, while casual and adjustment groups may have a completely uncontrolled agenda. Most member interaction in the action and policy groups is impersonal in nature, while interaction in casual and adjustment groups is extremely personal.

Obviously any one group may fit into several of these categories at one time since there are no firm boundaries between the categories. A classroom group can be, at once, an adjustment and policy-making as well as a learning group. (One hopes it is seldom a casual group.) In fact, when a classroom learning group has some power to decide policy and establish procedures in areas in which it has had little or no responsibility in the past, catharsis (adjustment) almost inevitably accompanies the policy-making activities. Because of this overlap, it is often more meaningful to think of a group as being predominantly an action group, instead of simply an action group, since it has other functions at different times. For the same reason, the casual-adjustment or the policy-action label is often more accurate than rigid adherence to any one category allows.

We can also divide groups into categories on the basis of where the group task or majority of individual member tasks (for nonpurposive

---

[3] See Barry Collins and Harold Guetzkow, *A Social Psychology of Group Processes for Decision-Making* (New York: John Wiley & Sons, Inc., 1964), pp. 74–87.

groups) is located. Two categories are thereby generated. The tasks of some groups are internally contained in the group itself, and the tasks of other groups are external in that they entail acting on the outside environment of the group in some way. Viewing group tasks in this way permits a reclassification of the above five categories in terms of "psychological geography." We may assess where the task is located in relation to the boundaries of any particular group. Policy and action groups are definitely formed to work on the external environment and therefore have a task locus outside the group itself. Casual, adjustment, and even most learning groups exist primarily for the immediate rewards of group interaction and, as such, have their task locus within the group. Of course, classroom learning groups do hope to obtain an "A" in the course or a degree from the university and to extract a living from the external environment eventually. But even these special learning groups are more directly concerned with internal, immediate, class-centered events and goals than they are with future external goals, and they tend to act as though immediate group membership is (or had better be) sufficient unto itself.

Deviating from a discussion of group goals for a moment, we see that an individual's goals, whether volitional or unthinking, may also be characterized by any of these group classification systems. In Barnlund's system,[4] for example, an individual whose goal in a classroom learning group is adjustment illustrates this to-be-expected incongruency of the goals of certain members with that of the group. A certain member may not be interested in the goal of an action group. Perhaps he never intends to support or to help implement the planned march to city hall but is in the group solely for the stimulating company he finds there. One can think of other examples of individual purposes which depart so far from the group goal that they may more accurately be characterized by other goal categories. If one deviates too far from the goal of a highly motivated group and the group is aware of this, his opinion will no longer be sought in the group unless he is also contributing or is in control of some resource that is vital to the group effort.

Another way to look at group type is to ask whether group membership is relatively voluntary or is prescribed by a boss, spouse, or circumstances. May a person who is already in the group leave of his own "free" will? Many groups are set up by an outside authority, and persons are appointed to membership. Other groups—like an open discussion session on a social issue, a local chapter of the American Civil Liberties Union, or the John Birch Society—may be joined and left quite voluntarily in keeping with the dictates of one's own conscience and other personal considerations. The degree of choice concerning membership

4 Barnlund, "Our Concept of Discussion: Static or Dynamic," pp. 8–14.

or nonmembership in a group is an important determinant of a person's attitudes and behaviors while in that group. A group can also be classified in terms of minimum or maximum choice with respect to the relative control that other members have over one's membership status. In addition to the choice level of a particular group, individuals may have several different choice levels foisted upon them within the same group. A voluntary group may contain members who would leave the group were it not for pressures from individuals or circumstances which discourage their doing so.

Group life expectancy is another basic way of differentiating among group types. Temporary groups meet once or twice and never again. Members of these groups may behave very differently from members of more permanent groups just because they know that they will not meet (as a group) again. Groups that meet frequently, like families and classroom groups, are usually permanent. However, a family reunion in the last few minutes, as mother cries and so forth, may appear to an outsider to be a temporary group. Similarly, on the last day of school, classroom groups from the elementary to the university level change somewhat in climate and in the relationships among all the group members. One reason for the difference between temporary and permanent groups is that members of temporary groups, knowing that they will soon be out of reach of other members, are free to act more honestly with one another than members of permanent groups are. Threats from powerful members (like teachers), status differences, and other determinants of member relations are not relevant factors in the anticipated futures of the temporary-group members.[5] Although there are more similarities among temporary and permanent groups than there are differences, the member behaviors which make a difference or are important to the group vary somewhat in the two group situations. In grade school, the substitute teacher often bears the brunt of group misbehaviors simply because, in a permanent group where one leader is very important, the substitute is only a temporary leader.

Consider, for a moment, the following groups: a student seminar; the President's cabinet; a businessman's luncheon club; the executive council of the Americans for Democratic Action; birthday party-goers; a religious study group; participants in a dormitory beer blast; a small, local Ku Klux Klan; a family at dinner; a student council committee at a university; and strategists for a CORE demonstration. Each of these groups may be described in terms of each of the several category sys-

[5] For example, see E. Paul Torrance, "Some Consequences of Power Differences on Decision Making in Permanent and Temporary Three-Man Groups," in *Small Groups: Studies in Social Interaction,* eds. A. Paul Hare, Edgar F. Borgatta, and Robert F. Bales (New York: Alfred A. Knopf, Inc., 1966), pp. 600–609.

tems presented above and many more. Table 1 summarizes the criteria and corresponding group types.

TABLE 1: GROUP TYPE

Types	Dimensions of Types
Purpose	One common group goal ...... Complete diffusion of member goals
Organization	Planned .... Spontaneous
Nature of shared goal	Casual ..... Adjustment ..... Learning ....Policy-making ....Action
Task focus	Internal task .... External task
Membership arrangement	Voluntary .... Prescribed
Group life expectancy	Temporary .... Permanent

By starting with a very brief description of one group, we may see how these classification systems apply. Every Monday morning at eleven o'clock Professor X goes to a meeting of the Student Scholastic Standing Committee, which is attended by three other faculty members and one dean, all of whom draw their salaries from Perilous State University. This committee reviews petitions from students who wish to change their status in the Liberal Arts College of old PSU. The substance of the committee's work is accepting or denying petitions from students who wish to drop or add courses to their term schedules after the deadline and referring certain cases to similar committees or administrators in other colleges of the university. A criterion statement set forth in the University Senate rule book governing academic matters at the University guides the committee. His department chairman placed Professor X on this committee. No rule explicitly provides for getting off the committee, although Professor X receives a form once a year on which he is asked to rank his top three preferences out of approximately 20 committee titles. The relationship between this process and his eventual placement on a particular committee is not quite clear to X.

This group is a (1) purposive, (2) planned, (3) permanent, (4) action, (5) external-task-focus, (6) prescribed-membership group. All these classifications are important only to the extent that member behaviors are effected by them. It is important to note some ways in which even this rather formal group defies the rigidity of several of the above classifications. The group in question is only rather permanent since it takes on some characteristics of a potentially temporary group as the end of the academic year approaches and the chance of a reshuffling of committee assignments looms in the mind of a particular member. The attendance record of one member may cause an observer to think that the group's meetings are more spontaneous than planned. Certain segments of the group discussion may sound like that of a casual or social group, and at times individual members may make statements that are predominantly cathartic in nature, reflecting their own personal frustrations and biases rather than pertaining to the task of the group. All these behaviors are very normal ways in which groups repeatedly evade our attempts to pigeonhole them.

GROUP LEADERSHIP

Our position is similar to that of the writer who maintains that leadership is probably the most overworked topic in discussion and is more properly relegated to the status of a secondary function: "Training in discussion should place primary emphasis on the *nature* and *process* of discussion" instead of on leadership.[6] Unfortunately, much attention has, in the past, centered on the notion of the one-man leader, who, because of great talent or experience or other personal characteristics, leads a group to dispose successfully of the task at hand. Stereotypes of what a leader should be have evolved from this notion and have led to a mythology of leadership.[7] In our view belief in this folklore has resulted in a loss both of creative solutions and of a maximally effective use of group deliberation in organizations whose functioning depends largely on group problem-solving. Regardless of the probable reasons for the past emphasis in discussion on a separation between the leader and his followers, it is important to understand that thinking about group processes in this way inevitably leads to an impractical and inefficient use of the vast human potential residing in many small groups.

Many groups have a formal chairman or boss who is the leader because of his status outside the group (foreman at the plant, president of the club, etc.), because he was appointed by the boss or elected by the group members, or because he took over when the group needed some direction or organization. The very existence of these formal leaders in a group may cause one to stop thinking analytically about just what the term *leadership* implies. One is tempted to equate leadership with the one man who is the leader and thereby to avoid grappling with the meaning of leadership at all. "Leadership is what the leader does; sometimes he does it well—sometimes, not so well;" so goes the evasion.

Our approach to leadership begins with an attempt to find out how leadership affects a group. We start by defining leadership as any behavior in the group which makes a difference in the group's activity and

[6] Robert Cathcart, "Leadership as a Secondary Function in Group Discussion," *The Speech Teacher,* 11 (September 1962), 221–26.
[7] For a discussion of several bases of the mythology, see Thomas Gordon, *Group-Centered Leadership* (Boston: Houghton Mifflin Company, 1955), pp. 22–45.

thinking to the extent that it affects the goal or product which the group is striving to accomplish or produce. This statement is much too nebulous to help us in defining what kinds of activities we must consider; but it does indicate our interest in any leadership act, regardless of its source. A leadership act originating from a quiet, new, low-status group member is just as important in our notion of leadership as one emanating from a high-status, highly talkative, assertive, formally designated chairman. One advantage of this leadership-act approach is that we do not overlook those aspects of leadership which a formally designated leader does *not* contribute in a particular group. An equally important advantage of this view over the one-man approach is that a leadership act may be studied in the context which it arises—namely, the task of the group and the elements in the larger environment which govern important aspects of group interaction. When leadership is viewed as the personal magic of one man or a few men, this objectification is not likely to occur. A third and very practical advantage to this view of leadership pertains to attempts to improve group effectiveness. Group members may use knowledge about group processes to assess which leadership acts will be desirable or undesirable for the group's goal achievement. They may then attempt to encourage leadership acts which are positive for the group goal and inhibit those acts whose effects are negative.

On the other hand, if leadership is equated with one or another individual or chairman, then the above advantages are precluded. To encourage or inhibit an act can be interpreted by group members as a necessary demand of the task, while to encourage or inhibit whole individuals is to reward or to punish the undifferentiated acts (both good and bad) that usually come from any single personality. The above discussion of group process indicated that one of the primary advantages of group deliberation over individual efforts is the verification process; the critical-thinking apparatus of different members check the faulty reasoning and information of others in the group.[8] When group members view leadership as synonymous with one leader or even several leaders (as opposed to acts), the false is accepted with the true, the stultifying and the mediocre with the creative and the brilliant. Group members are likely to engage in disruptive behavior when their one-man leader does not behave the way they expect a leader to behave.[9]

Of course, an appointed, elected, or emergent one-man leader or chairman is not necessarily harmful to the goals of a particular group. On the contrary, many groups could not function effectively without a

[8] For a good summary and interpretation of the research pertaining to the error-checking functions of small-group discussion, see Collins and Guetzkow, *A Social Psychology of Group Processes for Decision-Making*, pp. 18–30.

[9] Peter J. Burke, "Authority Relations and Disruptive Behavior in Small Discussion Groups," *Sociometry*, 29 (1966), 237–50.

formally designated leader. Certain aspects of the task situation may even demand a highly directive leader—for example, when a condition of stress requires immediate decisions and structuring of member roles and activities for member action.[10] The values to be gained and those to be lost by this kind of structuring of the leadership role must be balanced against one another. It is necessary only that the members and the leader be alert to potential leadership acts by nonleaders. When one man, by his presence or position in the group, produces an atmosphere in which others give away their initiative and willingness to contribute potentially positive leadership acts, the group task suffers immeasurably. Peripheral members in a group can afford to avoid responsibility and the burden of task success and can blame the central person for task failure.[11] The above problems, together with notions on the part of the leader of how he should act in his leadership role, often add nothing and subtract much from the potentiality of the group as a whole.

Some students of group discussion support a modified one-man theory of leadership. They feel that it helps groups if one person plays a guiding role in which he exerts direction for the group primarily in the area of suggesting or enforcing procedures which the group will follow in their interaction—procedures such as setting up the agenda, moving the group onto a new topic at an appropriate time, and resolving conflicts. This school of thought maintains that the substantive work of the group is still entirely in the hands of the group members. The leader does not interfere except to perform his guiding functions. We do not support this theory for two reasons. First, it is rather difficult for us to imagine how one man can pre-empt all the procedural insight in a group, unless he is so much more experienced, trained, or gifted than the rest of the group that he could do more on his own than could the combined group. If this is the case, group deliberation is not necessary in the first place. When your group task is to solve a difficult problem in mathematics and there is an "Einstein" in your group, go home and take a nap; you simply are not needed. Second, procedural matters are closely tied to both interpersonal relations and the nature of the group task. A leadership act in one area affects activities in all the others if the act is a significant and influential act at all.

The leadership-act approach assumes that people are so dynamically different anyway that each group member has to work with certain givens—his personality, past experiences in groups, and the like. Within

[10] John A. Sample and Thurlow R. Wilson, "Leader Behavior, Group Productivity and Rating of Least Preferred Co-Worker," *Journal of Personality and Social Psychology*, 1 (1965), 266–70.
[11] Herman Medow and Alvin Zander, "Aspirations for the Group Chosen by Central and Peripheral Members," *Journal of Personality and Social Psychology*, 1 (1965), pp. 224–28.

the bounds set by what he is and what he knows, he may be able to develop certain insights into the lawful and predictable facets of group interaction. People are so different and group tasks so varied that one group member is not likely to respond to or be led by the same person or method so effectively as another member may be.[12] A fruitful approach is to focus on a knowledge of the processes or workings of persons in groups.

We define leadership acts in terms of whether they significantly enhance or impede the activities necessary for the group to approach its goal. In this perspective it is easy to see that an act that is desirable in one group may be undesirable in another. Similarly an act may be helpful at one stage in a group's life and may considerably thwart the group's purpose at another stage. For example, assume that member *A* voices several very insightful criticisms of member *B*'s proposed solution to a problem. If the group should reject all inadequate solutions among many proposed at this point, the act must be judged to have a positive effect on the group task. However, if the problem requires that many solutions be proposed before any are evaluated, then member *A* is doing a disservice to his group by, among other things, (1) wasting valuable time in which other solutions could be heard, (2) scaring off other potential solutions by his thorough criticism, and (3) causing the group to discount a whole idea when parts may have been put to use by others in the group. Situation and timing are very important elements to consider when judging the value of a particular act. In this respect one may talk about positive and negative leadership acts as defined by their effects on group direction. Restraining negative acts may be as important a part of leadership as promoting positive ones; the past emphasis on what a leader ought to do has somewhat obscured this perspective.

If one insists on thinking about leadership as a characteristic of various human individuals, we suggest the following definition. Leadership is the art of knowing what the situation (group type, member needs, kind of task, time requirements, etc.) requires and then seeing to it that what is required is provided either by one's self or by others in the group. We may consider this functional or shared leadership quite independently of whether a designated leader is present in the group. Leadership may be shared whether or not one man is called *leader*. The designated leader requires considerable skill and insight to avoid having his formal designation affect other group members. One can know what the situation requires only by developing his insight, by par-

---

[12] Dean Barnlund, "Consistency of Emergent Leadership in Groups with Changing Tasks and Members," *Speech Monographs*, 29 (1962), 45–52.

ticipating in many groups, and by systematically observing those aspects of group communication which he should know about.

Ross and Hendry describe how research on leadership began with a preoccupation with (1) the traits of a leader (consistent with a one-man view of leadership) and soon expanded to consider (2) the characteristic structure of a group built from member needs and interaction patterns and (3) the elements in the environment of the group including its task and total situational context.[13] Ross and Hendry indicate that most students of group leadership now consider all these foci necessary for an understanding of leadership phenomena. In his interpretation of the research on the effects of leadership on group problem-solving, Hoffman concludes that a single leader may be helpful or harmful to group productivity depending on whether he permits minority opinions to be heard, uses the group resources artfully, and the like, or dominates, ignores potential contributors, etc.[14]

We have suggested so far that leadership must be a shared endeavor among all the group members, regardless of whether a leader-person is in the group. In most problem-solving groups there is too much to do for one man to (1) see what is needed at every moment in group interaction and (2) see that it gets done all the time. But the underlying dynamics of leadership—who does what in a group—are not so simple as our few introductory comments imply. A topic closely related to an understanding of both group leadership and group process is that of who does what consistently. Haiman terms this topic the *specialization* of roles and functions in a group.

Developing an analogy of the small group to society, Haiman cites individual differences, the need for personal stability, and a natural division of labor as three forces which bring about specialization in a group.[15] First, the fact that persons bring different abilities, personalities, knowledge, likes, and experiences in other groups to a group means that certain functions are more readily performed by some members than by others. The behaviors arising out of these individual differences cause specialization of roles and functions within a group. Some members simply like to do certain things more than others. Because of previous group experiences certain group members are highly capable in performing a number of necessary group activities.

Second, every person needs a somewhat stable set of expectations; he needs to be able to depend on certain features in his relations to others

13 Murray Ross and Charles Hendry, *New Understandings of Leadership* (New York: Association Press, 1957), pp. 17–31.
14 L. Richard Hoffman, "Group Problem Solving," in *Advances in Experimental Social Psychology*, Vol. 2, ed. Leonard Berkowitz (New York: Academic Press Inc., 1965), pp. 99–132.
15 Franklyn S. Haiman, "The Specialization of Roles and Functions in a Group," *The Quarterly Journal of Speech*, 43 (1957), 165–67.

around him and in the relations among those others. Human beings must classify their experiences and situations. They must classify people also for this is the way they attempt to understand happenings in the world. They must feel that they can expect certain behaviors from certain group members; they must be able to predict what will happen, in part. This ability to arrange a more or less stable world is probably a very basic part of man's ability to cope with his environment, and it is certainly an ingredient of what has come to be known as "mental health." Because I think I know that lightning will not strike me about ten times at irregular intervals throughout the day, because I know that the floor is not likely to crumble under me as I read a book or eat my breakfast, I can free myself for a concern with other matters in my environment. This need for stability in "my world" is responsible for some of the anxiety and minor tension that many people experience in a room full of strangers. One asks one's self not only, "What are they going to do?" but also, "What are they thinking about me?" What am I supposed to do?" and, "How do I fit into this situation?" Ambiguous situations and unclear role relations are more frightening or frustrating or both for some individuals than for others, but everyone resolves this stability problem in his own way by gradually (sometimes too quickly) acquiring a way of thinking about the strangers as their behaviors label them for him.

This need for individual stability explains why stereotyping of people and of situations plays such a large part in our social world. In a group one quickly identifies the joker, the leader, and the fact man. Frequently, this labeling process actually affects the behavior of members other than the one applying the label. If everyone in a group expects someone to be witty and treats him as though this were his only function in the group, he is likely to maintain that role and avoid all others. He knows he is rewarded by laughter and attention for being funny. Why risk rejection by contributing other acts to the group task? This topic is closely connected with norms and expectations in interpersonal communication, which were considered at length in previous sections.

Third, a division of labor occurs in the group in the same way and probably for many of the same reasons that it occurs in society. A keeper of the minutes is one example applicable to many groups. If everybody in the group takes minutes, their attentions are all divided. Besides, some notes are illegible, and some writers are not able to keep up. If one member already possesses shorthand skill, this person may keep minutes for the whole group and with experience may become more efficient than anyone else at this task, thereby providing a valuable service to the group and freeing everybody else's full attention for more substantive matters.

These three forces automatically tend to differentiate roles and functions, irrespective of the formal roles imposed on the group from within or without—roles like leader.   For this reason, a leadership role is almost superfluous in most groups unless it is confined to certain narrow functions.   Enforced, superficial role rigidity just adds to the problems created naturally by specialization of roles and functions.[16]   Our earlier discussion of the restrictiveness of heavily formalized role sets contained a description of role-distance behavior, which, by its widespread occurrence, signifies the necessity for human communicators to maintain some flexibility and to escape from the excessive expectations of elaborated roles.   The simple specialization of functions complicates the peer relationship of any two group members; it detracts from the solidarity and the cohesiveness of the group.   Furthermore, although the secretary role may be necessary in a group, if the functions of secretary are too encompassing, the secretary is, in effect, removed from the group as a potential contributor.

Some observers have argued that the specialization of roles and functions simply means that each group member is dependent on other members, just as in society shoemakers and shoe buyers are mutually dependent.   They argue that the realization of this interdependence should increase group harmony.   This assumption would be correct providing everyone (1) specialized in exactly his preferred role, (2) was completely satisfied with the resulting status system and distribution of rewards, and (3) could compensate for the barriers to communication which specialization brings about.   Unfortunately, these utopian conditions do not exist in groups or in societies that we have observed—at least, not all at once or all of the time.

Haiman describes a cycle of circumstances which begins with the division of labor in a group.   Either one of the two other forces for specialization (individual differences and the need for stability) could also initiate the cycle; it probably results from all three forces described here and from other sources as well.

1. Division of labor leads to specialization.

2. Some specialties are more important to the group than others, and a higher value is therefore placed upon them.

---

[16] Comparisons of the effectiveness of natural or emergent leaders with that of appointed or elected leaders support this view. We refer to the distinction between a clear superimposition of a leader role on a group in the latter types of leadership and the evolution of a leader through his behavior, as with emergent leaders. If a leader is elected after a warm-up discussion, this distinction is not applicable; he wins the election because he is an emergent leader. For example, see Morton Goldman and Louis A. Frass, "The Effects of Leader Selection on Group Performance," *Sociometry*, 28 (1965), 82–88; Calvin D. Mortensen, "Should the Discussion Group Have an Assigned Leader?" *The Speech Teacher*, 15 (1966), 34–41.

3. Rewards and prestige are granted in accordance with the value of the specialty, and hence inequalities of wealth and influence are developed.

4. Specialization also creates a need for coordination, and the coordinator must be given power and authority; thus hierarchy is created.

5. Differences of rank erect barriers to communication, and the more sharply defined these barriers become the greater is the interference with feelings of comradeship and *esprit de corps*.[17]

By now it should be obvious that leadership (acts) is synonymous with the very complex process of communication within the group. Leadership is a fine sounding word that probably has done as much to mislead group members as to aid them. To provide beneficial leadership acts and to inhibit negative ones for a particular group working on a specific task at a particular time in a particular situation require far more than a few bromides about leadership can provide. These actions require insight and knowledge into the workings of groups of various types in various situations. There are no short cuts to effective leadership. Effective leadership and effective participation are one, and they (or it) assume a knowledge of the dynamics of the group-communication processes.

GROUP AS INFORMATION SYSTEM

It would help very much if students of group communication could be given a precise course of action or a how-to-do-it guidebook that would apply to all or even to many of the group situations that they eventually encounter. Since we know of no one who could write this book, given the present stage of knowledge on group communication, we have tried to select the best alternative. We propose that thinking about the group as an information pool provides a framework in which a member can ask the best questions concerning what behaviors he should contribute to the group in a given situation. Quite simply, a participant or an observer should consider that the group contains a wealth of resources consisting of various kinds of information. The member task or the group task is to extract from the group that information which is relevant and necessary to its goal. Another part of this task is to leave in or to avoid information possessed by the group that is superfluous or potentially destructive to its goal achievement.

Potential information is the whole range of human behaviors in the

17 Haiman, "The Specialization of Roles and Functions in a Group," p. 169.

form of either verbal (usually spoken) or nonverbal activity that might occur or that have already occurred in a particular group. An event or member comment does not have to "happen" to qualify as potential information. One member may be in possession of a fact, feeling, attitude, or personal quality which is never known to the group. This is still potential information. The pool of potential information is vital and unique for every group. It is limited by the information and abilities of the individual members in the group at a given time and by the physical resources available. For example, we do not worry whether, at the end of our classroom discussion, one or several group members will produce a full-size battleship. Furthermore, we do not consider that swearing in Swahili is a potential behavior or piece of information if we know that no one in the group possesses a knowledge of Swahili. Potential information in our usage then is nothing more than the behaviors which could occur in the group; some of them do and some of them do not actually occur. Members can never know for sure all the potential information contained in their group. They can only guess. Some behaviors are potential because an individual could produce them, and some, because they could conceivably result from a series of complicated interactions among several members in the group. This last class of behaviors is characterized by a mutuality and reciprocity of stimulation and reaction, respectively, among members as they interact together. These behaviors are especially important since they are the only products of group action which make a group effort (as opposed to an individual effort) worth anything at all.

Potential information divides into two parts that are extremely unequal in amount of content—manifest information and latent information. *Manifest information* consists of those elements in the potential-information pool which occur in a group at some time. *Latent information*, the larger class of information, consists of those behaviors which have not become part of the group's knowledge at a particular point in its history. What does happen is manifest; what has not happened but could conceivably be brought about by persons or circumstances is latent. Since only a very small fraction of what can be said or what can occur ever is or does in a particular group, the pool of latent information is always vast.

Referring to the earlier discussion of positive and negative acts, one may think of positive acts as those which (1) search for and encourage latent information which is likely to help the group solve its problems and (2) discourage manifest information which blocks a satisfactory resolution of the group's present or future problems. Information presented to the group may still be latent—for example, the quiet suggestion which is ignored because of its source or the way one unnoticed member leans back in his chair and looks at the ceiling every time another member speaks at length. Also, information which was manifest at one point and was recognized by the group may be forgotten when most relevant, perhaps much later in the life of the group. For all useful purposes this is latent information. Manifest information ceases to be manifest when it ceases to be used—when it ceases to affect the group process. But it remains in the potential pool waiting to be extracted again when it is needed or not extracted at all. Of course, the largest class of latent information is that which is never manifest on the surface in the group.

Information can be about people or ideas, procedures or social objects. Information can be about events that happened far away or within the group itself. It can be about feelings. It can tell what a group member thinks about his country, his dog, or the person sitting next to him. Information can also be facts—about a member's country, his dog, the person sitting next to him, or the group's task. Opinion information and factual information concerning people and events outside the group are often necessary for the work of any task-oriented group. Information concerning feelings which group members and nonmembers have toward one another is also very vital to a group's well-being and efficient functioning. On the other hand groups do digress into themes irrelevant to the task. After content-analyzing the themes from 124 three- to eight-man discussions, Berg found that one-eighth of all introduced were irrelevant to the task and accounted for 6.7 per cent of the group's total discussion time.[18] But some investigators feel that a certain amount of irrelevancies is inevitable and even necessary for the interpersonal adjustment required for successful work on the group task.[19]

Those verbal and nonverbal forms discussed in the first section of Part II convey information in a group. As in dyadic communication sight and sound are the predominant but not exclusive channels for conveying information. We shall suggest that other channels are also important in certain group situations by pointing out only that in some groups the combination of alluring perfume (smell) and a pretty pair of knees (sight . . . or touch) has probably played a great part in promoting interpersonal relations and retarding task accomplishment.

In addition to the several forms of sensory perception, the climate of the group conveys information. This climate consists of the memories of past happenings in the group, the tone of the acts of the group members,

[18] David M. Berg, "A Descriptive Analysis of the Distribution and Duration of Themes Discussed by Task-Oriented Small Groups," *Speech Monographs,* 34 (1967), 172–75.
[19] Robert F. Bales, "Adaptive and Integrative Changes as Sources of Strain in Social Systems," in *Small Groups: Studies in Social Interaction,* eds. A. P. Hare, E. F. Borgatta, and R. F. Bales (New York: Alfred A. Knopf, Inc., 1966), pp. 127–32.

the norms that establish the acceptable and the expected and distinguish these from the unacceptable and the unexpected, a host of immediate impressions from the physical setting in which the group is working, and the interpersonal character of member behaviors in the group. Immediate manifest information can change the climate or reinforce the old climate—can change what is acceptable and expected or further entrench the norms already present in the group.

Range of Potential Information

Viewing the group as an information *system* is of importance here. For the most part, it is an open system. However, during the course of any one meeting, it is closed in that the members are stuck with their pool of information; they are limited by their membership and interaction possibilities. But the group is often free to bring information back to the next meeting, to bring in new members, to tap new information resources, and otherwise to expand its pool of potential information. In this sense the system is somewhat open. Another characteristic of this system is that any occurrence in one part is likely to affect a member behavior in another part. The *range of potential information* contained in the group is therefore very important and may vary from extremely limited to extremely extensive. The more differences among the members of a group—differences in factual information, point of view, remembered experiences, personalities, verbal behavior, values, etc.—the larger the potential information of that group. An entire group is *homogeneous* (similar) or *heterogeneous* (different) with respect to all these various attributes.

A completely heterogeneous group would have the largest repertoire of information. However, since no two people in this group would to any extent share factual or opinion information, feelings, style of communicating, personality characteristics, and associated values, the potential information in the group would be extremely hard to control to enhance task achievement. That is, it would be exceedingly hard to obtain the agreement or cooperation needed to elicit the relevant information from the information pool. If two people do not have the same facts, their group benefits to the extent that both persons are capable of contributing unique, vital information to the group. But if no two people in the group have the same facts, the group is in trouble. The heterogeneous group can cooperate and use potential information only if members share some goals and agree on some procedures. Having a large potential (latent) body of information upon which to draw is not helpful if no one can agree on what is relevant.

In the opposite case all group members' skills, knowledge, values, and experiences would be so homogeneous that the range of potential information on which the group could draw would be extremely narrow. A group like this is fine for casual or social purposes. The private club allowing only a select group into its chambers or some fraternities whose rush practices are geared to a particular brand of middle-class pledge are examples of overly homogeneous groups. Since values, personalities, and backgrounds are so similar, members of these groups are mutually supporting, and cooperation is at a maximum. However, for a work group to have such an extremely homogeneous membership is detrimental since the reduced potential information and points of view represented by the members curtail creative solutions and real interchange of information.[20] There just is not much to exchange beyond small talk, mutual support, and fellowship. According to an old saying, "When two people agree on everything, one of them is unnecessary."

We have discussed the simple cases of extreme group homogeneity and heterogeneity across all member characteristics. In reality, the members of a particular group are rarely extremely heterogeneous or extremely homogeneous in more than one or two respects. For example, members of one group may be well balanced in several characteristics (socioeconomic backgrounds, etc.) but extremely heterogeneous with respect to their individual motives for being in the group. The classroom group of undergraduate upperclassmen at a resident university is frequently just such a group. After two or three years of living in a rather common environment, people develop a common slang vocabulary, a body of shared perceptions and attitudes toward objects in the environment, and the like. The overly cooperative group and the overly competitive group stem from homogeneity/heterogeneity imbalance in some basic respect.

Another way to view the range of potential information of a group is in terms of the degree of overlap in information brought in by individual members. An extreme overlapping of information and an extreme divergence of information are end points on a scale of mutuality of information in which the preferred amount of shared information is somewhere in the middle; the amount varies from one end of the continuum to the other according to the nature of the group task, the demands on interpersonal relations in the group, and the work environment. In the best situation, a group possesses enough divergence in information for intermember argument, stimulation, and creativity and enough overlap for minimal agreement and cooperation on group

[20] Hoffman, "Group Problem Solving," pp. 113–14. But see Collins and Guetzkow, who argue that tasks requiring minimal organization and use of group resources but maximum group harmony are more effectively performed by groups with member homogeneity in personality and background. *A Social Psychology of Group Processes for Decision-Making,* pp. 100–106.

goals—for rewards from interpersonal satisfaction through mutual support and expressed appreciation.

Noise Sources

Noise, as we discussed earlier in this book, refers to interference with information flow. In treating group communication, it is helpful to define *noise sources* as any factors which tend to convert permanently the useful potential information of a group into latent information (information from which the group will never benefit). These noise sources limit the manifest information produced by the group at any particular time. The consequence of noise is a loss of relevant information of potential value for group task performance.

Member differences in potential information

Members enter a group with certain differences in their potential to make contributions to the manifest information pool. As noted above, each group member possesses attitudes, knowledge of facts and opinions, past experiences with related problems, and a value system which differs in many respects from that of every other member. These member differences are noise sources to the extent that members have difficulty in reaching or fail to reach agreement on such matters as procedures for approaching their task and methods for resolving group conflict and for assessing what facts and values should be considered in group sessions. In the extreme case individual differences in the group are so great that the members do not perceive the same problem or seek the same group goal. Quite often, failure to discuss problems separately and one at a time leads to wasted time and frustrated members. How many groups have we been in in which members, when working on a task or procedural problem, attempted to discuss at once both criteria for solutions and the solutions themselves? Failure to define in advance what factual or other information is needed also can result in the noise of chaos and member withdrawal and frustration. Frustration, apathy, and interpersonal hostility result unless this problem is overcome or until the group can find some aspect of the problem that serves as a starting point upon which to build a common perspective. Certain member differences may not be so important as they seem to be to the members who differ. Often another member can point out similarities or move the discussion to a different topic if postponement is in keeping with group goals.

Another way member differences in factual information can inhibit potential information from entering the system is exemplified by the individual who possesses a fact which is highly relevant to the group problem but who is reluctant to divulge this to the group because it does not seem to fit in with information others in the group have been contributing. Similarly, if one point of view or perspective on a task or interpersonal problem predominates in a group, an overly cautious member may withhold a potentially valuable and creative perspective. This loss may be minimized if group members make it clear that the viewpoint or argument that they have not heard may be the one they most need. If group members habitually reward the contributions of infrequent contributors with their attentiveness and appreciation, the returns in information may be quite worth the effort; they may produce very worthwhile ideas as well as serve as a check on discussion that might just be in a rut. It is difficult for group members who are in the heat of an argument or fast paced discussion to keep the needs of the group task uppermost in their minds and not allow their individual needs to mold their behavior into a blind rush that tramples potential information from others. But, groups whose members temporarily can put aside self-oriented needs in favor of group-oriented needs win higher task achievement for their effort.[21]

If one member possesses a great deal more factual information on a task topic than any other member possesses, the group may allow an inordinate amount of its time to this member, while potential contributions pertaining to procedure and interpersonal relations or even other factual information may be lost to the group. This situation occurs frequently, perhaps because of the value our society places on getting the facts. While one must not discount the importance of factual information for any group task, an uncritical preference for factual contributions over all other potential information may not coincide with the immediate needs of the group. Testing facts for relevance, reasoning processes, procedural suggestions, and interpersonal problems all may take precedence over a fact at any given time in a particular group. Any time one member speaks at length, other members think of comments that they would like to make, and, if they cannot, apathy or resentment probably results. Anyone who must spend a lot of time on the receiving end of a communication is likely to become restless, frustrated, and then hostile because he does not have a chance to speak, ask questions, criticize, or somehow reply.[22] Scheidel and Crowell content analyzed the discussions of five problem-solving groups and found that 35 per cent of total dis-

[21] N. T. Fouriezos, M. L. Hutt, and H. Guetzkow, "Measurement of Self-Oriented Needs in Discussion Groups," *Journal of Abnormal and Social Psychology*, 45 (1950), 682–90; Bernard M. Bass and G. Dunteman, "Behavior in Groups as a Function of Self, Interaction, and Task Orientation," *Journal of Abnormal and Social Psychology*, 66 (1963), 419–28.
[22] Harold J. Leavitt and Ronald A. H. Mueller, "Some Effects of Feedback on Communication," in Hare, Borgatta, and Bales, pp. 434–43.

cussion content consisted of feedback processes. Feedback was characterized primarily by clarification and agreement.[23] The need to respond
can certainly be observed to some extent during lectures in college classrooms and much more so in a small-group meeting, where group members expect some amount of equity in participation. This phenomenon
is just a manifestation of a broader principle in group communication:
Any manifest information, because it occupies time, displaces other
potential information that might have been forthcoming from each of
the other members of the group.

Member differences in values and attitudes may also be noise sources.
When predominantly one attitude prevails in a group with respect to
a particular topic, a member who differs on that topic may default in
presenting an extremely important fact or argument because of the
pressure of the group or his fear of the group's possible reaction.

Member differences in personality

We might have included this discussion of personality differences in
the above subsection since those features of member personality that are
communicable to a group are as much a part of the group information
pool as facts and member attitudes. However, determining how much
of one's personality is actually capable of being translated into interpretable information through one's behavior is very difficult and justifies a
separate and special treatment for this particular noise source. Some
individuals are aggressive and verbally proficient. Others are aggressive
and not so verbally proficient; others are quiescent and verbally skilled;
still others, quiescent and unskilled in oral expression. Other individual
differences such as dependence on authority and lack of confidence
immediately come to mind when personality traits are under discussion.
Some people avoid conflict, while others are combative in nature. It
is easy to see how the effects of one member's personality can constitute
noise for other group members. A shy member finds it difficult to challenge an idea espoused by an aggressive, fluent member. A group in
which most members seek dependence on some authority figure or great
leader accepts many leadership acts uncritically. Accepting poor suggestions is often less threatening for these members than struggling for self-
direction in a difficult problem-solving situation in which members have
much freedom to make choices about how to proceed toward their group
task.

A group which contains extremely homogeneous personalities has a
difficult time accomplishing any challenging task. Imagine the noise

[23] Thomas M. Scheidel and Laura Crowell, "Feedback in Small Group Communication," *Quarterly Journal of Speech*, 52 (1966), 271–78.

which would ensue from a group whose members were all excessively aggressive or dependent on authority or comic-minded or serious-minded or exceedingly cooperative. The last trait calls for some explanation since the very nature of the discussion ideal is misleading in one respect. Discussion necessarily assumes a minimal amount of cooperation. However, some members may feel, from observing television panel shows, planned public symposiums, and other discussion performances, that cooperation is the most desirable commodity of discussion. This is not true, of course. Task accomplishment is the most desirable commodity to be gained from small-group communication, and an inferior product results when group members avoid honest disagreement and critical evaluation of member contributions. The potential values that the creative use of conflict and competition among group members holds for problem-solving groups have been passed over to a considerable extent in discussions of group methods. It is becoming increasingly clear that controlled competition within groups can be an asset to those groups' task achievements.[24]

Finally, we all are familiar with the slightly paranoid member who takes offense at every negative evaluation of his contributions and with the insensitive member who does not separate the idea he is criticizing from the person who presented it. These group "problem children" waste much precious group time if insightful group members do not recognize and circumvent these noise sources.

Individual differences in interest

Other differences may also contribute noise which suppresses potential information. Group members are rarely interested in the same problem or subproblem to the same degree. Members who are disinterested or less interested obviously do not feel so responsible or so motivated to contribute to group problem-solving or to the main task as the highly interested and involved group members do. Valuable information is also lost in another way because of this variable member interest. Participation and involvement usually produce heightened involvement, interest, and responsibility on the part of the participants. The discrepancy between the involvement of the participants and that of the silent noncontributors increases with the passage of time. Abstaining members also tend to feel less responsible for the group product as time goes by since others are carrying on the discussion and whatever happens can be blamed on them. When a great disparity of participation persists, increasingly more group resources become lost to the domain of latent information.

[24] For example, see James W. Julian and Franklyn A. Perry, "Cooperation Contrasted with Intra-Group and Inter-Group Competition," *Sociometry*, 30 (1967), 79–90.

Groups must find ways of breaking this cycle of disinterest-disengage-ment-withdrawal if valuable information is to be used. Fortunately, people are most likely to be interested in those topics that they know the most about, so we may expect some inequality of participation at any given time. Unfortunately, these inequalities tend to have halo effects, and groups tolerate them long after the very informed and the very interested members have contributed their unique information. In most cases we may attribute these halo effects to the status of the contributors.

Individual differences in status

Sometime when you are in a group which can spare your services for a minute, observe who is being looked at most of the time by all the group members. It is important to observe who people look to both when they are talking and when they are silent. In most small groups one person more than any other is the focus of attention. He is the high-status man in that group. When a member starts to talk, he usually looks at the member whose comment preceded his own or at the member whose comment produced his reaction. Frequently however the speaker shifts his glance directly to another person in the group a moment after he has begun his commentary. Again, this focal person is the high-status member in the group. There are exceptions to this observation. Some-times a member who has very little status in the group becomes the focal point for a time—the deviate or the holdout, for example, whose refusal to go along makes him the center of the group's efforts to change his mind. But over several group meetings—usually in one meeting—the high-status person is easy to identify by this method. Even in the case of the above exception, the high-status person probably leads the attack and still captures about as much attention as the deviate. It is only natural that most member attention be paid to the high-status person in the business conference, the board meeting, and the faculty committee meeting since this status usually indicates that the holder is a source of considerable power; the support of power is always sought in order to have one's proposal adopted, one's position secured, or because of other less intentional behavioral determinants.

In a small group the high-status person has his position because (1) he earned it by obtaining high group approval (achieved status), (2) he was elected or appointed leader, chairman, or president (positional status), or (3) his reputation outside the group was favorably evaluated by the group members. More than one of these brands of status may apply at the same time to one or several members in a group. The very existence of different levels of status produces noise in a group since it means that some members obtain more group attention and other members' potential information is slighted. Let us consider some of the ways in which this noise occurs for each of the three kinds of status.

Achieved status comes to a member when he acts and talks in a way that causes the group to look to him for guidance and support. A member can achieve status in many ways—from efficiently handling a conflict in the group to contributing much factual knowledge on a topic. In the former example he informs the group (1) how to handle conflicts of this kind in the future and (2) that he is capable of performing certain behaviors that are valuable to the group.

Since so much information comes so fast in group interaction, members must distort and oversimplify their observations of what has happened in order to retain anything from the interaction. Since John was so effective and made sense in situation X, the group is likely to view John as an effective and sensible person in general. Thus, much admiration may accrue to John, who, incidentally, may have no other positive information to contribute to the group problem at all. But, since our information must be simplified and organized, we are likely to uncritically accept John's mediocre overtures in other aspects of the group problem. John may have achieved his status by simply talking more than anyone else at a time when others had little to say. However, regardless of how he achieved his status, once he has it, members will address more remarks to John than to lower-status group members, who may have real information.

The simple mechanics of eye contact can be very important in group communication. The likelihood that John will speak at a particular time in a group depends in part on the extent to which he feels he is expected to speak. When someone addresses John and looks at him, he can hardly fail to respond if given the chance. Conversely, if John is never addressed directly by anybody, a certain combination of motivating forces within and around John must conspire to produce an utterance from him. He will slip increasingly into the role of listener, until, at last, he knows that the sound of his voice would so startle his fellow group members and so violate their expectations for his silence that he would almost "rather die" than speak. Differential member status thus assures that some members are ignored more than others, thereby relegating important information to the trash pile of latent information forever.

Differences in status or social rank curtail by their very existence the possible interaction patterns that might occur in a particular group. Low-status persons in a group usually speak to members with higher status rather than to other low-status persons. Once the status hierarchy is stabilized, high-status persons usually speak to other high-status members. When these facts are considered in light of the effect of physical directness on member participation, it is easy to see how much valuable potential information is inevitably lost to every group that ever gathers around a conference table.

Being elected leader, chairman, or president further rewards the group member who achieves high status. His new *positional status* further entrenches the communication barriers just discussed. Positional status is found in most small groups. Frequently the boss or supervisor or some other higher-up from the group's environment (factory, corporation, etc.) has the responsibility for leading or chairing the group. Positional status does not refer only to transplanted power from outside-the-group sources however. The boss may appoint a member to lead the group or his peers from within the group itself may elect him. Positional status derived from outside sources is frequently a very loud noise factor because the added power of the company or corporation or university administration is behind the supervisor or leader. In addition to this relationship-distortion factor, the leader's qualifications may bear no relation whatsoever to the skills demanded by the group task. The noise is only slightly muffled when positional status comes from an appointee since the boss or a power figure usually does the appointing. We have already discussed the special case of achieved status being transformed into positional status within the group. Positional status, like achieved status, ensures that certain information will be lost because of the mechanics of individual motivation and attention previously described.

When a group relies on one member a great deal because of his reputation elsewhere, that member has high *reputational status*. Here again noise is produced when overreliance on this high-status person results in the loss of other, more crucial information and procedural direction which this person is not capable of giving the group. If the reputation is impressive enough, group members find it difficult to evaluate as non-crucial or erroneous something that the high-status person says, even though it may indeed be. Less noise occurs in this situation if the high-status person gained his reputation in activities closely related to the task of the present group. But, if the group task is to solve the water shortage in Chicago and our star obtained his reputation from his research in nuclear physics or from his winning the race for student body president or from his prowess in running a jack hammer, group faith has been sadly misplaced. He may add to the information pool, but he is unlikely to live up to the superhuman capacities group members may attribute to him. Alas, when the member's reputation glows to completely outshine the group's rational thinking capacities, the group honors him with additional positional prestige and the functions and power associated with that position. Noise is compounded with noise. Throughout the above discussion we have considered only one top-status role. Of course, in most groups status is spread among various members who form a status hierarchy. Groups do not confer achieved status only on the man who takes over. We may often define fairly unambiguous gradations of status for several people in groups and for all members in quite a few small groups. Positional status applies to the secretaries, the sergeants at arms, the seconds in command, and the fourths in command as well as to the chairmen. Reputational status is a very important phenomenon in the real world, largely because so many small groups work within the framework of a large organization and so many group members are known quantities. Any status differential produces noise in the group information system, and all groups develop some form of status hierarchy.

We should qualify the rather dismal picture painted above. We know of groups in which holders of achieved status artfully decline to get mileage out of their preferential role; of other groups in which chairmen wisely use their positional power to make potential information in the group manifest; and of still other groups in which experts rightly disclaim the expertness with which they are inadvertently credited. Having said this, we still have our stated task in this section, which was not to list group successes but to analyze causative factors in old failures.

Noise from situational sources

Certain noise sources which do not fit under the several topics considered thus far are important enough to merit some attention at this point. The specialization of roles and functions in a group, described above, causes several serious disturbances to effective group functioning. In the above discussion of positional status as a noise source we dealt with one way in which specialization creates noise. Natural specialization in a group constitutes, by its very nature, a basic noise source related to all other sources discussed so far. Communication problems created by specialization in a small group are often manifested in complete withdrawal, partial nonparticipation, and subgrouping within the group itself. The very fact that the different functions may not be performed by the members most capable of those functions is an immediate problem. The division of labor may not be so efficient as group members believe it to be. In addition, dissatisfaction with a special role, envy, jealousy, or irritation with another's role behavior may result from the hierarchy created by specialization. Specialization in a group is more subtle than specialization in society. Since a large part of the behavior in small groups is verbal behavior, much specialization manifests itself in members' limiting themselves to certain kinds of statements whose relevance is primarily task-oriented, primarily interpersonal, or primarily procedural. Some members may confine themselves to even narrower behavioral roles, such as attacker, joker, supporter, fact man, or just listener.

A particular brand of noise results from specialization when one man, because of the situation, pre-empts an important group resource. If the task calls for a highly technical or manual skill, like knowing Latin or taking shorthand, and if only one member can perform this function, certain powers and responsibilities fall to this person in other areas as well. For instance, if a group needs rather detailed information on its proceedings, what the recorder selects or leaves out may produce noise. Also, the group may accept the recorder's direction and advice in other areas since he controls a badly needed resource. His special function gives him special access to information, and therefore he has an edge over other members if he wishes to use it to dominate or influence discussion for some reason.

If only one person has done his homework or research in a particular area in which knowledge is indispensable to some phase of group problem-solving, that person is an indispensable man. Equally crucial, that prepared individual is the only person in the group capable of assessing just how indispensable his information is. All other members must rely on his judgment, and because of this reliance his power increases. We may liken this pre-emption of crucial resources to a monopoly in society. It creates dependency and accords more power to the monopolist. Furthermore, if something goes wrong with the monopolist in the group, the group is not prepared to replace him.

In small-group communication, as in dyadic communication, the setting of discussion may be quite influential for what occurs in the group. An example of this tends to operate in certain social and even in many noncasual groups; members (especially in an unfamiliar situation) are sometimes loathe to challenge the comment of a host upon whom they depend for coffee, tea, milk, beer, or whiskey. Although this kind of self-inhibiting behavior may seem silly and illogical, resource pre-emption does have a powerful effect in this and more formal group settings.

Of course, a leader may exert much control over the behavior of group members and task activities as a monopolist if he pre-empts, because of his behavior, his title, or his status, a certain leadership function for himself. Without him the dependent group members may cease to function as they are supposed to. We may describe all member resources in this way. Thus, when any important piece of group machinery breaks down, other machinery must be ready to take its place. Specialization of functions, if allowed to proceed to the extreme, would probably result in the most inefficient group functioning conceivable. In this hypothetical group any information would be pertinent to only one specialist at a time, and responsibility would be divided into distinct individual zones instead of being shared by the group; every man would be indispensable to the group and no one would be responsible or capable beyond his own narrow niche.

Almost every textbook treating discussion includes a section on communication networks, or paths, along which information is permitted to or tends to flow within a particular group.[25] The wheel, the inverted-Y, the circle, the chain, and the open network are among the most frequently discussed patterns. Figure 7 illustrates these networks. Since,

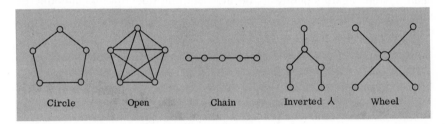

Fig. 7. Communication networks.

in all our lives, we have never been in or observed small, face-to-face groups which even slightly resembled the circle or the chain designs, we shall briefly discuss only the other three patterns. Presumably, if everyone speaks loudly enough, all groups conform to an open network, in which what one person says is heard and is responded to by potentially every person in the group. On the other hand, we may also consider communication flow in terms of the intended recipients of various comments made during group interaction. Analyzing groups with respect to these who-to-whom patterns usually produces much more complicated and asymmetrical patterns than any of those presented here. Frequently members seem to be addressing the whole group. Any pattern is possible in small-group discussion. The range of possibilities is limited only by members who will not talk to particular others, by members who will not talk at all, and by the number of people in the group. The wheel is probably the most frequent pattern that occasionally can be seen operating in a group since, as we pointed out earlier, group interaction

[25] For a recent review of communication network studies, see Marvin E. Shaw, "Communication Networks," in *Advances in Experimental Social Psychology*, Vol. 3, ed. Leonard Berkowitz (New York: Academic Press Inc., 1966), pp. 111–47.

frequently centers for a time around one man—a temporary deviate, a high-status person, a holder of resources, a coordinator of member activities, or a source of critical information. The inverted Y has meaning for us only when an outside-the-group person or persons are included in the network. The isolated dot at the top of the inverted-Y pattern represents, for example, the boss who gives information and directions to a group leader and receives reports from him on group progress. There are no physical barriers in the open-network, face-to-face group, but a number of both psychological and social noise sources may limit the flow of information along certain paths or among certain people in the group. When the interaction of a group temporarily turns into several private conversations among pairs and trios of group members simultaneously, a common, central focus must break this pattern before an open system again operates. Because finding the optimal amount of manifest information is the seeking-searching-trading process that it is, a potentially open network is most desirable for most small-group tasks.

Summary

We may think of noise as a phenomenon which produces a more random selection from the potential information pool than would be produced by a well planned, rational selection of elements that are positive for a group's goals. In this sense noise is a nonselective process through which more useless and fewer useful units of information become manifest information in the group. Many people who conduct discussions and group problem-solving activities think that all that is needed for success is a good, "strong" leader and several willing and cooperative followers. More often than not, these group efforts produce manifest information that is only slightly more relevant and productive than that which would be produced by any group of strangers selected at random and given a random problem to solve.

One may liken the potential information of a group to a large bag of marbles of various colors. Of all the marbles, only the red ones are helpfully employed at a given time. One may plunge his hand aggressively and repeatedly into the bag and with a show of much confidence come up with a handful of nonred marbles and an occasional red one. Or one may attempt to assess by holding the bag up to the light or by other such opportunistic moves just where a cluster of red marbles may be located. The texture of the marbles may provide a clue to the selector. Furthermore, once nonred marbles have appeared out of the bag (manifest information), one may selectively reject them as expeditiously as possible according to some set of criteria (light waves reflected, effect on group climate, etc.). The plunger will never find many more red marbles than what chance allows. The group which searches actively for clues as to where the red marbles (positive information) are located will probably improve the odds. And this group most certainly will not be satisfied to probe the top of the bag and assume that what it finds there is all there is. The measure of a group's success is the extent to which the members, by employing thoughtfully selected criteria, can overcome the noise sources which randomize manifest information. These criteria enable members to produce increasingly more positive manifest information from the bag of potential information.

Information Type and Group Function

We may classify any single unit of behavior which occurs in a group or which could occur in a group (potential information) on the basis of (1) its basic function within the total group process, (2) the purpose of the group member exhibiting the behavior, and (3) the effects the behavior has on the group members who observe it.

Basic function of a unit of information

Dividing the potential information of a group into (1) task-relevant information, (2) interpersonal information, and (3) procedural information has certain advantages for the practitioner of group discussion. Task-relevant information and interpersonal information serve complementary functions in all groups. No group can move ahead and get down to business on a problem of any importance without dealing with interpersonal information along the way. On the other hand, if all a group's time is devoted to its internal interpersonal relations, no progress will be made on the group task.

A third class of potential information in the group is procedural information. This class is tied to both task and interpersonal information; yet it describes functions distinct enough to constitute a third perspective on potential information. Procedural information consists of those guidelines which members may be able to employ to help (or hinder) the group in its approach to both task and interpersonal problems. Manifest procedural information usually comes in the form of an explicit appeal, suggestion, or demand to the group as a whole. Statements concerning whether the group should have an agenda, what kind, who the leader should be (if anybody), what his powers should be, what method should be used for resolving conflict should it arise are all examples of procedural information.

Frequently, group members adopt a procedure automatically and unthinkingly just because they started doing things that way. This is often a serious mistake. Procedural information must be conveyed explicitly to the group so that (1) later misunderstandings can be avoided, (2) members can be given a chance to object, and, most important of all, (3) the underlying need (if any) for a particular procedure can be outlined. Such a discussion often clarifies the group's goal and other important issues. We are not saying that decisions on desirable procedure cannot or should not be postponed in many cases. Often, a group can operate on very few procedural givens. A group can quickly agree on "in case of fire . . . jump" at the very beginning of its life. Such low-cost rules may save the group much hassle and noise later on at a crucial stage in task accomplishment.

One question that students often ask in a classroom discussion about group leadership is, "Isn't procedure an area in which one highly skilled member of the group should provide leadership and guidance?" We considered this comment in a previous subsection and saw that the information-system point of view offers another resolution. If one man has a larger amount of positive, potential procedural information than the entire group has, then that man certainly should handle all the procedural direction for the group, providing his capacity for contributing negative procedural comments (ones that would hurt the group) is very low.

In this case X is the only person in the group who can make positive procedural suggestions, and, since the other members in the group may make negative procedural suggestions, X gets the job. This kind of intellectual monopoly is extremely unlikely to exist. Furthermore, one can only guess at the potential information in a group or where it is located. Therefore little can ever be gained by forcing all the other group members to withdraw from the field.

Many groups seem to be automated only when it comes to selection of appropriate procedures. That is, discussion groups often follow some procedure for no reason other than familiarity—it seemed to work before or it is the only method they know. But if the procedure in question was used to solve a different kind of group problem in a different setting, the same method could be more harmful than if the group were just to plunge ahead with no procedural considerations whatsoever.

Purpose of behaver

We may regard manifest information from the point of view of the *behaver*, who, by talking or doing or both, turns some formerly latent information into manifest information. The behaver does some things intentionally and other things unintentionally, purposefully and nonpurposefully. He may talk to the group as a whole or look at one member and talk loud enough so that the group can hear him. He may smile or grimace to show his approval or disapproval of others' contributions or of the way things are going in general at one particular moment. He may state a fact, state his own opinion, report an opinion of another, or present a line of reasoning which supports or attacks an idea presented by another. He may tell his philosophy of life or cry or punch someone in the nose. He may look at one individual while directly addressing another group member by name. These can all be purposeful acts from his behavioral repertoire—from his personal store of information. He gives this information to the group to use as it may. But many of these same behaviors—this same manifest information—may occur when the behaver is not aware that he is informing.

Unintentional behaviors produced naturally may also constitute a very important part of the manifest pool of information in a group. X may address the group while casting a glance toward a power figure or a pretty girl or a member with whom he is in competition. There may be an edge to his voice which he does not realize is there, or perhaps he realizes it but can do nothing about it momentarily. X may inform the group by his silence, especially if he has been a particularly talkative member in most circumstances or if another member in the group has just directed a comment at him. He may become defensive and inform the group of this by a more assertive attitude and more vocal force than the situation merits. He may become angry and inform the group of this by an uncharacteristic, too rapid, arhythmic speech. He may use a polysyllabic word where a simpler expression would be sufficient and so inform the group of his desire to impress. All these are unintentional behaviors, of which he is not aware or over which he has no control. He conveys information to the group in excess of that which he means to convey.

The examples so far have been instances of neutral or undesirable traits or feelings of the individual behaver. But people inform unintentionally about desirable qualities also. Sometimes a quiet, simple statement informs not only about substantive facts on a topic but also about the well ordered mind of the speaker. The way in which one member argues with another may inform the group of his stability and fairness as a person. By observing a conflict, the group may notice an ability of one member to develop creative ideas out of disagreement in addition to noticing any substantive progress made on the issue in contention. So-called *bad* characteristics of a group member, whether intentionally or unintentionally revealed by him, can constitute a positive piece of information for the group. The tendency of one member to exaggerate his "facts" is very valuable information. The trait itself may be bad, but knowing about it is advantageous to the group if reliance on facts is important to its task. Certain other ways in which a member can inform unintentionally about himself can be observed only over a long period of time. Tendencies to give support to others, to attack others, to contribute predominantly task-relevant or interpersonal or procedural information are just a few of the traits that a behaver may communicate to his group over a long history of member interaction.

Effect on observer

The other end of the behaver's frame of reference is, of course, the perspective of the several group members who are observing, listening to, and watching him. By this time you are aware that what is received in human communication is never exactly the same as what was sent. Because of this and because we can cheerfully sacrifice consistency to attain relevance, we now approach the group members who are observing or receiving the information or behavior entirely differently from the way we discussed the behaver himself. Responses elicited by the behaver's actions may be (1) affective, or emotional, and (2) ideational, or informative in the narrow sense of that word. Affects such as anger, pity, shame, envy, sympathy, elation, depression, enthusiasm, and embarrassment occur together with ideational reactions in an observer. Likewise ideation rarely occurs without some trace of emotionality. Therefore, we are not suggesting in the following discussion that the two modes of response can be separated in any one person's reaction to a given behavior or even that it makes sense to speak of two modes. But, because they aid our attempts at explanation, we shall rely on the notions of predominantly affective and predominantly ideational member responses.

A particular behaver may elicit in an observer ideational processes which cause the observer to remember an event or idea similar to the one described. Perhaps, through a chain of only slightly understood thought associations, the observer remembers an idea completely unrelated to the stimulating remark. Another frequent ideational response focuses attention on certain aspects of the ideas presented, and the observer, by combining these aspects with his interpretative and rational evaluative thought processes, puts together a different idea or shifts focus from the idea initially presented. Any behavior observed, whether by listening or watching, alone or in combination, adds new information to the potential information store of the various individual observers in the group. New elements in the observers' repertoires become potential ingredients for the observers' manifest information if and when they contribute to the group.

To facilitate explanation we presented the earlier discussion of the behaver as though a person turns his behavior on and off. This is incorrect, of course. A group member is always behaving whether he talks or not. However, we are interested only in that information which crosses the actual threshold and becomes manifest in a group so that most members can take it into their own internal store of information. *Behavior* here includes only the potentially useful information which does become part of the information of the whole group. Of course, individuals notice different things during their group interaction and, having noticed something once, may forget all or part of it. We are not suggesting that manifest information occurs all at once or never within a group. The threshold for what is noticed may be different for any two observers at a given time. Some group members derive meaning from a particular member behavior which others do not notice in more than a casual way. In addition to this, interpretations of the same behavior by two group members often vary so much that each attaches a different meaning to the behavior.

In all the examples of ideational reaction above, individuals added to their stores of potential information and thereby increased their repertoires of potential remarks and actions in relation to a particular subject. However, many of these ideational reactions are not so simple in their effect on the individual's potential information as these examples may imply. For one individual, a new piece of information or an intriguing suggestion may displace momentarily or for the duration of the group's life a particular piece of potential information. Thus, certain information is lost, temporarily or permanently, to the latent domain. If X has something to say on a topic and someone shifts the topic before he says it, his information is lost to the latent domain. Also ideational processes stimulated by another's behavior may cause a member to reevaluate the worth or appropriateness of an idea he was going to present, and this information too is then lost. In any group one never has enough time to say more than a very small percentage of what one is thinking. Therefore that information which an individual group member selects is limited by such factors as opportunity, personality, and the nature of the new information emerging in the group at the time.

A member may also consign potential information to the latent pool when he decides that one or several others have already said what he intended to say. He may feel that his slant is so similar that to present it would be redundant and would leave him open to negative criticism. This process is constantly a factor in the ideational responses of group members to the behaviors of other group members. Fortunately, this verbal self-editing process saves much time. Unfortunately, a self-restrained member may withhold an occasional piece of valuable information with a different twist. When in doubt, contribute.

The above examples suggest observer responses to only ideational or factual information. However, a group would probably be incapacitated if members did not frequently respond ideationally (with a minimum of emotion) to affective behaviors of other members. Information about degree of interest, self-confidence, certainty of judgment, directed hostility, or friendliness is affective information that a behaver can convey intentionally or unintentionally and that other group members can respond to. In the university classroom, students and professors are constantly evaluating, quite objectively, the emotional overtones that they observe in one another. They put this ideational information to constructive use as they attempt to establish the stable pattern of expectations and role relations so important to any human association.

We may well have treated the predominantly affective, or emotional, reactions produced in group members under noise since factual and analytical information and solutions which evoke anger, uncritical sympathy, or other automatic emotions on the part of an observer provide little useful information to the group and often use up valuable group time. On the other hand, conviction and involvement are necessary ingredients of real confrontation. And, if a group member is involved in his task, a fact can stir his emotions as much as a favorite poem or a hated object. Communication of one's wholehearted support of an attitude or of an idea espoused by another requires a modicum of emotional involvement on the part of the supporter.

Affective reactions to member behaviors most often produce noise when the reacter's emotion comes from a failure to separate ideas from the human beings who present those ideas. One should remember that a group member is much more than what he says and does in a group. His manifest behaviors in a group reveal only a minimum of what he is. Affective reactions also produce noise when ego-involvement with one's own words and defensive, hold-fast attitudes to maintain an image in a group bypass real reasoning processes and consign valuable information to the latent domain. Our description of how new ideational information expands an observer's potential information also applies to affective information. If one can become aware that he reacts with an emotional affinity to some member personalities and with repulsion or irritation to other member personalities, he may adjust somewhat to his humanness, pledging a more critical evaluation of the ideas of the former and a more accepting evaluation of the behaviors of the latter in all future group deliberation.

Summary

Awareness of the subtleties of the ever-changing manifest information in a group, of the fact that manifest information expands the potential information of a group by stimulating new perceptions in the information stores of its members, and of the way some manifest information by its existence drives other information to the latent sphere represents the insights that group members should have in order to avoid noise factors that inhibit useful manifest information. Knowledge of the complexity of group processes should foster an attitude of careful experimentation and discourage an arrogant, know-it-all attitude in all the members. The potential information of each group member, and therefore of the group as a whole, is constantly fluctuating from the first moment of group life. The manifest information which must be drawn from the dynamic group information pool is limited and complicated by the various factors considered in this section and by many others. Manifest information can tell the group an outside-of-group fact or opinion about a group member, or it can convey feelings about a member. In short, information can be about people as well as about things and ideas.

The problem of noise in a group is serious because many group failures are never thought of as failures. A noise source—status, for example—interferes in a myriad of ways with optimal manifest information, but group members accept it uncritically and unconsciously because it is so much a part of the way things are that they do not even question whether things could be different. What further audacity it would take to suggest an actual departure from traditional, established group procedures concerning leadership, uses of the agenda, and others! A group must be aware of its own information system and even analyze some of its characteristics. Members may then realize that effective group communication requires them to make conscious choices from among their available behaviors and to establish procedures which improve the quality of the results of their deliberations.

GROUP COMPOSITION, TASK DEMANDS, AND INSTRUMENTAL FORMS

What should one do in a discussion group to assure the best possible task achievement? We certainly have not answered this question thus far in our consideration of group communication; and we do not feel that it can be answered at all. We have indicated the effects of certain conditions under which groups are formed, the characteristics and effects of several kinds of leadership, and the basic nature of the group information system. We even stated our preferences in some of the above matters based on the evidence available. However, in almost every instance we have been forced by the evidence to qualify our generalizations drastically. So, for example, we maintain that highly directive or autocratic leadership is much more effective when the group task permits only one solution and requires only one kind of information from the group members. But, when the task requires varied information and approaches, nondirective leadership produces the best outcomes.[26]   As another example, we maintain that a group that is highly cohesive performs its task better than a less cohesive group. But, a highly cohesive group does poorly on a task that requires heterogeneous and conflicting contributions because extremely high cohesiveness in a group homogenizes individual performance levels and contribution contents.[27]   In other words it is not possible to provide one adequate answer to the above question without more information than that question contains.   It always depends.   In the next few pages we shall discuss the art of asking answerable questions of one's self and of others who may be available concerning small-group communication; we shall simultaneously present an alternative conception through which to approach decision-making discussion activity.

$$\text{group composition} \times \text{task demands} \times \text{instrumental forms}$$

$$= \text{group output}$$

We shall explore briefly the terms of the above equation and the relationships among the terms.   Group composition and task demands are givens; that is, we assume that they are relatively stable and unalterable. One is stuck with his group members and with his group task in most cases.   Instrumental forms is the unknown quantity in the equation.   It is a blank check that must be filled in or identified either through knowledge of the group members or, as in many cases, through habitual forms or accident.   This term represents the only area in which one may exercise choices in the group discussion; it is the only facet of small-group discussion in which decisions may be made.   The term on the right side of the equals sign is in reality unknown until the group has completed its task and has received an evaluation of the quality of its product.   But we shall treat this term as a given and equate it with high task quality or most effective solution possible or the like.   In every group the three terms on the left combine to produce a result or outcome, the group task. As we shall define them, group composition, task demands, and instrumental forms subsume every variable phenomenon or characteristic that enters into a small-group discussion and upon which the eventual excellence, mediocrity, or failure of the group output depends.

[26] Marvin Shaw and Michael Blum, "Effects of Leadership Style upon Group Performance," *Journal of Personality and Social Psychology*, 3 (1966), 238–42.
[27] C. J. Lammers, "Stratification in a Small Group," *Human Relations*, 20 (1967), 283–300.

We shall not specify the long list of instrumental forms here but shall indicate that this list includes the procedures for resolving conflict, the various kinds of agenda (including no agenda), the physical arrangements possible for member discussion, the modes and styles of leadership available, and the numerous other techniques and alternatives for dividing labor in the group; in short, instrumental forms cover any means that the group could use to structure goal-directed interaction out of the numerous and rather randomly available behavioral possibilities that members can provide.

In too many groups, instrumental forms are never considered deliberately but just occur because members often make automatic assumptions about what are proper and what are improper procedures. This is probably one reason why criteria-oriented groups are more successful on group tasks than solution-oriented groups are.[28] Groups which have the foresight to delineate criteria for a problem are also likely to deal explicitly with procedural matters before rushing for solutions. In many other groups forms are not discussed. In these groups, members select and discard forms not on the basis of what they know about their group composition and about the task demands but on the basis of one member's naive generalizations from previous group experience which brought him to favor or discredit a particular method as being the best or the worst one possible. As we have seen throughout this section, group communication processes are not so uncomplicated that one method or procedure is good (or bad) all the time in all circumstances. In all areas of instrumental forms—leadership, division of labor, and the like—a group must select from among the many alternatives those forms to use and those forms to add or omit as problem-solving progresses. The only basis for selection of one procedure over another is an analysis of the given terms in the equation—a thoughtful analysis of the prescribed elements of group composition and task demands.

When group meets task what forms should be used to achieve maximum group output? We shall look first at the elements prescribed by the first given, group composition. We have already seen how every group is unique and contains various member personalities, levels of member training in discussion, member experience in dealing with similar tasks, member possession of task-relevant information, and many of the elements discussed in a previous section. Even though every group possesses a unique combination of member resources, every group also may be described as possessing more or less of a certain element of group composition. Homogeneous or heterogeneous levels of information,

[28] N. R. F. Maier and A. R. Solem, "Improving Solutions by Turning Choice Situations into Problems," *Personnel Psychology*, 15 (1962), 151–57.

skill in problem-solving, opinion and attitude resources are all aspects of group composition. Members have different perspectives on the task. One member may have a reputation others know about. Two members may be old friends or enemies. The group may contain four or five or 20 members. The group may consist entirely of males or females or be mixed in sex composition. Member backgrounds may be similar or varied. Age levels represented in the group are important composition elements if the task is one which people of different ages perceive quite differently. Group members may have varied or similar motivations for joining or being in the group and resultant levels of apathy or commitment to the group task goal. Is the group voluntary or prescribed? Does it have a temporary or rather enduring life expectancy? All of these group and member characteristics and resources should be considered in selecting instrumental forms.

Some facets of group composition are visible at first. Perhaps, after some group work, patterns of member attraction and member conflict emerge, and changes in forms may be in order. Group composition offers many clues for selection of desirable task-facilitating forms for any given group. Research has uncovered several stable relationships between elements of group composition and the instrumental forms most likely to facilitate that group's task. We have discussed a limited number of these relationships throughout the section on group communication.

Many of our conditional statements regarding leadership and other forms were qualified by the nature of the group task. We now turn to the second given in our equation—task demands. Like group composition, every group task has unique properties. And like group composition, uniqueness notwithstanding, the task may be described in terms of its several elements or demands. Roby and Lanzetta have defined task demands, indicating that "the distinctive features of particular tasks will be the degree to which they require certain group behaviors for adequate performance."[29] We shall include the influence of the environment in which group discussion takes place within the realm of task demands. Suffice it to say that for some groups and for some tasks, an important and consequential factor in the resulting group product is whether the deliberation occurs in a private, quiet lounge or in the busy corner of a crowded office building. This very incomprehensive but suggestive list gives examples of task demands which may be critical to consider in selecting instrumental forms for structuring the group problem-solving activity.

[29] T. B. Roby and J. T. Lanzetta, "Considerations in the Analysis of Group Tasks," *Psychological Bulletin*, 55 (1958), 95.

Is time critical?
Is technical information required?
Is the task complex multistage or single stage?
Is a variety of different kinds of information needed?
Are parts of the problem similar or different?
Is a synthesis of information required?
Is an integration of information or creativity required?
Is total member agreement required?
Does the task involve implementation in addition to oral decision-making?
Does the task imply a necessary order of precedence of its several stages?

At present, there is little prescriptive information on what various tasks require of group members for effective action. Investigators have just begun to develop a system for classifying different tasks on the basis of the particular combinations of demands unique to those tasks.[30] But beyond that, group members must be analytical and draw inferences according to their best reasoning capabilities. Most task descriptions contain much information from which wise groups can profit. For example, consider a group whose task is to recommend to a town council a solution to a water-shortage problem. An immediately apparent task demand is that the group eventually must by some means agree on a set of statements to be included in the recommendation. It must find a locus of agreement with respect to an unknown number of issues. But reaching this kind of agreement is not a demand of all other group tasks. Some groups, like the synectics groups of Gordon[31] and the brainstorming groups of Osborn[32] may fulfill their group task with a minimum of formal member agreement.

In the above example, no means of arriving at agreement is implied in the task. So the group has a wild card, or choice of forms, with which to work toward agreement. If the task is such that members have to implement the solution themselves, total consensus is the desirable level of agreement toward which to work. Consensus, when achieved, means that every member is somewhat committed and in support of the decision. Therefore, members are likely to cooperate during the implementation of the solutions. They are eager to defend it to outside-of-group critics and have an investment in making it work. For the same action group, forms which facilitate equality of member participation and

---

[30] For example, see Roby and Lanzetta, "Considerations in the Analysis of Group Tasks," pp. 88–101; Marvin E. Shaw, "Scaling Group Tasks: A Method for Unidimensional Analysis," Technical Report #1, University of Florida, July 1963.
[31] William J. J. Gordon, *Synectics* (New York: Harper & Row, Publishers, 1961).
[32] A. F. Osborn, *Applied Imagination* (New York: Charles Scribner's Sons, 1953).

influence are desirable in the planning stage because future member satisfaction and cooperation are furthered by maximum member participation and shared responsibility for the decisions. However, if the water-shortage task implies other demands—for example, if the group need not implement their solution and if time is a critical demand—different forms will be more effective.

Group tasks rarely specify most of the forms which the group must absolutely use, and they quite frequently specify no forms whatsoever, even though choices of the appropriate instrumental forms are aided by a knowledge of the task demands, as indicated above. Some tasks, of course, do tell group members precisely which method they must use in certain areas of deliberation. For example, juries have the explicitly stated task of trying to arrive at a consensus. In this example, the method of agreement is specified as an integral part of the task itself. Jurors are limited to that level of agreement-seeking before they even start. But, of course, they have a considerable number of decisions to make in all the other instrumental areas, including the character of their leadership, other special roles and divisions of labor, and methods of obtaining optimum feedback in their deliberations.

Ascertaining what is not a critical demand of a task can be very important to selection of the appropriate forms. Unfortunately, many groups plunge into their tasks with a back-breaking load of restrictive and superfluous assumptions concerning the "proper" forms—assumptions derived from limited personal experience in group problem-solving of dissimilar tasks and from everywhere else except from the nature of the present task itself. To carry the water-shortage example a step further, if members know they must agree on certain things, time may be saved and interpersonal strife avoided by making it clear to all at the outset just how much agreement is necessary. Members might begin by stipulating what will constitute a significant disagreement as inferred from the reigning set of task demands. Like group composition, task demands should reflect on all aspects of group interaction. Task demands and group composition provide clues to which instrumental forms are most appropriate and valuable for a task.

The excellence of the final output depends on the ability of the group members to recognize the elements in group composition and task demands and to consciously select the best instrumental forms available in the repertoire of the group. Members must select forms which connect the two givens, group composition (resources) and task requirements, most harmoniously. Armed with an analysis of task demands of a particular group task and an analysis of group-composition elements, group members are better able to answer the question posed at the beginning of this section, "What is the best procedure for our group?" With such a focus group members are able to choose procedures consciously and deliberately in their attempts to guide their discussion toward goal attainment.

We have discussed the two givens in the group equation separately here only because books are restricted to linear exposition. But groups are faced with composition and task-demand problems at the same time and must select their methods from an analysis of the interaction of both. Group members should make judgments at every point in their work with respect to these important matters.

CONCLUSION

In Part II we have covered topics pertaining to the social basis for communication, dyadic communication, and group communication. Inevitably, many important aspects pertaining to each area were not included because of space limitations. Certain other important topics were treated only briefly. What was presented was an integration of the important features of the communication behavior of small numbers of people in face-to-face communication settings. Topics were emphasized in relation to the relative importance we place on them, of course. But, in addition, other topics were given a measure of attention in direct proportion to their absence in other discussions on speech communication, not only because we deemed them important but also to avoid needless duplication in our own academic division of labor.

Because material presented in the many areas here scratches only the surface, and necessarily so as pointed out above, the interested student may want to supplement these materials by referring to other sources that address dyadic and small-group communication. Suggestions for further reading in these areas are in the Postscript at the end of the book.

In the first section of Part II we saw that it is difficult to separate the nature of the human communicator from the nature of the interpersonal relationships in which he communicates. Next we discussed ways in which the silent agreements communicators make with one another come to govern large segments of their communication behavior in dyads. Finally, small-group communication was described from several different angles: (1) the type of small group one may find himself in; (2) the kind of leadership a member may select for his group; (3) a look at the small group as an information system; and (4) the outline of a strategy for making procedural decisions in small-group deliberations.

We have said throughout the discussion of group communication that groups are more than just environments in which work gets done—that groups also are or can be important sources of pleasure and individual satisfaction even as work on the group task goes forward. But groups are even more than sources of satisfaction. Groups serve societal communication processes in a very important way as the repositories of social attitudes and sometimes even of values for the individual who is usually a member of many small groups. Many groups reinforce, change, and shape in various ways the attitudes of their members. Small-group norms and attitude constellations, when taken from many groups, become what we refer to as *public opinion*. These topics and many more will be discussed from the perspective of public communication in Part III.

ALTMAN, IRWIN, and WILLIAM HAYTHORN, "Interpersonal Exchange in Isolation," *Sociometry*, 28 (1965), 411–26.

BACKMAN, CARL, PAUL SECORD, and JERRY PEIRCE, "Resistance to Change in the Self Concept as a Function of Consensus Among Significant Others," in *Problems in Social Psychology*, eds. Carl Backman and Paul Secord. New York: McGraw-Hill Book Company, 1966.

BALES, ROBERT F., "Adaptive and Integrative Changes as Sources of Strain in Social Systems," in *Small Groups: Studies in Social Interaction*, eds. A. P. Hare, E. F. Borgatta, and R. F. Bales. New York: Alfred A. Knopf, Inc., 1966.

BARNLUND, DEAN, "Consistency of Emergent Leadership in Groups with Changing Tasks and Members," *Speech Monographs*, 29 (1962), 45–52.

———, "Our Concept of Discussion: Static or Dynamic," *The Speech Teacher*, 3 (1954), 8–14.

BARTH, JOHN, *The Sot-Weed Factor*. Garden City, New York: Doubleday & Company, Inc., 1960.

BASS, BERNARD M., and G. DUNTEMAN, "Behavior in Groups as a Function of Self, Interaction, and Task Orientation," *Journal of Abnormal and Social Psychology*, 66 (1963), 419–28.

BERG, DAVID M., "A Descriptive Analysis of the Distribution and Duration of Themes Discussed by Task-Oriented Small Groups," *Speech Monographs*, 34 (1967), 172–75.

BOIS, J. SAMUEL, *The Art of Awareness.* Dubuque, Iowa: Wm. C. Brown & Co., 1966.

BURKE, PETER J., "Authority Relations and Disruptive Behavior in Small Discussion Groups," *Sociometry,* 29 (1966), 237–50.

BYRNE, DONN, and RAY RHAMEY, "Attraction as a Linear Function of Positive Reinforcements," *Journal of Personality and Social Psychology,* 2 (1965), 884–89.

CATHCART, ROBERT, "Leadership as a Secondary Function in Group Discussion," *The Speech Teacher,* 11 (1962), 221–26.

COLLINS, BARRY, and HAROLD GUETZKOW, *A Social Psychology of Group Processes for Decision-Making.* New York: John Wiley & Sons, Inc., 1964.

COMBS, ARTHUR, and DONALD SNYGG, *Individual Behavior* (rev. ed.). New York: Harper & Row, Publishers, 1959.

DARLEY, JOHN, and ELLEN BERSCHEID, "Increased Liking as a Result of the Anticipation of Personal Contact," *Human Relations,* 20 (1967), 29–40.

EKMAN, PAUL, "Differential Communication of Affect by Head and Body Cues," *Journal of Personality and Social Psychology,* 2 (1965), 726–35.

FOLLETT, MARY PARKER, *Creative Experience.* New York: David McKay Co., Inc., 1930.

FOURIEZOS, N. T., M. L. HUTT, and H. GUETZKOW, "Measurement of Self-Oriented Needs in Discussion Groups," *Journal of Abnormal and Social Psychology,* 45 (1950), 682–90.

FROMM, ERICH, "The Nonproductive Character Orientations," in *Readings in the Psychology of Adjustment,* eds. L. Gorlow and W. Katkovsky. New York: McGraw-Hill Book Company, 1959.

GAMSON, WILLIAM, "Experimental Test of a Theory of Coalition Formation," *American Sociological Review,* 26 (1961), 565–73.

GERGEN, KENNETH, and BARBARA WISHNOV, "Others' Self Evaluations and Interaction Participation as Determinants of Self Presentation," *Journal of Personality and Social Psychology,* 2 (1965), 348–58.

GOFFMAN, ERVING, *Encounters.* Indianapolis: Bobbs-Merrill Company, Inc., 1961.

———, *Interaction Ritual.* Garden City, New York: Doubleday & Company, Inc., 1967.

———, *The Presentation of Self in Everyday Life.* Garden City, New York: Doubleday & Company, Inc., 1959.

GOLDMAN, MORTON, and LOUIS A. FRASS, "The Effects of Leader Selection on Group Performance," *Sociometry,* 28 (1965), 82–88.

GOODE, WILLIAM J., "A Theory of Role Strain," in *Problems in Social Psy-*

chology, eds. Carl Backman and Paul Secord.   New York: McGraw-Hill Book Company, 1966.

GORDON, THOMAS, *Group-Centered Leadership.*   Boston: Houghton Mifflin Company, 1955.

GORDON, WILLIAM J. J., *Synectics.*   New York: Harper & Row, Publishers, 1961.

GROSS, EDWARD, and GREGORY STONE, "Embarrassment and the Analysis of Role Requirements," in *Problems in Social Psychology,* eds. Carl Backman and Paul Secord.   New York: McGraw-Hill Book Company, 1966.

HAIMAN, FRANKLYN S., "The Specialization of Roles and Functions in a Group," *The Quarterly Journal of Speech,* 43 (1957), 165–74.

HASS, HAROLD, and MARTIN MAEHR, "Two Experiments on the Concept of Self and the Reaction of Others," *Journal of Personality and Social Psychology,* 1 (1965), 100–105.

HEIDER, FRITZ, "Consciousness, the Perceptual World, and Communications with Others," in *Person Perception and Interpersonal Behavior,* eds. Renato Tagiuri and Luigi Petrullo.   Stanford, California: Stanford University Press, 1958.

———, *The Psychology of Interpersonal Relations.*   New York: John Wiley & Sons, Inc., 1958.

HOFFMAN, L. RICHARD, "Group Problem Solving," in *Advances in Experimental Social Psychology,* Vol. 2, ed. Leonard Berkowitz.   New York: Academic Press Inc., 1965.

HURLOCK, ELIZABETH, *Adolescent Development.*   New York: McGraw-Hill Book Company, 1955.

JOURARD, SIDNEY M., *The Transparent Self.*   Princeton, New Jersey: D. Van Nostrand Co., Inc., 1964.

———, and RICHARD REMY, "Perceived Parental Attitudes, the Self, and Security," *Journal of Consulting Psychology,* 19 (1955), 364–66.

JULIAN, JAMES W., and FRANKLYN A. PERRY, "Cooperation Contrasted with Intra-Group and Inter-Group Competition," *Sociometry,* 30 (1967), 79–90.

KRETCH, DAVID, and RICHARD CRUTCHFIELD, *Theory and Problems of Social Psychology.*   New York: McGraw-Hill Book Company, 1948.

LAMMERS, C. J., "Stratification in a Small Group," *Human Relations,* 20 (1967), 283–300.

LEAVITT, HAROLD, and RONALD A. MUELLER, "Some Effects of Feedback on Communication," in *Small Groups: Studies in Social Interaction,* eds. A. P. Hare, E. F. Borgatta, and R. F. Bales.   New York: Alfred A. Knopf, Inc., 1966.

MAIER, N. R. F., and A. R. SOLEM, "Improving Solutions by Turning Choice Situations into Problems," *Personnel Psychology,* 15 (1962), 151–57.

MEDOW, HERMAN, and ALVIN ZANDER, "Aspirations for the Group Chosen by Central and Peripheral Members," *Journal of Personality and Social Psychology*, 1 (1965), 224–28.

MORTENSEN, CALVIN D., "Should the Discussion Group Have an Assigned Leader?" *The Speech Teacher*, 15 (1966), 34–41.

MOWRER, O. HOBART, *The New Group Therapy*. Princeton, New Jersey: D. Van Nostrand Co., Inc., 1964.

MULLAHY, PATRICK, "Some Aspects of Sullivan's Theory of Interpersonal Relations," in *Readings in the Psychology of Adjustment*, eds. L. Gorlow and W. Katkovsky. New York: McGraw-Hill Book Company, 1959.

NEWCOMB, THEODORE, "Aspects of the Acquaintance Process," in *Science and Human Affairs*, ed. Richard Farson. Palo Alto, California: Science and Behavior Books, Inc., 1965.

———, *The Acquaintance Process*. New York: Holt, Rinehart & Winston, Inc., 1961.

OSBORN, A. F., *Applied Imagination*. New York: Charles Scribner's Sons, 1953.

RIECKEN, H. W., "The Effect of Talkativeness on Ability to Influence Group Solutions to Problems," *Sociometry*, 21 (1958), 309–21.

ROBY, T. B., and J. T. LANZETTA, "Considerations in the Analysis of Group Tasks," *Psychological Bulletin*, 55 (1958), 88–101.

ROGERS, CARL, *On Becoming a Person*. Boston: Houghton Mifflin Company, 1961.

ROSENBERG, B. G., and JONAS LANGER, "A Study of Postural-Gestural Communication," *Journal of Personality and Social Psychology*, 2 (1965), 593–97.

ROSS, MURRAY, and CHARLES HENDRY, *New Understandings of Leadership*. New York: Association Press, 1957.

RUESCH, JURGEN, "The Role of Communication in Therapeutic Transactions," *Journal of Communication*, 13 (1963), 132–39.

———, and GREGORY BATESON, *Communication: The Social Matrix of Psychiatry*. New York: W. W. Norton & Company, Inc., 1951.

RUESCH, JURGEN, and WELDON KEES, *Nonverbal Communication*. Berkeley, California: University of California Press, 1961.

SAMPLE, JOHN A., and THURLOW R. WILSON, "Leader Behavior, Group Productivity and Rating of Least Preferred Co-Worker," *Journal of Personality and Social Psychology*, 1 (1965), 266–70.

SARBIN, THEODORE, "Role Theory," in *Handbook of Social Psychology*, ed. Gardner Lindzey. Reading, Massachusetts: Addison-Wesley Publishing Co., Inc., 1954.

SCHEIDEL, THOMAS, and LAURA CROWELL, "Feedback in Small Group Communication," *Quarterly Journal of Speech*, 52 (1966), 271–78.

SCHOPLER, JOHN, and MARJORIE MATTHEWS, "The Influence of the Perceived Causal Locus of Partner's Dependence on the Use of Interpersonal Power," *Journal of Personality and Social Psychology*, 2 (1965), 609–12.

SEGAL, MARSHAL H., DONALD T. CAMPBELL, and MELVILLE J. HERSKOVITS, *The Influence of Culture on Visual Perception*. Indianapolis: Bobbs-Merrill Company, Inc., 1966.

SHAW, MARVIN E., "Communication Networks," in *Advances in Experimental Social Psychology*, Vol. 3, ed. Leonard Berkowitz. New York: Academic Press Inc., 1966.

————, "Scaling Group Tasks: A Method for Unidimensional Analysis," Technical Report #1, University of Florida, July 1963.

————, and MICHAEL BLUM, "Effects of Leadership Style upon Group Performance," *Journal of Personality and Social Psychology*, 3 (1966), 238–42.

SHERIF, MUZAFER, and CAROLYN SHERIF, *Reference Groups*. New York: Harper & Row, Publishers, 1964.

SHERWOOD, JOHN J., "Self Identity and Referent Others," *Sociometry*, 28 (1965), 66–81.

SIEGEL, ALBERTA, and SIDNEY SIEGEL, "Reference Groups, Membership Groups and Attitude Change," in *Group Dynamics: Research and Theory* (2nd ed.), eds. Dorwin Cartwright and Alvin Zander. New York: Harper & Row, Publishers, 1960.

STAGNER, ROSS, *Psychology of Personality*. New York: McGraw-Hill Book Company, 1961.

SULLIVAN, HARRY STACK, *Clinical Studies in Psychiatry*. New York: W. W. Norton & Company, Inc., 1956.

————, *The Interpersonal Theory of Psychiatry*. New York: W. W. Norton & Company, Inc., 1953.

SUPER, J., "Self and Other Semantic Concepts in Relation to Choice of a Vocation," *Journal of Applied Psychology*, 51 (1967), 242–46.

TAGIURI, RENATO, "Social Preference and Its Perception," in *Person Perception and Interpersonal Behavior*, eds. Renato Tagiuri and Luigi Petrullo. Stanford, California: Stanford University Press, 1958.

TAYLOR, HOWARD F., "Balance and Change in the Two-Person Group," *Sociometry*, 30 (1967), 262–79.

THELEN, HERBERT, *The Dynamics of Groups at Work*. Chicago: University of Chicago Press, 1965.

THIBAUT, JOHN, and HAROLD KELLEY, *The Social Psychology of Groups*. New York: John Wiley & Sons, Inc., 1959.

TORRANCE, E. PAUL, "Some Consequences of Power Differences on Decision Making in Permanent and Temporary Three-Man Groups," in *Small Groups: Studies in Social Interaction*, eds. A. P. Hare, E. F. Borgatta, and R. F. Bales. New York: Alfred A. Knopf, Inc., 1966.

TUCKMAN, BRUCE W., "Interpersonal Probing and Revealing and Systems of Integrative Complexity," *Journal of Personality and Social Psychology*, 3 (1966), 655–64.

TURK, HERMAN, and C. ROBERT MILLS, "Authority and Interaction," *Sociometry*, 27 (1964), 1–18.

WASHBURN, DONALD, "Intrapersonal Communication in a Jungian Perspective," *Journal of Communication*, 14 (1964), 131–35.

III

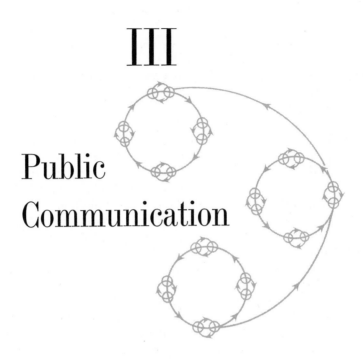

Public
Communication

So far we have studied the process of communication on the level of the individual. This study enabled us to concentrate on various human neurological and psychological elements of behavior as they combine to produce the communicative act. We discovered that the human being is a highly complicated system of interacting physiological and symbolic capacities. These capacities are activated by the human's need (1) to understand and cope with his environment, (2) to secure and maintain contact with others of his species in order to obtain both security and self-identity, and (3) to maintain as much balance and order as possible both in himself and in his surroundings.

The desire to identify and interact with others leads to the development of various human groupings, which in turn add new dimensions to communication behavior. Even though individual members compose a group, we discovered that a group is more than the sum of its parts. Groups develop unique standards of behavior, value orientations, and patterns of communication. In other words groups take on the characteristics of systems too; they strive to maintain their balance, struggle for enhancement, and become involved in interactions, either complementary or disturbing, with other groups. If we remember that it is only one point of view, we may perceive society as many interacting groupings of people, most of whom are busy communicating with each other and all of whom keep a check on internal order and harmony through a network of communication channels.

Society itself is a system once again larger than the sum of its parts and equally dependent upon maintaining balance and order. Somehow, despite the potential for chaos and breakdown (and ample evidence shows that both can occur on the societal level), many societies manage to maintain coherence and stability. Communication between one segment of society and another and, indeed, in some respects the institutionalization of communication are important elements contributing to such an achievement.

In this section we shall examine communication from what we shall call the *public perspective*. Most of the principles discussed earlier regarding individual and group communication are relevant to the public-communication process. Language remains the primary symbol system for conveyance of the message; the psychological phenomena of reception, information-processing, and transmission are inherent in any communicative act; and the various pressures and influences associated with human interaction occupy a central place. Consequently, in our study of public communication we shall necessarily concern ourselves with many of the interests and questions that have already arisen in connection with the communication of individuals and groups. But, to fully understand and appreciate public communication, we must discuss these and other elements in an enlarged context and with a somewhat different focus.

In the following pages we shall delineate what we mean by the term *public communication*. Because the theoretical basis for our study is located in the traditional study of rhetoric, we shall take a brief look at the historical development of rhetoric to better understand the continuities and differences between the traditional approach and the contemporary viewpoint. Next we shall examine the elements, or variables, that constitute a public-communication transaction, and finally we shall discuss the functions and possible effects of public messages on an audience. We hope the reader, after completing Part III, will have a better understanding of the complexities, patterns, and vagaries of the multiplicity of public messages which bombard him in modern society.

The Public-Communication
Perspective

Let us begin by describing, at least in a general and preliminary way, the dimensions of public-communication situations which differentiate them from individual- and group-communication situations. The word *public* moves the messages we are going to be dealing with beyond the sphere of individual privacy. Of course, persons may respond to a public message either individually or in private. But the messages we are talking about either are intended to reach many people or, in the case of private messages which receive public exposure, have the potential of reaching many people.

To say that a message is intended for widespread public consumption or even for the consumption of a few score persons implies certain things about the nature of the message. Generally a public message concerns matters that have relevance to a group or groups of people; it contains meaning that is in the public domain. The concept of *public,* as we have just used it, is necessarily a complicated one which we shall explore further at various points in our discussion. We cannot easily maintain a distinction here between public and private; certainly the usual superficial distinctions will not do. While it may usually be held that such topics as sexual behavior are of a private nature, the legitimate theater, movies, television, magazines, novels, published scientific reports which have been popularized, and the growing public discussion of population control have all focused widespread attention on various aspects of sex. One can turn to almost any area of behavior which may be considered private and find that public conversation has been conducted on it.

Perhaps an example or two will help us understand the nature of public interest. A teacher who decides to lecture a student on the vices of inadequate classroom behavior or improper study habits probably chooses to do so in the privacy of an office. The subject to be discussed, at this time, concerns only the student involved. To be sure, some of what is said may be generally applicable to the whole student body, but, for the moment, very specific and individual behaviors are the salient points of the discussion, and others need not discuss, evaluate, or vote on the matter. Similarly, when a group of corporation executives gather to discuss the proper marketing techniques for a new product, they refrain from airing their views in public. Once again, there is a public relevance because decisions reached in the discussion will affect the consumer. But, for the moment, the interests of the discussants do not include the production of messages for public consumption or for influencing public behavior.

Public messages are statements which are of interest to many people; the number may be 200 or several million. But the message must have a certain significance to a particular segment of the public before we can conclude that it is a public message.

In another sense, the language of a public message is more general than specific and more pluralistic than individualistic. Generally, public messages do not contain queries about personal health, murmurs of individual endearment, or the individual abbreviations one hears in a conversational setting. In private the language code tends to be very flexible and elaborate, filled with personal phrasing and connotation; but in public it is restricted so that the recipients' understandings of the message overlap. Of course the public language code may be technical and specialized and therefore somewhat mystifying to the average person. The terminology of psychologists or philosophers assembled in convention is highly technical. But, for the immediate public attending the convention, the code is understandable and a part of its lexicon.

Another dimension of the public-communication situation which differentiates it from interpersonal or small-group activity has to do with interaction between speaker and listener. In a public situation, the receiver of a message has less opportunity for interaction with the communicator than he does in a face-to-face or small-group situation. Consequently, the pressures to conform with the ideas expressed by the communicator are probably not so great, and the opportunities for influencing the communicator, at least the immediate opportunities, are not so prevalent. As we shall see later, communicator-listener interaction plays a significant role in determining the final effect of a public message.

No doubt you will be able to find various exceptions to the general distinctions we have just noted. One of the problems confronting any student of communication is that of knowing where to draw realistic boundaries—realistic in the sense that they do not distort the nature of the communication process too severely. We trust that our distinctions place the communication we shall be examining in this part of the book into a workable context; we make no claim that these boundaries are hard and fast.

One more distinction deserves notice. In the pages that follow we shall have to look many times at the process and effects of mass communication. The usual conceptualization of mass communication includes all the activities of the various media, such as radio, television, newspapers, motion pictures, and magazines, which do not rely upon personal contact. Thus advertising and entertainment are legitimate subjects for study by mass-media specialists. However, we shall not concern ourselves here with entertainment or advertising, though much of what we say applies to those modes of communication. Our major interest will be in exploring messages dealing with public issues, i.e., social, political, and economic issues related to public welfare.

Once again, we have drawn a tenuous distinction because many of the values expressed or implicit in advertising and entertainment reflect more serious matters and sometimes influence the way a public perceives social problems. Between the Civil War and World War I, for instance, the average American boy delighted in the escapades of the fictional heroes in Horatio Alger stories. The moral of the Alger tales was quite clear: If a boy demonstrated the sturdy qualities of diligence, perseverance, honesty, and thrift, he was assured of becoming a financial success. The unstated corollary was that he would become poor and downtrodden through stupidity or lack of will.[1] A firm believer in the Horatio Alger view of success either would not be prone to listen to or would not understand spokesmen of the later Progressive Era, who argued that society had to shoulder the blame for individual failure. In more contemporary times, it has been argued that the failure to include Negroes as fashion models in popular magazines or in television commercials or as characters in children's readers accounts for some of the misunderstanding and mistrust on the part of the white majority. Hollywood and advertising have both been castigated for portraying an overly glamorized, unrealistic way of living which leads to frustrated ambitions on the part of persons who may later vent their anger on various issues of social import.

Nevertheless, we shall not attempt to include such elements of influence in our descriptions of public communication because to do so would require another book. But we must remember that all kinds of messages affect the response to any particular message and that a person's response is always holistic and not compartmentalized.

Many of the characteristics and problems of public communication are pertinent to both oral and written communication. Because man's ability to manipulate linguistic symbols makes both writing and speaking

[1] Frederick Lewis Allen, *The Big Change* (New York: Bantam Books, Inc., 1961), pp. 56–58.

possible, we would distort reality by treating them as distinctly separate processes. This is not to deny that there are differences. For most of us it is easier to speak than to write, and consequently we can produce more words per unit of time when we talk. But generally our oral behavior is less efficient than our written in that we are more repetitive and rambling and produce fewer ideas per phrase unit.

In addition we receive and internalize written and spoken messages in different ways. We can take our time analyzing written discourse, but spoken discourse (discounting electronic voice recordings) tends to come at us quickly and only once, so that we react more holistically and subjectively than analytically. And, if we do insist upon exercising a critical attitude as we listen to oral discourse, we risk losing part of the message as our thoughts linger on and we meditate about certain ideas. Also, in oral communication we are often in the presence of the communicator, and his mannerisms and personality may have much to do with how we react to what he says. But, insofar as both spoken and written communication involve man's attempt to convey meanings, ideas, attitudes, and information to his fellows through the use of linguistic symbols, we can expect many similarities. We shall center our attention on oral communication, for the most part, in the pages that follow, but the reader should be able to apply much of what is discussed to both oral and written communicative situations.

The theoretical beginning for our study is classical rhetoric. The ancient Greeks, fathers of much of Western thought, were as interested in the problems of oral communication as they were in philosophy, drama, athletics, and politics. Never content to allow important aspects of their lives to go unexamined, a number of important Greek thinkers undertook to describe and prescribe principles for successful public speaking. The interest in rhetoric remained strong through the Roman period and was one branch of the tripartite division of knowledge called the *trivium* in medieval times. Later other disciplines and interests eclipsed and denuded the study of rhetoric, but in modern times communication has emerged as an area of investigation of central importance to the humanities and social sciences. In many cases we see little resemblance between modern communication research and the ancient, traditional study of rhetoric, and we are tempted to say that rhetoric has become irrelevant to our lives. But a more accurate explanation is that modern times have promulgated new problems and altered old ones, and as a result the study of oral communication has taken on new colorations and has expanded in fresh and interesting ways to cope with modern needs. Unlike the dinosaurs, rhetoric is not extinct but is constantly displaying new mutations and strengths.

It may help us to understand both the focus of this part of the book and the reasons for the focus by reviewing rhetorical theory in terms of its response to historical demand.

THE RHETORICAL TRADITION

We shall first recall the circumstances which necessitated a systematic body of knowledge about oral communication for those circumstances forged the guidelines by which theory was molded.   Strong vestiges of the guidelines may be found today in many of the textbooks on oral and written communication.

In the fifth century B.C. citizens on the island of Sicily deposed Thrasybulus, Tyrant of Syracuse, and established a democratic form of government. Along with the new freedom came a new problem, the distribution and establishment of ownership of land which had been confiscated by the Tyrant. Courts were established to adjudicate the various claims, but there were no professionally trained advocates. So a citizen had to plead his own case in the hope of persuading the judges that he possessed legal rights to a designated piece of land.

Because a problem almost inevitably causes someone to take advantage of the resulting need, someone undertook to formulate a body of principles for presenting claims convincingly. Corax is generally given credit for beginning the systematic body of theory on oral discourse. Since documentary evidence establishing prior ownership was not available, Corax of necessity based his rhetorical theory and precepts on the process of reasoning by inferences based on probability and outlined what he felt to be the proper partitioning and organization of a judicial speech. Tisias, a pupil of Corax, may have been the first ghost-writer as he followed the guide lines of his teacher in writing some judicial speeches to be delivered by others.

About 427 B.C. Gorgias, an ambassador from Sicily to Athens, so impressed the Greeks with his mastery of oratory that he created great interest in the art of oral discourse and became a highly successful teacher of the principles of rhetoric. The Athenians provided fertile ground for the development of rhetorical theory because their society depended upon oral communication. Greek literature in the form of epics and drama was presented orally, and speeches by various characters played a prominent part within that literature. Greek political life was based on the efficacy of speaking. Athenian citizens served occasionally on juries to hear pleadings by other citizens, and the whole legal structure was ultimately responsible to the Assembly of citizens, in which every man who was not a slave was eligible to serve. One of the most profound characteristics of the Greeks was that they enjoyed talking and listening to talk. They were more inclined to talk and argue and cajole verbally than they were to fight, at least within the confines of their own city-state. The Greeks had a strong agonistic sense of play; they often praised verbal skills in debate and dialectic as they did athletic prowess on the field.[2] And so it was personally satisfying, politically necessary, and eminently practical for every citizen to be able to communicate in public discussion. Thus the art of speech-making came to have a prominent place in Greek interests.

We shall not attempt to detail the full history and development of Greek rhetorical theory; the reader can find ample sources on the subject should he so desire. We note in passing, however, that such renowned scholars as Plato and Isocrates undertook investigations and discussions of rhetorical principles and practices, and Aristotle attempted a fairly complete explication of the subject in his *Rhetoric,* which is still the most influential treatise on the principles of oral communication. Thus, the Greeks, in general, concerned themselves with the role of speech-making in their society, with the personal characteristics required of the citizen in the fulfillment of his political obligation through speaking, and with the technical and artistic requirements of an effective public speech. The primary Greek emphases were on the citizen as public speaker and on the glories of skillful oral play.

One of the greatest contributions of Rome was the preservation of the legacy of Greece. The Romans were not great innovators, but they were remarkably successful in transplanting and assimilating many of the Greek ideals, customs, and teachings. Therefore it is not surprising that, as Rome became the center of the civilized world, Greek teachers of rhetoric continued to instruct the citizens of the Republic.

From the beginning the political climate in Rome differed from that in Greece and inevitably affected the practice of oral communication. Athenian political life was shaped by the city-states, small entities in which every citizen could actively participate in civic affairs. The procedure for decision-making, based as it was on public discussion and argument, promoted cooperative behavior and rational judgment but not speed and efficiency. The conditions of Roman rule, however, placed a higher premium on efficiency than on democratic procedure. As the Republic turned to Empire and the fortunes of the Roman world came to depend on the whims of the emperor, civil liberties declined and with them went any prospect for meaningful public discussion.

Rhetorical practice did not die however but assumed a new mode. Speech-making became fully developed as an artful demonstration with primary emphasis on style rather than on substance. The deliberative, or judicial, speech, which focused on existential problems, gave way to

[2] For an interesting discussion of the play element in Greek culture and rhetoric, see Johan Huizinga, "Play-Forms in Philosophy," in *Homo Ludens* (Boston: Beacon Press, Inc., 1955).

academic oratorical exercises known as *suasoriae* and *controversiae.* In these, brilliance of performance rather than civic contribution was the criterion for success.

To say that the loss of political freedom alone hindered the development of meaningful rhetorical practice may be an overly simplistic analysis of the situation. George Kennedy offers the following explanation to complete the picture.

> The entire educational system under Greek influence had been directed toward producing orators for public life in the city-state: war and peace, the dangers of tyranny, and the like. By the time the Romans learned to speak with an elegance up to Greek standards a considerable number of problems no longer existed and especially the problem of war between city-states. One might take the pejorative view that liberty was lost, but one might equally well say that the original problem had been solved by the institution of empire. What happened then was not so much political oppression but a frustration between thinking that one must speak and not having anything worth saying. No great political causes arose to demand eloquent expression. What the Romans failed to do was to turn to other areas where discussion and oratory might have been possible, to spreading Roman ideas among the provinces, to developing policies of civil administration, to humanitarianism, or to the revision and extension of national ideals.[3]

Despite all handicaps, rhetoric did not lose its popularity. Speech activities in the form of declamatory performances and exercises flourished. Herbert Muller explains this development this way:

> Thought was smothered under oratory and rhetoric; eloquence was never so prized as when it ceased to serve any real need, merely concealing the fact that great public issues were no longer being debated.[4]

Cicero and Quintilian wrote extensively on rhetorical theory and practice. Even though the circumstances for meaningful discussion were not present, they both continued to treat rhetoric in the Greek tradition; that is, they were concerned with advising and training public speakers for political leadership and with prescribing methods for rhetorical success.

The writings of Cicero continued to be extremely influential in the Middle Ages for Latin was the language of the educated minority, but the practice of public speaking remained unimpressive. The great cohesive force of the Middle Ages was the Church, which inspired and influenced philosophy, science, art, and political theory, and attempted

---

[3] "Two Problems in the Historical Study of Rhetoric," *The Pennsylvania Speech Annual,* XXI (September 1964), 20–21.
[4] *The Uses of the Past* (New York: Oxford University Press, Inc., 1959), pp. 216–17.

to prescribe morality. The age was a bawdy, sensual one in many respects, but, intellectually, medieval man was constrained by the extreme formalism of his religion. The logic of the schoolmen was deductive, based on theological premises which were never questioned and which allowed no fresh discoveries of thought. As Muller explains, "One reason why the Dark Ages were dark was that there was no thought worthy of the name of heresy."[5]

We are not surprised that, under these circumstances, the tradition of scholastic declamation started by the Romans continued in medieval schools. The scholastic speaking of the age took place in a contest atmosphere, in which the dialectical skill of the speaker was emphasized and the subject matter was devoid of much practical impact. "Once the ardor and daring curiosity of the twelfth century had staled, the schoolmen settled down to endless dispute over the choice of horns in dilemmas."[6]

The increased emphasis on written communication further diluted the oral tradition. Such emphasis was necessary because, in addition to being intellectually religious, medieval man was a great initiator of trade and commerce. As letters came to play an important part in the transaction of the business, the study of the art of letter-writing became a practical matter and absorbed some of the energy formerly devoted to the study of oral rhetoric. Essentially, then, rhetoric became dialectical skill in scholastic declamation and became letter-writing in business.

St. Augustine, bishop of Hippo, wrote the most important work of rhetorical theory and precept during the medieval period. Augustine's writing reflects the fact that the most potent force during this time was the Christian church, which demanded adherence to its doctrines and influenced the destinies of its subjects to a great extent. Augustine's four-volume work, *De Doctrina Christiana*, deals mostly with a proper understanding of the scriptures, but he devotes the fourth volume to the principles of Christian rhetoric. We can understand the major thrust of Augustine's writings by noting the purposes he set down for this rhetoric: (1) to instruct to righteousness; (2) to conciliate to righteousness; (3) to stir to righteousness. Rhetoric was not concerned with discovering the truth or with arguing about what the truth was or even with persuasion based on probabilities. Truth was to be found in the scriptures, the unalterable words of God. The Christian duty was to spread and explain the word of God and to convert the heathen. With his truth in hand, the Christian should attempt to speak with eloquence, said Augustine, and if he could not achieve eloquence he should speak with wisdom. But, if wisdom was not possible either, then at least the

[5] Muller, *The Uses of the Past*, p. 247.
[6] Muller, *The Uses of the Past*, p. 252.

Christian should lead a good life and be an example, so that his life could be as a "flowering speech."

The theological bias of the Middle Ages provoked the rationalistic counterreaction of the Enlightenment, and with rationalism came an interest in rediscovering the nature of man rather than in futilely exploring the essence of God and angels. Greek humanistic values came into prominence but were never made relevant to practical living as the Greeks had made them. In fact, the rationalism of the sixteenth and seventeenth centuries had all the characteristics of a closed metaphysical system, and in this respect it resembled the conceptualizations of the thirteenth century.[7]

A second intellectual development was more practical: Advances in science were a kind of reaction to consistent rationality. The tradition of Aristotle, medieval disputation, and deductive logic came under increasing attack and received perhaps the greatest blow from the pen of Francis Bacon, who urged an empirical approach to the acquisition of knowledge. We may think that the birth of true scientific inquiry brought with it a new probing into the fundamental problems of man and a renewed desire to solve some of those problems through discussion. But such was not the case for the interest in science did not bring political freedom for the average man. The age of Enlightenment was also the age of Monarchy, with its exclusive and limited ruling classes. Hence, freedom for full political expression was not enjoyed by Renaissance man as it was by the citizen of the Greek city-state. Consequently, there was no practical necessity for the diffusion of knowledge and for the development of effective oral-communication skills. However, the interest in written communication continued from the medieval tradition as the spread of literature became extensive in the eighteenth century and a literate middle class emerged.

In the development of rhetorical theory, trends started in the Middle Ages continued into the Renaissance. Generally, we may delineate three approaches to teaching and theorizing about rhetoric: the traditional approach, still based on the writings of Cicero and other Romans, encompassed all the classical divisions of rhetoric from invention, or the discovery of arguments and appeals, to delivery; the stylistic approach concentrated on the use of various linguistic devices such as schemes and tropes to the exclusion of all else; the Ramistic approach, established by the Frenchman Peter Ramus, conceived of rhetoric only as style and delivery. Two notable contributions during this period were those of Thomas Wilson, who preserved the full Ciceronian tradition in his *The Arte of Rhetorique*, and of Francis Bacon, whose writings gave invention

[7] See Carl Becker, *The Heavenly City of the Eighteenth Century Philosophers* (New Haven, Connecticut: Yale University Press, 1960).

prominence over style and delivery.   Despite these writings of substance, in popular usage rhetoric was basically the study of linguistic style.

In eighteenth-century England the emphasis on style rather firmly established rhetorical study as literary criticism in the written tradition and as elocution, emphasizing dramatic delivery, in the oral tradition. The most influential work in the literary tradition was Hugh Blair's *Lectures on Rhetoric and Belles-Lettres.*   More firmly in the classical tradition (in the sense of treating the full scope of rhetorical study) and more imaginative in treatment was George Campbell's *The Philosophy of Rhetoric.*   Campbell wedded his rhetorical theory to the new psychological theories of the time, placed logic firmly within the scope of rhetoric, and indicated that rhetoric was concerned with informing and delighting as well as persuading.   Richard Whately's *Elements of Rhetoric,* which appeared in 1828, returned to the Aristotelian tradition by treating rhetoric as an offshoot of logic.   Whately concentrated upon argumentation composition and emphasized the role of logical principles in argument.

Courses in rhetoric continued to be a part of the school curriculum, and in the nineteenth century England developed a strong tradition of Parliamentary debate.   Agitation for social reform swelled at various times from the citizenry.   But the presence of a solid traditional ruling class composed of the landed nobility assured that a well developed class consciousness, the strong control of Parliament by the aristocracy, and a general fear of radicals demanding political reform would all prevent the average man from having any chance to assume the responsibilities of full citizenship.   Consequently, speech-making was never the problem for the average Englishman that it was for the Greek commoner.

In his survey of classical rhetoric, Corbett remarks that the "classical strain of rhetoric came to an end with Whately."[8]   In one sense this is so, but in another it is not.   Classical rhetoric no longer occupies the central position in the curriculum that it once did, and no one has written a complete contemporary rhetoric based on classical precepts.   But the twentieth century has nevertheless witnessed a renewed interest in the classical tradition.   This interest is particularly noticeable in America, where in the 1920s some scholars felt that the literary emphasis on forms and composition of discourse failed to account for the dynamics of oral communication.[9]   The first step in the rejuvenation of rhetoric was the

[8] Edward P. J. Corbett, *Classical Rhetoric for the Modern Student* (New York: Oxford University Press, Inc., 1965), p. 566.
[9] See Carroll C. Arnold, "Rhetoric in America Since 1900" in *Re-Establishing the Speech Profession* (State College, Pennsylvania: Speech Association of the Eastern States, 1959), pp. 3–7.

rediscovery of the great classical writings on oral communication. From 1920 on, studies have examined the classical tradition and have attempted to reconstruct the meanings of Aristotle, Cicero, and others and to explain their significance for modern times.

But influences other than the classical ones permanently colored the development of rhetorical theory. Such men as James Winans and Charles H. Woolbert incorporated the new developments in psychology, for instance, into their writings on public speaking. Methods were developed for the controlled study of human behavior, and gradually the results of such studies entered the literature dealing with oral communication. In recent years the social sciences have produced a great quantity of research data relevant to the study of human communication. The addition of such data to the body of rhetorical knowledge is a significant departure from classical tradition for the early Greeks and Romans were not great empirical investigators. They were far more interested in prescribing than in describing, and, as we have seen, later writers followed and fostered their prescriptive tendencies. But the development of scientific methodologies for the study of human behavior brought the opportunity to test classical theory. The inevitable result has been the alteration or rejection of several prescriptive formulations which were not based on the way we actually behave. New conceptualizations of human communicative behavior have been established; new theories have replaced the old ones; and new terminology, some of it precise, some of it vague, has come into popular usage. In sum, we are currently experiencing a knowledge explosion which, if it does not overwhelm us, promises to provide a far more accurate picture of man as communicator than any we have heretofore possessed.

In addition to encompassing a descriptive approach based on empirical and experimental research, rhetorical enquiry now covers a diversity of communicative acts. Classical tradition concentrated on public-address situations, in which one speaker personally confronted his audience. The public-address situation was a paradigm for later writers on oral communication. The number of courses which the American educational curriculum offers with public address in the title indicates our continuing interest in the efficacy of public persuasion. Such an interest is not at all surprising in view of our historical heritage, which includes the great debates leading to the birth of the United States, the Civil War dialogue epitomized in the Lincoln-Douglas debates, the chautauqua movement, the impassioned oratory of religious revivalism and of the great social movements such as women's suffrage, and the occasional congressional debate which captured the attention of the nation. In a very real sense we have put much faith in public speaking, just as the fifth-century Athenian did.

But we also realize that oral communication plays a significant role in many situations other than the public one.   As we saw earlier, we are now aware that the acquisition of speech is an integral part of our personality development; that it facilitates building the web of personal relationships which are so important to our well-being; and that we often find ourselves in small groups, in which, talking and acting together, we accomplish much of the world's work or at least lay the foundation for that work.[10]

New fields of academic study and research, such as semantics, linguistics, speech audiology and pathology, group dynamics, and communication, explore and analyze the myriad human experiences in which oral communication plays a fundamental part.   As Wilbur Schramm notes, communications research "is one of the busiest crossroads in the study of human behavior, which is understandable because communication is a—perhaps *the*—fundamental social process."[11]   We realize increasingly that more behavioral similarities than differences underlie the various communication experiences.

Modern society has wrought changes in public communication which have caused us to revise, expand, and sometimes break away from the classical paradigm of the face-to-face speaker-audience situation.   Today public communication has as much or more impact than it did in ancient societies.   With mass media and instantaneous electronic transmission, communicators can address the world if they so desire.   We no longer center our lives in small communities, in which, largely free from daily outside interference, we can rise to address our fellow inhabitants with some reasonable expectation of influencing the course of events.   We are now a part of a mass society, affected by events occurring not only across our continent but across oceans and indeed around the world.

Our present channels for communication have greatly increased the distances voices can travel, and hence the potential audience for a speaking event is much larger than it ever was before.   Furthermore, transmission can be instantaneous, with no significant lapse of time between the initiation of communication and the reception of it by people around the world.   Early Greek orators were restricted in distance by the power of their lungs.   To spread news from region to region or polis to polis, runners had to be dispatched.   We are so accustomed to learning about events in Europe or Asia or Africa almost as they happen and are so used to hearing such speeches as the President's Inaugural Address or

[10] An excellent and enjoyable book describing the various functions of speech is Charles T. Brown and Charles Van Riper, *Speech and Man* (Englewood Cliffs, New Jersey: Prentice-Hall, Inc., 1966).
[11] "Communication Research in the United States" in *The Science of Human Communication*, ed. Wilbur Schramm (New York: Basic Books Inc., 1963), p. 1.

State of the Union Message as they are delivered, no matter where we live, that we cannot comprehend any other state of affairs. Our modern mass-communication systems expose us to many more messages than our predecessors ever heard. Thus, we have the opportunity to be much better informed than were the citizens of any other historical age. And we are subjected to many more persuasive points of view than our grand-parents were. Statesmen and demagogues, public servants and hucksters find their task of reaching audiences easier than it was previously. The average man listens to his leaders more easily and efficiently than ever before, and at the same time his leaders have an easier time feeling the pulse of public opinion than they used to.

Twentieth-century man benefits from a more efficient communication system than that which his forebears had and so should have a more accurate picture of the world around him. There should be more under-standing, less misinterpretation, fewer cases of falsification and distortion than ever before. Unfortunately, we know that such is not the case and that misunderstandings and distortions are as often enhanced and mag-nified as they are minimized. As Brown and Van Riper point out, the belief that conquering communicative space and time diminishes com-munication problems is an illusion. In fact, the reverse is true, for the larger the communication system, the more people who get into the act.

> If we double the distance, density of population remaining constant, we quadruple the number of people who get into the "conversation." If we triple the distance we add nine times as many people, and on it goes at this accelerating rate.[12]

If we remember the old party game of passing a rumor down a line of people to see how distorted it becomes, we can begin to comprehend the magnitude of some of the problems presented by our "efficient" mass-communication network.

Many of us will find opportunities during the course of our lives to stand up before various groups of people and to address them for an extended period of time. The better we are able to communicate at such moments, the better we fulfill our obligations as useful citizens of the world. This observation is as true today as it was in the time of the early Greeks, who undertook the first great experiment in an open society. But, for the most part, we citizens of the modern world can be charac-terized better as receivers of public communication than as public com-municators. We sit in audiences more than we stand on platforms facing them. We listen to public statements of important officials on radio and T.V., catch portions of important speeches on newscasts, read re-

---

[12] Brown and Van Riper, *Speech and Man*, p. 74.

ports of and comments on public utterances in newspapers and magazines, and listen to our friends discuss the remarks of a speaker they have
heard. The mass-communication media are a primary source of our
understanding of what is happening in the world around us. We find
our attitudes and beliefs affected by what we see and hear and read, and
we take action, e.g., vote, picket, purchase, on the basis of our attitudes
and beliefs. Consequently, we must understand how and why we, as
receivers, behave and react as we do in communicative situations.

THE RHETORICAL PRESENT

We shall round out our perspective on public communication by examining briefly some of the contemporary dimensions of public communication which are a direct result of mass media and mass society to
see how they differ from their Athenian counterparts. To begin, we
must recognize that the mass-media channels themselves have a major
influence on the nature of a communicative act. Radio messages, for
example, depend greatly upon voice quality for their success. Certainly,
some speakers project more vibrant, warm, reassuring personalities than
others project. One of the factors, perhaps the outstanding factor, contributing to the success of Franklin Roosevelt's radio addresses to the
nation was his dynamic, confident voice. We cannot appreciate the
strength of Roosevelt's messages by merely looking at the manuscripts.
We must listen to recordings of his speeches to begin to sense the rhetorical power possessed by the former President. Whether the nation
would have been adversely affected by constantly viewing the crippled
Roosevelt on crutches, as he was during his years in office, is a matter
for speculation.

Television also places its unique demands and bestows its unique
blessings on those who use it. Some individuals find it easy to project
on camera, others do not, even though they may be perfectly amiable in
person. Some persons are naturally more handsome or beautiful than
others. These and other factors must be tossed into the communicative
pot as variables likely to influence the ultimate success of a T.V. appearance. We need only remember that a portion of Richard Nixon's
failure in the televised 1960 presidential debates was attributed to a
naturally heavy beard and that President Lyndon Johnson preferred
that only one side of his face be shown on camera to realize the impact
the so-called *T.V. image* is thought to have.

We now realize that another element of a communicative situation
which has been altered by the nature of mass communication is what
classical theorists referred to as *ethos*. Ethos is the speaker's personal

characteristics, such as authoritativeness, honesty, perspicacity, and good will, which make him more or less believable and trustworthy in the eyes of his audience. Obviously, if we know a communicator personally and have had dealings with him and opportunities to observe his behavior in various circumstances, we are better able to judge his character than we are if we have not had much personal contact with him. The small world of the fifth-century Athenian allowed early teachers of rhetoric to treat the concept of ethos within this personal framework.

But our twentieth-century world requires a totally different framework because we seldom have personal knowledge of or dealings with public communicators. We therefore base our image of a communicator on second-hand impressions gained from observing him through the mass media, from reading various commentaries and reports about him, and occasionally from seeing him in person on public occasions or from listening to the comments of acquaintances who have seen him. We shall discuss the nature and influence of a communicator's image more thoroughly later, but we note here several external factors which can have much to do with how we estimate a communicator's character.

As we noted earlier, the channels of the mass media themselves can construct images for us. Television enhances the persuasiveness of some individuals and diminishes the effectiveness of others. A television image may be inaccurate and misleading of course, but nevertheless its potential for image-building is considerable. And, when an image gains wide popularity, many public officials try to become associated with it.

The era of John F. Kennedy offers an interesting case study of the interaction between a strong personality and the mass media. Kennedy was a natural object for the mass media, not only because he was an important public figure but also because he had a youthful, vigorous, and interesting personal style. He came from a forceful family, which surrounded him with equally interesting personalities, and his wife and children were attractive and charming in their own right. Journalists and broadcasters quickly fastened on the salient characteristics of Kennedy's style and played them for all they were worth, sometimes to the exclusion of other facets of his behavior.

Kennedy's image became full blown during the 1960 presidential campaign and was considerably enhanced by the television debates with Vice President Nixon. But the image-making was well under way before that campaign began. In 1956 Kennedy narrowly missed the Democratic Party's vice presidential nomination, but he became a national political figure at the same time. From 1957 to 1959, national magazines discovered that the Kennedy clan was excellent copy. *Saturday Evening Post, Time, Redbook, McCalls,* and *U.S. News and World Report,* to mention only a few, carried stories on the senator and his family. In

1959, pollsters found that people around the country were describing Kennedy as "energetic," "intelligent," "good looking," "aggressive," and "dynamic." The groundwork for Kennedy's presidential image was thoroughly laid by 1960, largely through the efforts of the mass media. Those controlling the mass media did not decide to build a national reputation for Kennedy but, typically, merely took advantage of ready-made and salable copy; the image was later magnified as publicity fed on publicity.

Examination of descriptions and discussions of the Kennedy administration clearly indicate the power of the Kennedy image. The whole coterie of New Frontiersmen, from cabinet officials to secretaries and errand boys, were portrayed as being dynamic, pragmatic, and forceful. And, in addition, various potential Republican leaders such as Governor George Romney of Michigan,[13] Governor William Scranton of Pennsylvania,[14] and New York City mayorality candidate John Lindsay[15] were no doubt undismayed to find themselves described in the familiar New Frontier terms or in some cases labeled Republican John Kennedys. We cannot determine with certainty the cause for the popularity and wholesale adoption of the Kennedy image, but we cannot deny that the image was extremely influential and that the mass media played an important role in its formulation and maintenance.

Because we are personally removed from most public communicators and because we, as humans, need to identify, interpret, and evaluate incoming information in a meaningful way, we tend to associate communicators with institutions and interests. Greek society also had institutions and interests, but the few thousand members in a polis had a much easier time than we do today judging a person on his own qualities. In modern society we tend to identify Walter Reuther with labor unionism, General Maxwell Taylor with the military establishment, and Secretary of State Dean Rusk with the Johnson administration. In some cases, such identifications are meaningful. Government officials, for instance, are often required to clear their public statements with the President because in a real sense they do represent or are taken to represent the whole administration. In a mass society comprised of a multitude of interest and institutional groupings, our impersonal separation from public communicators foster our natural tendency to generalize and associate. Under these conditions, external ethos becomes an important factor; e.g., we distrust Reuther because we dislike labor union power, or we refuse to grant credibility to the statement of a physician on social legislation because he represents the American Medi-

13 *Newsweek*, February 19, 1962, p. 20.
14 *Newsweek*, January 27, 1964, p. 20.
15 *Newsweek*, May 31, 1965, p. 26.

cal Association. In other words, public communicators often either benefit or suffer because our image of them is colored by our image of the
institution or interest they represent. Thus, our contemporary concept
of ethos must be modified and enlarged to include a number of external
factors which early classical rhetorical scholars did not have to notice.

As we can see from our previous discussion, we must not overlook
the impact newspapers and news magazines have on our perceptions of
the world around us and hence on our reception of oral communication.
The printed news media report the comings and goings of various public
officials and most of their public statements. Since the majority of us
read at least one newspaper and occasionally leaf through news magazines, part of our image of a public communicator is based on what we
read. And, as we shall see in the next section, our image of a certain
speaker may have much to do with how we react to what he says.

We need to be aware that we do not often get a complete picture of
either public leaders or their statements through the journalistic media.
Most of what we read is opinion and interpretation rather than straight,
factual reporting. The press often exaggerates a story to make it more
exciting for its readers, and in some cases it manufactures news when
there is none. Editorial policies of various papers and magazines influence the way a certain story is reported, and studies show that editors
have much to do with the nature of local, national, and international
news stories through selection and editing.[16]

Since most papers and magazines do not carry the complete text of a
public speech, we have only certain selected excerpts and paraphrases
which may or may not accurately reflect the speaker's intended meaning.
Because of the tendency of the press to emphasize the dramatic, we may
miss the qualification or reservation expressed by a speaker and receive
only an assertive generalization. In other words, newspapers and magazines play a significant part in the great conversation of our society and
influence to some extent the way we receive and interpret various public
statements.

A most important difference created by the mass media of course is
the nature of the audience. Greek and Roman audiences were small and
localized, a condition the invention of the printing press rapidly altered
later. Today it makes more sense to talk of audiences rather than audience for the world audience whose existence is made possible by modern
communication systems is really composed of various national and
cultural groupings all with their own interests and points of view. And

[16] For instance, see David Manning White, "The 'Gatekeeper': A Case Study in the
Selection of News," pp. 160–72, or Walter Gieber, "News Is What Newspapermen Make It," pp. 173–82, both in *People, Society, and Mass Communications*,
eds. Lewis Anthony Dexter and David Manning White (New York: The Macmillan Company, 1964).

even within the boundaries of one particular country there are numerous and fairly distinct groupings based on nationality, culture, geography, interest, purpose, and so on. For a communicator, preparing his remarks with a small, fairly homogeneous audience in mind is quite different from attempting to determine how peoples throughout the nation or the world will react to what he says. The attractiveness of the opportunity to speak to more audiences simultaneously is tempered by the realization that the risks of incurring displeasure and misunderstanding are multiplied.

An inevitable result of the existence of various audiences with divergent points of view, all of whom may receive the same public message in one form or another, has been the extensive and sophisticated use of ambiguous language. To avoid unwarranted or unwanted interpretations or, more probably, to allow for the widest possible range of interpretation, many prominent communicators feel the need occasionally to couch their statements in vague language. Former Korean ambassador Ben C. Limb acknowledges the necessity for ambiguity.

> Oftentimes his [the ambassador's] main concern is not to set down in clear and simple language a statement of facts so obvious that it cannot be misunderstood. Quite to the contrary, his purpose often is to concoct an ambiguous composition which—no matter how carefully it may be analyzed—will add up to no real meaning whatsoever.[17]

The politician who wishes to say something to the members of a labor union without antagonizing management officials feels the same need for ambiguity.

In addition to wanting to avoid the firm commitments of specific statements, public communicators often want to allow for as many future alternatives as possible. It may be advantageous, for example, to appear to be planning firm action without describing what form such action may take. We see this intent in such statements as: "If the American imperialists step up their military activity in Southeast Asia there will be grave consequences," and, "The United States will make an appropriate response to further Communist infiltration." As Oliver states:

> Diplomacy must transmute "say what you mean" into "say something that can be interpreted to mean whatever may prove to be convenient in circumstances that cannot be foreseen."[18]

[17] From Ben C. Limb, "Speech: The Life of a Diplomat," in *Culture and Communication*, ed. Robert T. Oliver (1962), p. 30. Courtesy of Charles C Thomas, Publisher, Springfield, Illinois.

[18] Robert T. Oliver, ed., *Culture and Communication*, (1962), p. 66. Courtesy of Charles C Thomas, Publisher, Springfield, Illinois.

Intentional ambiguity may also be used to evoke powerful emotional responses. Modern mass-communication systems have greatly increased the potential for creating identification patterns on a large scale. These patterns carry with them categorical judgments that guide and direct thought. Images called to mind by such terms as communist, Wall Street, liberal, conservative, radical, free enterprise, and others can hinder or obstruct meaningful public discussion by clouding important issues with strong emotion. In sum, ambiguity has no doubt always been a problem whenever and wherever men have communicated with one another, but modern means of propaganda and mass communication have multiplied and intensified the problem.

We have not exhausted all the differences between the act of public speaking as it is pictured in classical writing and the contemporary nature of the process of public communication. But our discussion has demonstrated that our mass society and our modern technical know-how have combined to alter the classical public-speaking paradigm in important ways. In the next section we shall take a close look at the various elements constituting and surrounding public communication in order to gauge their influence on our behavior.

The Variables of
Public Communication

In the next section of our study we shall come to grips with the problem of assessing the effects of public communication and the reasons for those effects. But first, let us look closely at the variables which combine to make up the act of public communication. Essentially, public communication, like any other act of communication, is a transaction between communicator and receiver. The transaction is dynamic, on-going, ever subject to change, and therefore difficult to describe accurately. To understand it, we must discuss the highly active communication process as if it were somewhat static, both because our language forces us to and because we enhance our knowledge of the total process by closely examining the individual phenomena which constitute it. In this section we shall talk about the various elements, or variables, of public communication as if they were somewhat discrete and isolated. If we remember that the distinctions suggested in the following discussion are not real but are made for purposes of analysis only, we can hope to keep distortion to a minimum.

THE COMMUNICATOR

Let us begin our analysis of the public-communication process by assessing the role and influence of the communicator, the speaker who presents the message. Common sense tells us that the perceived character of the speaker is one of the factors which shape an auditor's response to a verbal message. All of us know certain individuals who command our respect for one reason or another and other individuals whom we hold in comparatively low esteem. We tend to grant a certain amount of credibility to the statements of people we respect, but we are likely to discount the opinions of those individuals we hold in low esteem. As a result of this understandable human behavior, the respected person has an easier time convincing us that his point of view is correct than does someone we do not like.

Aristotle listed ethos, the character of the speaker, as one of the three means of artistic persuasion in speaking. He explained that a speaker's character is the cause of persuasion

> when the speech is so uttered as to make him worthy of belief; for as a rule we trust men of probity more, and more quickly, about things in general, while on points outside the realm of exact knowledge, where opinion is divided, we trust them absolutely. . . . We might almost affirm that . . . character is the most potent of all the means to persuasion.[1]

The concept of ethos has occupied a central place in the study of oral communication ever since Aristotle proclaimed its potent, persuasive force. In recent years studies on the influence of a speaker's personality, character, or authoritativeness have provided empirical confirmation of the early Greek observation. Various studies in psychology, sociology, speech, education, and communication deal with differing aspects of ethos. Andersen and Clevenger, in their excellent summary of experimental research in ethos, state that the findings are neither sufficiently numerous nor sufficiently sophisticated to enable one to draw definite conclusions about the operation of ethos. They do however conclude the following:

> The finding is almost universal that the ethos of the source is related in some way to the impact of the message. This generalization applies not only to political, social, religious, and economic issues but also to matters of aesthetic judgment and personal taste.[2]

Clearly Aristotle did not think it desirable to judge the character of the speaker on the basis of any prior impression. Rather, he felt the speech itself must contain the elements by which an auditor decides that the speaker is good or evil, credible or fraudulent. Nonetheless, it is equally clear that auditors do allow prior impressions to influence their reaction to a message, so we must include more in a realistic concept of ethos than Aristotle was willing to include. We need first to draw a distinction between genuine ethos and perceived ethos.

Obviously, the more we know about an individual through personal contact, the better able we are to make judgments of his honesty, sincerity, geniality, humanitarianism, and so on. When people with whom we are familiar express their opinions, we have some idea of whether

[1] Aristotle, *Rhetoric*, trans. Lane Cooper (New York: Appleton-Century-Crofts, 1932), pp. 8–9 (1356a).
[2] Kenneth Andersen and Theodore Clevenger, Jr., "A Summary of Experimental Research in Ethos," *Speech Monographs*, XXX (June 1963), 77.

they are objective or biased, realistic or visionary, probing or superficial. In other words, we have some insight into their real character.

Auditors of public communication are seldom in a position to render judgments based on intimate knowledge. Consequently many different factors, some genuine signs of character and some spurious and misleading, influence the image, or perceived ethos, of a speaker. Andersen and Clevenger[3] suggest the term *image* because it refers to the ideas an auditor has about the character of a speaker, whether those ideas are correct, partially correct, or totally erroneous. An auditor may accept what a communicator says because he has heard the communicator described as an expert on his subject. Or the communicator may be a member of the same political party as the auditor or share the same religious viewpoint or express the same biases during the course of his statement or just be good looking. For any of these and similar reasons an auditor may tend to accept the statements of the communicator without serious question. On the other hand, if a communicator belongs to an opposing political party or interest group, possesses a differing ethnic background, expresses "unacceptable" biases or values, or is slovenly in personal appearance, these facts may provide justification for dismissing his statements summarily. As human beings we may deplore an auditor's reasons for liking or disliking a speaker, but as students of communication we must realize that the image of the speaker held by the auditor for whatever reason in some measure affects the auditor's response to the speaker's message.

Second, we need to be aware that ethos, the auditor's image of a speaker, is not a static concept but is subject to constant re-evaluation and change. Unless the speaker is totally unknown, an auditor has some image of him before he begins to speak. This initial image exerts its influence on the auditor's reception of the message from the very outset, so we need to consider the impact of antecedent ethos. But, because communication is such an extremely dynamic process, the continuing impression made by the speaker may create a new image, and thus the auditor's impressions before and after the communicative act may be very different. Consequently, we must consider those image-changing elements intrinsic to the communicative situation—what the speaker says, how he says it, the sincerity of his demeanor, and his demonstration of qualities of expertise. The residual image—that is, the image that remains in the mind of the auditor after the speaker has finished his message—readily reactivates itself to become the antecedent image in the auditor's mind when he next hears the speaker. Of course, intervening factors, such as reports on the activities of the speaker or subsequent

[3] Andersen and Clevenger, "A Summary of Experimental Research in Ethos," p. 59.

public statements uttered by him and reported in various ways, cause alterations in an auditor's residual impression and result in the formulation of a new image. Image formulation is a complicated process which is often difficult to trace accurately and sometimes impossible to verify.

Several research studies, however, successfully illustrate the influence of antecedent ethos on auditors' reactions to a message. In one instance, Haiman presented a 15-minute, tape-recorded, persuasive speech favoring national compulsory health insurance to three groups of auditors. The speech was introduced differently before each group. One group was told that the speech was given by Eugene Dennis, secretary-general of the American Communist Party. A second group was told that the speech was delivered by Dr. Thomas Parran, surgeon-general of the United States; included in the introduction was a listing of Parran's professional qualifications. The third group was told the speech was delivered by a Northwestern University sophomore. Before hearing the speech each auditor was asked to indicate on the Woodward shift-of-opinion ballot his initial attitude toward compulsory health insurance. After hearing the speech, the auditors again recorded their opinions on the speech subject. Results showed that the speech attributed to Parran caused a significantly greater shift of opinion than the other two speeches.[4] Since each group of auditors heard the identical speech, we may reasonably conclude that the auditors' attitudes toward the communicator, established before hearing the speech, significantly influenced their reaction to the speech content itself.

Kelman and Hovland conducted another study which attempted to measure the impact of antecedent ethos. They presented a speech advocating lenient treatment of juvenile delinquents to three groups of high school students. Three different introductions were made: one group believed the speaker to be a judge of a juvenile court; the second group believed the speaker to be someone picked from the audience; the third group believed the speaker to be a person with a criminal record who had been a juvenile delinquent. In a post-experiment questionnaire, the student auditors rated the speaker on the fairness and impartiality of his remarks. As we might expect they felt the "judge" gave a fair presentation over twice as many times as they thought the "juvenile delinquent" did. Opinion change in favor of lenient treatment for juvenile delinquents occurred to a significantly greater degree in the group which heard the "judge" than in either of the other two groups.[5]

[4] Franklyn Haiman, "An Experimental Study of the Effects of Ethos in Public Speaking," *Speech Monographs,* XVI (September 1949), 190–202.
[5] K. C. Kelman and C. I. Hovland, " 'Reinstatement' of the Communicator in Delayed Measurement of Opinion Change," *Journal of Abnormal and Social Psychology,* XLVIII (1953), 327–35.

Notice that in both cases reported above neither the content of the message nor the way in which it was delivered varied from group to group. The variable was the image of the speaker cast in the introduction. This antecedent image influenced auditors' reactions to the message itself.

The results of the influence we have been discussing appear so far to be fairly straightforward. If an auditor conjures up a negative image of a communicator for some reason, he tends to reject the communicator's message or at least is not moved by it; if an auditor pictures the ethos of a communicator in a positive light, he is disposed to accept what the communicator has to say. To describe influence in this manner, however, is to talk only in terms of fairly general responses and to say more about the direction of the response than about its precise qualitative nature. Because human attitudes are extremely complicated, varied, and often ephemeral, any description of gross, directional attitude response is likely to conceal a variety of individual response differences. Much work remains to be done in terms of ferreting out and describing such differences, but several studies have done so fairly successfully.

One of the specific questions we may ask concerns the way in which we hear and remember the content of persuasive messages. When we are listening to the arguments of an advocate with whom we disagree initially, do we accurately perceive his message? Several studies reveal that most individuals practice what we may call *selective exposure;* that is, when allowed to exercise a choice, they expose themselves to "favorable" messages and refuse to heed "unfavorable" ones. But, what happens when they do pay attention to unfavorable messages, as may occur when two opposing advocates present contrasting or contradictory points of view in a public debate?

The results of a study undertaken to answer just such a question are very interesting. The procedure for the study was as follows: Twelve passages were chosen from the Kennedy-Nixon televised debates of 1960; they represented positions the candidates had taken on 12 key campaign issues. A panel of experts judged six of the passages to be ambiguous; they judged the other six to be unequivocal. The passages were recorded on tape and played to 70 subjects, 35 Republicans and 35 Democrats randomly selected from the party rolls in Lafayette, Indiana. The subjects were told which candidate was speaking; they listened to each passage as a separate statement and then explained to an interviewer their interpretation of what was said. Later, a content analysis was made of interviewee responses to determine the meanings reported for the various passages and the extent of agreement on any one passage. For the results let us quote directly from the study:

Results of the content analysis as applied to the interviewee responses indicated that members of a political organization often found meaning in a message spoken by a speaker whose political affiliation was congruent with their own; when the source of the political message was incongruent with the listener's party, many listeners tended to report that the speaker failed to offer any information. When the speaker represented the *same* party as the listener there was an average of three (out of a total of 70) responses that reported the speaker never gave his position. When the speaker represented a *different* political organization the average jumped to 11 responses. . . . In substance, people tended to read meaning into a message spoken by a favorable source and report a lack of meaning for an unfavorable source.[6]

Another study, which also examined audience response to the Kennedy-Nixon debates, asked the same general question in a slightly different way: Did the format of the debate, which placed the two candidates in a face-to-face situation, succeed in exposing auditors to opposing views? The subjects were 60 Republicans and 60 Democrats from four neighboring California cities. To measure relative exposure, the subjects took a 16-item information test which had eight items for each candidate; the test was based on statements made in the first T.V. debate. Specifically, the test attempted to determine whether subjects recalled more information given by their preferred candidate than by the opposition candidate. Results showed little difference in recall among subjects who thought both candidates made effective arguments or among subjects who said only their candidates made effective arguments. But recall was higher for the subject's candidate when the subject thought neither candidate had made an effective argument. Interviews conducted after the first, second, and fourth debates revealed that subjects were more likely to say the opposition candidate had made no effective argument than they were to admit their own candidate was ineffective.[7]

What these studies clearly indicate is that an auditor's total response to ethos includes a number of components such as listening, perceiving, attributing meaning, and recalling. It is well established that an auditor's image of a communicator is often an important determinant of the auditor's total response to the message.

While we still have the Kennedy-Nixon debates before us, let us refer to one more study. The findings here tell us something about the changing image of a communicator. A small-scale panel study of 95 New York

[6] Larry A. Samovar, "Ambiguity and Unequivocation in the Kennedy-Nixon Television Debates," *Quarterly Journal of Speech*, XLVIII (October 1962), 278–79.

[7] Richard F. Carter, "Some Effects of the Debates," in *The Great Debates*, ed. Sidney Kraus (Bloomington, Indiana: Indiana University Press, 1962), pp. 253–70.

viewers focused on new perceptions of the candidates arising from television exposure. Each subject was interviewed at length in September
before the first debate, immediately after the first debate, and once more
after the fourth debate. The dramatic improvement which occurred in
the Kennedy image as a result of the debates was particularly noticeable.

> The image of Kennedy was transformed from that of an eager, affable,
> young, and ambitious political aspirant into one that emphasized the
> competent, dynamic, and quick-thinking candidate.
>   "His debating techniques showed a quick mind."
>   "He was alert and interested at all times."
>   "He seemed to know all the time where to refute Nixon."
>   "He never fumbled."
>   "He presented himself as a doer, a leader, a positive thinker."[8]

One could well argue that the atmosphere surrounding political de-
bating, and for that matter campaigning in general, is more conducive
to the projection of a candidate's image than it is to a sober analysis of
his arguments. We can also note, particularly in connection with the
Kennedy-Nixon debates, that the average citizen simply did not possess
or have access to enough information to properly assess the argumentative claims advanced. In such a case, it is much easier to focus on
personalities than on issues. But these observations do not deny that
something about Kennedy's statements—the way in which they were
stated, the fact that they included much concrete supporting data, or
the confident assertiveness with which they were made—operated to
enhance his image in the minds of many who heard him. We can suppose then that at times Aristotle's desire that a speech influence a communicator's ethos is realized to some degree.

So far in our discussion we have done little to identify those characteristics of communicators which enhance or reduce ethos. We shall not
attempt such a task because the reasons for liking or disliking, accepting
or rejecting another human being are too numerous to mention without
becoming simplistic and tedious. Any listing of ethos factors is incomplete, unrealistically dichotomous, arbitrary in terms of definition,
and, on the whole, as useless as various listings of motivational factors
have proven to be. We can fairly safely assume some connection between the acceptability of a communicator as he is perceived by his
audience and those values, desires, and goals which the audience perceives as being important to them. We need to look at specific communicative acts before attempting any more definitive analysis.

---

[8] Kurt Lang and Gladys Engel Lang, "Reactions of Viewers," in *The Great Debates*,
    ed. Sidney Kraus (Bloomington, Indiana: Indiana University Press, 1962), p. 324.

THE MESSAGE

The message, that is, what the communicator says or writes, purports to be the central element in the transaction that takes place between communicator and auditor. We use the word *purports* deliberately because at times a message has less importance than does some other element of the communicative situation. We have just talked about occasions when our image of the communicator can determine whether we accurately perceive and evaluate a message. And we have seen throughout this book how past experience and knowledge stored in our memory system may cause us to misinterpret and misjudge the intent of a message. Personal predispositions, biases, and needs all influence the reception and processing of a message. And throughout the remainder of our discussion we shall examine still other variables which affect message reception.

Nevertheless, when human minds come into contact with one another during the course of communication, the message is one of the primary means of accomplishing that contact, and therefore it must always be considered an important variable.

We shall not attempt a detailed description of all the elements in a written or spoken message; a multitude of articles and books on speech, communication, and psychology discuss the various components of different messages. It is fair to say that of all the communication variables the message has received the most copious treatment. We shall instead summarize in a general way the major elements of messages and briefly consider their interactions.

Three basic elements of messages can be separated for analysis: the ideational, or content, element, i.e., the meaning; the organizational characteristics, or the form of the message; the linguistic element, or the language used to express the meaning. We need to remember that these elements are not perceived as discrete units by an auditor, even though we talk about them as if they were. Messages, particularly spoken ones, are perceived holistically, and we cannot realistically assess the impact of one element apart from the impact of the others.

When we ask, "What does the message mean?" or "What is the point of the message?", we are referring to the content element of communication. The communicator has certain ideas he wants to explain or express, a certain point of view about a subject he wants to project, or particular argumentative claims he wishes to have accepted. This is what the message is all about; it is the residual meaning the communicator hopes the receiver will remember when the communication act is over and all else is forgotten. In a well constructed message, the major ideas constituting the residual message stand out and are easily ascertained.

If the message is anything other than assertion, the communicator must include supporting ideas, illustrations, explanations, and other data to uphold the major ideas. In addition, nearly all messages, particularly those that are argumentative or persuasive in intent, either explicitly or implicitly express attitudinal stances, value judgments, ethical presuppositions, and other bits of emotional data. Obviously, the longer a message, the more secondary illustrative and supporting material it is likely to contain.

No matter how we describe message content, the important point is that meaning does not ultimately reside in the message but rather in the minds of receivers. The various ideas that make up the message, the examples, the statistics, the authoritative references, and the appeals all act as stimulators which trigger meaning in the minds of receivers. To the extent that the understanding and experience of the receivers overlap with those of the communicator, there will be identity of meaning. But to a significant degree meanings remain essentially individualized and private, human experiences do not precisely overlap, and the particular needs and values of one individual lead him to perceive a problem differently from the way his neighbor does. We often see what we want to see and hear what we want to hear in a message. Therefore it is difficult to generalize about auditor reactions to a message from an examination of the components of the message alone.

One of the areas of research which most clearly demonstrates the mistaken notion that certain elements of a message lead to predictable auditor response is that concerned with logical and emotional appeals. For a number of years logical and emotional responses were thought to be qualitatively different kinds of human behavior. A corollary assumption was that those elements within a message that appealed to logic were different from the elements appealing to emotion. Consequently, it was assumed that messages could be catalogued according to the logic or emotion they exhibited, and it was fashionable to speak of argument as a genre of discourse which emphasized logic and reason, while persuasive discourse was primarily emotional, nonrational, or irrational.

The impact of contemporary psychological theory led some researchers to question the validity of the logic-emotion dichotomy, and Ruechelle demonstrated clearly that audiences do not tend to respond to logical and emotional appeals as if they were at the opposite ends of a continuum.[9] Furthermore, he discovered no significant agreement be-

[9] R. C. Reuchelle, "An Experimental Study of Audience Recognition of Emotional and Intellectual Appeals in Persuasion," *Speech Monographs*, XXV (1958), 49–58. For a general discussion see Samuel L. Becker, "Research on Emotional and Logical Proofs," *Southern Speech Journal*, XXVIII, No. 3 (Spring 1963), 198–207.

tween speaker and listener judgments of the relative degree of logical and emotional appeals in speeches. What one person perceives as a logical appeal the person sitting next to him may well perceive as an illogical notion. How many of us have delivered what we thought was a perfectly reasonable statement only to find our listener treating our remark as if it lacked common sense?

Another example should suffice to make the point. Textbooks on argumentation and debate usually define evidence as data, such as facts and opinions, which bolster asserted claims. The primary purpose of such data, we are told, is to help "prove" the claims made. Thus, claims are to be evaluated on the basis of the evidence which supports them; evidence is the starting point, the raw material of which an argument is constructed. An assumption made by most debate textbooks is that those arguments which rely upon sound evidence are more effective than those which do not.

However, experimental studies which have tested the relative effectiveness of evidence in gaining favorable reception demonstrate that the ideal response suggested in textbooks is not always an accurate description of how receivers behave.[10] It appears that there are several psychological dimensions of reaction to evidence: certain predispositions may cause us to accept some data as strong support and to reject other data at once regardless of their actual merit; our image of the communicator may affect our response; a communicator may increase his stature in our eyes or diminish his authoritativeness because of the way he uses evidence; certain criteria for evaluating evidence, e.g., rejection of all apparently biased authorities, may cause us to misjudge actual credibility.[11] To function as evidence, data must be believed. Because there are many human reasons for believing or disbelieving and a variety of possible human responses to any single message element, we must conclude that drawing inferences about the causes of human response and behavior on the basis of message analysis alone is a risky venture;

---

[10] The reader who is interested in the role evidence plays in argument should read the following studies: D. C. Anderson, "The Effect of Various Uses of Authoritative Testimony in Persuasive Speaking" (unpublished Master's thesis, Ohio State University, 1958); Robert S. Cathcart, "An Experimental Study of the Relative Effectiveness of Four Methods of Presenting Evidence," Speech Monographs, XXII (1955), 227–33; D. L. Costly, "An Experimental Study of the Effectiveness of Quantitative Evidence in Speeches of Advocacy" (unpublished Master's thesis, University of Oklahoma, 1958); H. Gilkinson, S. F. Paulson, and D. E. Sikkink, "Effects of Order and Authority in an Argumentative Speech," Quarterly Journal of Speech, XL (1954), 183–92; James C. McCroskey, "The Effects of Evidence in Persuasive Communication," Western Speech, XXX (Summer 1967), 188–99.

[11] The psychological dimensions mentioned here are explored in more depth in Richard B. Gregg, "The Rhetoric of Evidence," Western Speech, XXX (Summer 1967), 180–89.

we need to know how the receiver perceived the message before making definite statements.

For analytical purposes, we may separate the form of a message—that is, the way in which it is organized for presentation, the order in which ideas are presented, and the placement of supporting data or evidence in relation to major ideas—and discuss it apart from the content. Various studies have been undertaken to determine whether one organizational pattern is more effective than another, either in terms of persuading or bringing understanding. The results of such studies are too varied or the attitude changes measured are too insignificant to allow the formulation of any meaningful generalizations. At times stronger arguments ought to be stated first, and at other times they are better left until last; sometimes both sides of an issue should be presented, and on other occasions only the favored side should be discussed, etc. We would be hasty to conclude, however, that the form in which a message is cast is meaningless. We may more wisely conclude that it does not make sense to measure the influence of form apart from content, situation, audience, and other variables. The human auditor tends to respond holistically, not compartmentally, and his reactions simply do not stand still for neat slicing. But it is precisely because the mind reacts holistically, abhoring the formless and imposing closure and pattern wherever possible, that the form of a message is an important ingredient in the total analysis. Thus, we may gain insight into the workings of a message by examining the formal skeleton shaping the content.

Without language, there would be no message as we are talking about it here; so it goes without saying that the linguistic element deserves our attention. There is general agreement that man's development of language, the symbol system he uses to convey meanings to his fellows, is one of the things which most clearly separates him from other animals. The very existence of language illustrates man's unique capacity to internalize his environment and to reproduce it in a symbolic form. Language not only represents external reality but also encompasses emotional responses to that reality; thus, when we examine the meanings contained in language, we are dealing with human reality or reality as man sees it. The reality represented in linguistic meaning may not, and in fact often does not, accurately portray what is in the external world. But language does convey symbolically what man believes is there, and that is what we must be concerned with.

We often think of language as the primary means of conveying meaning in communication, but this is not an accurate understanding of what linguistic symbols do. Rather than carrying meaning from one mind to another, language symbols evoke meaning in the minds of auditors. For communication to be successful in terms of achieving understanding, there must be some correspondence of meaning between the speaker who uses a symbol and the auditor who hears it. We assume a certain generality of meaning on the part of individuals who speak the same language, and correctly so because without this generality there could be no linguistic communication. But we must grant the general assumption with care because no two individuals have precisely the same experiences and they are not likely to have precisely the same meanings for words. Obviously the more abstract the term, the less we can assume similarity of meaning between communicator and auditor. The symbol *dog* probably evokes similar meanings more often and more easily than does the symbol *justice*. To compound the difficulty, language, as we have already seen, is attitudinal to a large extent. Linguistic symbols evoke emotional feelings which are as much a part of the meaning as any physical object to which the symbol may refer. Politicians, advertising agents, propagandists, and the like capitalize daily on the rhetorical aspects of language, that is, on the ability of language to evoke attitudes of value and judgment which can ultimately lead to action. Therefore it behooves those of us who are interested in understanding communication to be aware of the linguistic element of a message both for the meaning (or lack of it) evoked and for the attitudes engendered.

We have discussed message characteristics only briefly, but the reader should recognize by now that what humans bring to a message is probably more important than what the message contains. Thus, everything discussed in this book is ultimately related to human reaction to messages.

THE AUDIENCE

Traditionally, textbooks on speech and oral communication deal with communication from the standpoint of the speaker. In so doing they sustain the point of view of the Greeks and Romans, who were primarily interested in providing useful techniques for effective speaking. They did not overlook audiences, to be sure, because a communicator had to know something about the kind of audience he was speaking to, its interests and values, its sociological makeup, and other pertinent personal characteristics in order to compose an appropriate and successful message. The basis of the traditional point of view was the assumption that the principal initiator in a communicative act is the speaker. If he adjusts successfully to his audience, he can achieve his purpose. A corollary assumption was that a speaker who fails to evoke the intended response from his listeners has not successfully utilized or manipulated all the materials at his disposal in light of what he knows about his audience.

The traditional focus has some validity of course, but it is not the whole picture. In the past few years, researchers in communication have given increased emphasis to audiences, realizing that they are as influential in determining the nature and effect of a message as is any other element in the communicative process.

> Audiences . . . have, however, proved intractable. They make their own decisions as to whether to listen or not to listen. Even when they listen, the communication may have no effect, or it may boomerang. Increasingly, researchers have had to shift their attention to the audience itself to find out what sorts of people they are dealing with under what circumstances.[12]

Raymond Bauer, who wrote the statement above, notes that in many cases it makes more sense to describe a communicative situation as a "response-bound" situation than as a "stimulus-bound" one.[13] In other words audience influence is more important than speaker influence.

Anyone interested in understanding how man behaves during the process of communication must devote considerable time and effort to determining the nature of audiences for here he may discover his most useful leads. He must realize that an audience is not passive but makes demands of a communicator at the same time the communicator is placing demands on his audience. We may realistically describe a communicative act as a symbolic transaction involving a bargain between communicator and auditor; the interaction between the parties involved is never unidimensional but always reciprocal.

We describe audiences in various ways depending upon what characteristics we choose as being definitive. We may start with size. At one end of a continuum we place small audiences, such as local P.T.A. groups, civic clubs, or church groups. On the other end of the continuum we place the international audience because our rapidly developing systems of international communication make it possible for a multitude of persons from different countries to hear a public message or to see a public message or both. At various points along the continuum we place audiences of other sizes—local radio and T.V. audiences, large numbers of people gathered in one hall as at our national political conventions, and, of course, the national television audience, which changes in size depending upon the nature of the communicative event. Or we may devise a continuum based on similarity characteristics, grouping very homogeneous audiences at one end and extremely heterogeneous audiences at the other.

[12] Raymond A. Bauer, "The Communicator and the Audience," in Dexter and White, p. 127.
[13] Bauer, "The Communicator and the Audience," p. 127.

In either case, we are trying to discover those characteristics of an audience which cause certain response patterns to occur as a result of, or at least contiguous with, the reception of a message. If we adopt Bauer's conception of an audience as a system of "response potentials"[14] which can be triggered by a communicator and his message, then we can describe our task as one of trying to determine what those response potentials are and how they operate.

Several categories of sociopsychological phenomena describe response potentials. Generally, they refer to motivational attitudes, opinions, mind sets, and so on. When analyzing a particular audience in these terms, we must discuss those specific audience values, desires, and perceptions which relate to the communicator, the content of the message, and the situation surrounding the communicative act.

If we describe audience interests in this manner, several continua are very helpful. One is based on an affirmative-negative dimension. Is the audience favorably disposed to the communicator's point of view, or is it against his position? If there is disagreement, is it over basic values and conceptualizations, or is it about how to achieve an already agreed-upon goal? The latter determination is an important one because we know that the more a proposed change appears to threaten traditionally accepted values, the stronger the resistance to that change. This particular characteristic of human behavior accounts for the efforts of many communicators to convince their audiences that what they are proposing is not revolutionary but a modification of already accepted procedures in line with generally accepted goals.

A second dimension is that of homogeneity or heterogeneity in terms of audience beliefs, attitudes, goals, etc. Obviously, a communicator directs his messages more easily to those audiences with similar beliefs than to those with widely differing and divergent points of view. On one end of our continuum we may place audiences made up of small, local groups of people drawn together by a common interest, while at the other end we may again place the international audience, made up of groups of people in various countries who are interested in the subject matter of a message for one reason or another but who react differently depending upon their particular attitudes and goals. In between we may place audiences united by a general goal but still having sufficient differences over how to achieve the goal to account for differing reactions to the same message. The audience at one of our national political nominating conventions is a case in point; usually all delegates are united by a desire to advance the welfare of their party, but divergent local and regional problems may cause divisions on specific party policy. Obviously the more heterogeneous an audience is in terms of attitudes and beliefs,

14 Bauer, "The Communicator and the Audience," p. 127.

the wider the appeal of a message has to be to achieve its purpose; hence the more general and abstract its terminology is likely to be.

We may add a third dimension—that of audience interest and commitment. In terms of persuasive effect, audiences change their minds on the opinion level much more readily than they do on the level of deep and personal commitment. The more interested a person is in a matter, the more involved he is likely to feel, and, as Berelson and Steiner point out, empirical investigation reveals that "once a person commits himself to a position, that commitment itself becomes a barrier against change."[15]

A further useful dimension in which to characterize audiences concerns primary and secondary audiences. When a communicator is a public spokesman, he may, in addition to addressing an obvious, or primary, audience, also be addressing one or more secondary audiences. A United States senator, for example, may speak to a group of business leaders in a large city, his primary audience; but at the same time, aware that newspapers and T.V. are covering the event, he may include remarks intended for a larger, secondary audience. National spokesmen often issue statements to reporters knowing or hoping that representatives of foreign governments will receive particular meanings from them. In detailing the 1960 presidential campaign, Theodore White describes the several audiences any candidate must keep in mind as he tours the country. Because an entourage of reporters follows a presidential candidate, none of his remarks remains localized. Thus we have the national audience receiving daily reports in the press and on television and radio as to the nature of a candidate's actions and statements. We have the "strategic audience"—the audience in a particular state or region surrounding the candidate's specific speaking locale. As White points out, a speech delivered in St. Louis may receive only a paragraph's coverage in San Francisco but receives full-scale, front-page coverage in St. Louis and its environs. Knowing this, a candidate tries to acquire impact in those strategic areas in which he must accumulate votes in order to win. And we have the personal audience—those individuals who hear the candidate in person and who are the candidate's immediate sources of feedback.[16] The terms *primary* and *secondary* may not be sufficient to describe the audience potential, but the point is that, in terms of shaping a communicator's message, audiences which do not receive the message directly are often as important and are sometimes more important than those which do receive the message directly.

We have intimated all through our discussion that audiences do

[15] Bernard Berelson and Gary A. Steiner, *Human Behavior* (New York: Harcourt, Brace & World, Inc., 1964), p. 575.
[16] *The Making of the President, 1960* (New York: Atheneum Publishers, 1961), pp. 254–55.

affect communicators. We have concentrated so much in the past on the traditional, speaker-centered approach that very few studies investigate the nature of the audience as an initiator of influence. Most textbooks urge communicators at least to adapt their material to the anticipated audience. To achieve his purpose, the communicator must find out all he can about the audience he is to address and then, by picturing himself as one of them, decide how to present his material in the most favorable light. In this sense, even before it ever comes into being, an audience influences a communicator and hence the act of communication; its potential existence is affective before its actual existence is realized. Common sense supports this notion of antecedent influence; few persons consciously plan to communicate without considering—or at least acknowledging—an intended audience of some kind.

Several very interesting studies show that intended audiences may exert far more subtle influences than those suggested by the textbooks. In one study the experimenter traveled to several colleges and universities, presenting herself in classrooms as a representative of either the National Council of Teachers or the American Taxpayers Economy League, both fictional organizations. She explained each time that her organization was seeking speakers to address its members on the subject of teachers' pay and that she had arranged with the instructor for the students to write sample speeches the next week during class time. Next she read a short passage to each student group, favoring pay raises for teachers in one half of the cases for each intended audience (National Council of Teachers or American Taxpayers Economy League) and opposing a pay increase in the other half of the cases for each intended audience. Immediately after reading the passages the experimenter asked the students to write the passage she had just read to them from memory as accurately as they could. Returning a week later, the experimenter asked them to reproduce the passage again before writing the sample speech. The hypothesis that the subjects would be able to reproduce the passage more accurately when it was congruent with the intended audience than when it was incongruent was confirmed beyond the 0.01 level of statistical significance. In other words, a subject recalled material advocating increased teachers' pay if he were expecting favorable audience reaction better than if he were anticipating an unfriendly reaction.[17] A similar study conducted by Schramm and Danielson using different subject matter confirmed the hypothesis.[18]

Turning now to the possibility of an audience's influencing a com-

[17] Claire Zimmerman and R. A. Bauer, "The Influence of an Audience on What Is Remembered," *Public Opinion Quarterly,* XX (1956), 238–48.
[18] W. Schramm and W. Danielson, "Anticipated Audiences as Determinants of Recall," *Journal of Abnormal and Social Psychology,* XVI (1958), 282–83.

municator while he is communicating, we find again a dearth of empirical studies either substantiating or disproving the hypothesis that such influence occurs. Common sense once more tells us that the hypothesis is reasonable, and at least one study supplies justification. One of the purposes of this study (undertaken by C. F. Karns) was an investigation of the relationship between negative audience response and changes in speech content during the course of communication. Four experienced speakers each gave two, 15-minute, manuscript speeches on controversial topics. They presented one speech to a control group, the other to an experimental group prepared to react on cue by displaying either disagreement with what the speaker was saying or lack of understanding. Each speaker could modify his manuscript while speaking if he thought the changes would increase the persuasiveness of the speech. As predicted, audience reaction produced noticeable differences between the prepared content and the delivered content.[19] We expect this result to occur often during the process of communication.

Returning again to White's report of the 1960 presidential campaign, we find a vivid description of a speaker's reacting to audience response by gradually altering his message. White's passages portray the influence of an audience, both during and after the act of communication, and describe the modifications this influence caused in subsequent messages. White begins by talking about the first ten days of Kennedy's campaign, when Kennedy appeared to be very stiff and formal. Gradually, as he warmed to the crowds, Kennedy began to develop both his famous style and the theme of his campaign.

> What was more important than the slow growth of ease was the development in the humble all-purpose speech of the grand theme that was to dominate and shape his campaign to the end: *America cannot stand still; her prestige fails in the world; this is a time of burdens and sacrifice; we must move.*
>
> He began his first round with a loose collection of phrases and anecdotes that he jumbled into a pudding for the all-purpose speech; a collection of historical anecdotes; and then the standard phrases: "the importance of the Presidency"; "the world cannot exist half slave and half free"; "only the President can lead"; "farming is our number one domestic problem"; "automation can be a blessing or a curse"; "we must move"; "I ask your help."
>
> Then, gradually, as applause told him where he had hit and indifference informed him where he talked beyond the audience, the pattern began to shape itself into a theme.[20]

[19] "The Verbal Behavior of a Speaker as a Function of Certain Non-Verbal Aversive Stimuli Presented by an Audience in a Public Speaking Situation" (unpublished Ph.D. dissertation, University of Pittsburgh, 1964).

[20] White, *The Making of the President, 1960*, p. 256.

White goes on to detail various speaking occasions, then sums up the first ten days.

> The candidate had found his voice, had sensed a mood, had struck an attitude to the future and to the onward movement of America that would shape the rest of the campaign. He had come clear to himself and his audience. The sharpness of this single theme was to grow and grow, then communicate itself with the strength of simplicity.[21]

One conclusion from our brief attention to the nature of audiences is clear: The audience is an extremely important element in the communication process not only because it is the recipient of the message and will react to it but also because it can exert considerable controlling influence over the entire nature of the communicative act.

Our age has seen the development of sophisticated methods for data gathering, data analysis and processing, and computer simulation and projection. As a result, communicators in public life may now receive information on vast numbers of people efficiently and quickly. Pilot television shows are pretested by electronically recording the reactions of randomly chosen viewing audiences. Advertising messages are pretested in the same way. In both cases executives base decisions on the nature of the response received. Modern politicians have become expert poll watchers and takers and often choose to talk about certain issues on the basis of public-opinion analysis. The presidential campaign of 1960 witnessed the extensive use of advanced public-opinion sampling, and the use of computer simulation produced several remarkably accurate projections of voter attitude and behavior.[22] We can look forward to an ever-increasing reliance on data gathered through various means of audience analysis. In a later section of our discussion we shall examine more closely the nature of the phenomenon called *audience*.

CLIMATE OF OPINION

So far we have been focusing on the inherent elements of the act of public communication—the communicator, the message that is communicated, and the audience to whom the communication is directed. Now we must broaden our perspective to include those situational and social phenomena which exert their influence on any act of public communication. In so doing, we shall be dealing with a very nebulous and

---

[21] White, *The Making of the President, 1960*, pp. 258–59.
[22] See Ithiel de Sola Pool, Robert Abelson, and Samuel Popkin, *Candidates, Issues, and Strategies* (2nd ed.) (Cambridge, Massachusetts: M.I.T. Press, 1965).

immeasurable constellation of physical acts and events, social attitudes and values, and public moods and feelings which we call the *climate of opinion*. A climate of opinion inevitably surrounds every act of public communication, so it is necessary to understand the way in which this social milieu can substantially affect the impact of such communication.

It is difficult to delineate any pattern of climate-of-opinion elements which can be expected to hold from one communicative situation to another. Generally we can say that certain physical occurrences and events help to formulate the social climate of the times; attitudes both interpretative and evaluative form about the physical events and are reflected in public opinion; and certain cultural and social judgments and presuppositions always actively exert their influence by guiding perception and reflection.

All these elements combine to provide the social setting, or the climate of opinion, which acts as background for a specific communicative act. The climate of opinion heightens some attitudes, obliterates others, makes some considerations seem more important than others, calls forth certain values, and negates others. In public communication specifically, the climate of opinion causes some messages to be prominent and others unimportant, and otherwise affects the way in which messages are received and interpreted. The best way to understand both the nature and the importance of the climate of opinion is to examine some specific illustrations.

Among the most prominent public messages of our time are those Roosevelt gave when he assumed the presidency in 1933. To account for their full impact, one must appreciate the climate of opinion in which the statements were made. The physical effects of the Great Depression were of paramount importance at the time and were obvious everywhere. Shanty villages called *Hoovervilles* were thrown up by the unemployed in cities, bread lines formed throughout the land, businesses closed and boarded up their windows, and all across the country banks closed as the American banking system failed. It is difficult for those not alive at the time to appreciate the gloomy and despairing attitude that prevailed in the days prior to Roosevelt's inauguration. No clear way of working out of the economic morass appeared. Matters grew steadily worse between the time of Roosevelt's election and the day he took office, with the climax coming on inauguration day, March 4, 1933, when New York and Illinois, the last bastions of financial strength, proclaimed bank holidays.

The country wanted action and needed a leader in whom it could have confidence. As the time for the inauguration drew near, people around the nation turned on their radios to hear the words of the new Chief Executive.

This is a day of national consecration, and I am certain that my fellow Americans expect that on my induction into the presidency I will address them with a candor and a decision which the present situation of the nation impels. This is pre-eminently the time to speak the truth, frankly and boldly. Nor need we shrink from honestly facing conditions in our country today. This great nation will endure as it has endured, will revive, and will prosper. So, first of all, let me assert my firm belief that the only thing we have to fear is fear itself— nameless, unreasoning, unjustified terror which paralyzes needed efforts to convert retreat into advance.

Roosevelt went on to talk about the primary need of providing jobs for people and explained that if necessary he would assume broad executive powers to take action. In his chronicle of the 1930s entitled *Since Yesterday*, Frederick Lewis Allen recaptures the mood of the moment.

You can turn off the radio now. You have heard what you wanted to hear. This man sounds no longer cautious, evasive. For he has seen that a tortured and bewildered people want to throw overboard the old and welcome something new; that they are sick of waiting, they want somebody who will *fight* this Depression for them and with them; they want leadership, the thrill of bold decision. And not only in his words but in the challenge of the very accents of his voice he has promised them what they want.[23]

Almost immediately the climate of opinion across the United States became more hopeful. In the days that followed, the Roosevelt administration acted swiftly in an attempt to correct the nation's ills, and the fact that it acted at all was as important as the nature of the legislative innovations. As banks and businesses reopened and Roosevelt continued to pump confidence into the people with his fireside chats, the climate of opinion grew progressively more optimistic, and the optimism led to actions on the part of the people which further stimulated economic recovery. The history of the early New Deal provides a clear example of the influence of climate of opinion on the perception of and the reaction to public messages and shows how such messages in turn alter the climate of opinion.

Another striking illustration of the interaction among the climate of opinion, physical events, and public messages is the course of events related to the Soviet-United States test-ban treaty signed in October 1963. During the 15 years preceding 1960 the dominant view most Americans had of the Soviet Union was characterized by deep distrust. The government devoted itself to countering the threat of communism

[23] *Since Yesterday* (New York: Bantam Books, Inc., 1961), p. 85.

by standing firm in places like Berlin and Lebanon and by developing international alliances to thwart Moscow's offensive thrusts. During this period the development of nuclear weapons systems became a matter of great concern. In spite of the awareness of the devastating results of a nuclear war and hence of the need to control nuclear weaponry on an international scale, very little serious public opinion supported the notion that the Soviet Union could be trusted to uphold any agreement.

When Kennedy became President in 1961, he began to speak in urgent terms about the necessity of halting weapons testing and proliferation. For the most part the Kennedy statements ran counter to the prevailing climate of opinion, a hangover from the earlier period. In the fall of 1962, an event profoundly affected the climate of opinion. The United States government, discovering that the Soviet Union was surreptitiously supplying the Cubans with missiles capable of delivering nuclear payloads on American cities, imposed a naval quarantine around Cuba to intercept Soviet vessels and demanded the removal of missiles already in place on the island. For several fateful days, the world watched and waited while the two great nuclear powers confronted each other. Then, on October 28, the crisis was suddenly over as Premier Nikita Khrushchev agreed to withdraw the missiles and recall his ships. Clearly attitudes about nuclear weaponry and control, both in the United States and in the Soviet Union, were reassessed as a result of the crisis. Kennedy increased his efforts to reach an international agreement which would halt nuclear testing.

Just before the President was to deliver a commencement address at American University on June 10, 1963, Khrushchev agreed to resume a series of test-ban conferences. Kennedy gave considerable thought to his speech and decided to set forth an important statement on foreign policy, urging Americans to re-evaluate their attitudes toward the Soviet Union and to accept the notion that accommodation was possible with the Russians. In view of the new Soviet agreement, the address was particularly appropriate and brought unexpected results.

> The world response to this speech was amazing. Some called it the best speech since his inaugural address, and *Izvestia* and *Pravda* printed the text. More gratifying even than this was the secret word from intelligence sources that Khrushchev had been deeply impressed by the talk, that if Kennedy was willing to go before his own country, indeed the world, then he must be sincere. This was the beginning of the limited test-ban treaty which Kennedy would triumphantly sign in October, an achievement he rated second to none in his two and a half years in office.[24]

[24] Hugh Sidey, *John F. Kennedy, President* (New York: Fawcett World Library, 1964), p. 374.

When the test-ban treaty was signed, public-opinion polls indicated that 80 per cent of the people in the United States favored the agreement with the Russians,[25] proof indeed of a marked change in the climate of opinion surrounding United States-Soviet relations. Since the signing of the treaty, public messages have included an increased number of references to the benefits of expanding the détente between the two countries.

Our two examples are dramatic ones, chosen because they clearly reveal the significant interaction between climate of opinion and a communicative act. In many cases the elements of the drama are less noticeable and profound. But in every case, a climate of opinion surrounds and pervades the communicative act, and it demands inclusion in the overall conceptualization of public communication.

CULTURAL CONTEXT

We must finally broaden our focus to include those habitual mannerisms, customs, attitudes, and institutions that form the cultural patterns whose influence is a significant factor in human affairs. Each community possesses its peculiar cultural characteristics, which the larger cultural patterns of a whole people in turn subsume. These cultural patterns facilitate and strengthen both the communion and the communication of a people and at the same time control human behavior so subtly that they are often unnoticed. Anyone who has studied anthropology is aware of the influence of such cultural institutions as religion, family, home, and education. With these institutions we must include such cultural factors as patterns of behavior and manners, customs and traditions, and rituals and myths, which shape perceptions, attitudes, and judgments. All these and other factors form a *cultural screen* through which man receives his experience; thus man's perceptions of reality and consequently his behavior are already largely determined for him.

> There is a growing accumulation of evidence to indicate that man has no direct contact with experience per se but that there is an intervening set of patterns which channel his senses and his thoughts, causing him to react one way when someone else with different underlying patterns will react as *his* experience dictates.[26]

We do not mean to indicate here that man has no freedom whatsoever. We do, however, want to emphasize that man's behavior is controlled

---

[25] Arthur M. Schlesinger, Jr., *A Thousand Days* (Boston: Houghton Mifflin Company, 1965), p. 913.

[26] From *The Silent Language* (2nd ed.), by Edward T. Hall, p. 113. Copyright © 1959 by Edward T. Hall. Reprinted by permission of Doubleday & Company, Inc., New York.

far more by his cultural heritage than he is ever aware. As Edward
Hall explains:

> The man who is attracted to a woman may want to invite her out for
> a date. The choice as to whether he acts or not is his. What is not
> his to decide fully is the language he will use, the presents he can
> give her, the hours he can call, the clothes he can wear, and the fact
> that in the United States the woman has the ultimate say in the
> matter.[27]

It is impossible to categorize and illustrate all the ways in which
cultural differences can affect communication. Language differences
reflect cultural differences, and, since language controls thought processes
to some extent, there are obviously differences in patterns of thinking
from one culture to another. Different cultures attach varying meanings
to the same word and so interpret a communicative message in different
ways. They have differing images of what constitutes communicator
respectability and credibility; some cultures favor a thoroughly reasonable approach (by Western standards) when a cause or policy is being
advocated, while others are susceptible to a more intuitive, emotional
stance; some cultures place great value on the pragmatic workability of
suggested proposals and appeals, while others appreciate more idealistic
conceptions. And always, the common attitudes, beliefs, values, and
knowledge which accumulate through cultural influence largely account
for the success or failure of communication and the variations in audience response.

As with the concept of climate of opinion, several examples will illustrate the influence of culture on message reception better than a general
discussion could.

In the United States it is not at all unusual to find public spokesmen
delivering speeches of political import at various universities. Secretary
of State George Marshall first publicly announced the Marshall Plan for
economic aid to war-torn Europe in a speech at Harvard University.
Winston Churchill delivered his famous Iron Curtain address at West-
minster College in Missouri. Such persons as Martin Luther King, Vice
President Hubert Humphrey, Secretary of Defense Robert MacNamara,
and President Johnson have discussed the problems of racial relations
and of United States military action in Southeast Asia on a number of
college and university campuses.

But in Latin America, even though university students tend to be
more politically active than they are in the United States, tradition holds
that a politician should avoid politics when speaking on university

---

[27] Hall, *The Silent Language,* p. 112.

grounds. Certain American politicians, operating on the basis of their own cultural experience and unaware of Latin American tradition, have made the mistake of discussing politics at the wrong time and in the wrong place. Vice President Nixon, for instance, chose the University of San Marcos in Peru for a political address. In addition, Nixon's interpreter was a man dressed in full military uniform, a symbol of power and suppression to the Latin American students who sometimes riot against the military. Certain elements hostile to the United States took full advantage of the situation, and all parties concerned felt much discomfort and embarrassment.[28]

Language also varies from culture to culture; a number of interesting studies have been undertaken to determine the extent to which a linguistic system imposes a point of view on a communication. One such recent study carries important implications for international understanding. Edmund Glenn conducted a semantic analysis of parts of the printed record of meetings of the Security Council of the United Nations. Glenn's comparison of original statements and their translations into English, French, and Russian uncovered significant differences in meaning. The language of the translations revealed certain behavioral characteristics of the three nationalities: the Russian viewpoint tended toward universalism, which led to the expectation of politics directed toward the implementation of broad ideology and centralism; the English version exhibited a case-particularistic approach, with tendencies toward decentralization and the carrying out of policies by *ad hoc* bodies; the French translation revealed tendencies toward a compromise of the English and Russian points of view with a rationalistic approach.[29] We can easily see how misunderstanding and friction develop as national spokesmen gather around a conference table to resolve mutual problems.

When a communicator addresses audiences which share his cultural patterns of thought, he may disregard culture to a large extent. But, when he addresses peoples of a different cultural background, he must endeavor to express himself so that his message evokes proper understanding rather than misunderstanding in the minds of his listeners. With rapidly expanding intercontinental communication, when national leaders necessarily address a world audience, when the heterogeneity of the audience demands broad appeals, and when the ambiguities of diplomatic language are pregnant with possible meanings to which there

28 Incident reported by Edward T. Hall and William Foote White, "Intercultural Communication: A Guide to Men of Action," in *Communication and Culture*, ed. Alfred G. Smith (New York: Holt, Rinehart & Winston, Inc., 1966), p. 571.
29 "Meaning and Behavior; Communication and Culture," *The Journal of Communication*, XVI, No. 4 (December 1966), 248–72.

may come a variety of responses, the matter of cultural impact on communication demands increasingly more attention.

THE INTERACTION OF VARIABLES

Now that we have examined the basic variables that constitute and surround the process of public communication, we must picture them interacting with each other in order to arrive at a more holistic and realistic description of the total process. Each of the variables is present and influential whenever public communication occurs. But they do not all exert equal force on the receiver; some predominate over others, and the precise qualitative nature of each variable changes from situation to situation or even from moment to moment. How influential each variable is depends upon the particular perceptions of the individual receiver —his perceptions about himself, about his relationships to others, about his immediate needs in relation to the content of the message and the communicator, etc.

All these differences make it very difficult to understand exactly why a receiver hears, remembers, or behaves the way he does as a result of a specific message. We must draw generalizations concerning the influence of public messages with care and usually must state them in terms of probability or possibility rather than certainty.

In a national political campaign, such as a campaign for the presidency, several dominant variables may emerge. A faithful party voter who believes in political constancy listens to messages, reads appeals, judges candidates, and ultimately votes on the basis of party affiliation. His sense of loyalty takes precedence over all else, and the effect of a candidate's personality, his stand on various issues, his manner of message presentation, and all other factors have to pass through the filtering screen of the voter's loyalty.

An individual's perception of his relationship to an issue may become the dominant variable. For instance, a person who believes that the passage of certain taxation legislation will affect his own income listens very carefully to a candidate's stand on that legislation. On local issues, an individual's response to public statements is often based on his own perceptions of what he has to gain or lose by the intended action. In such cases the prestige of an authority may not be an important factor in the receiver's response; the more closely an issue seems to be related to his interests, the more firmly he is likely to hold his attitudes, and thus the chances for outside influence diminish. We know that at times an authority, held in high esteem by a receiver, utters statements supporting ideas inimical to the beliefs of the receiver, with the interesting result that the prestigious authority is disassociated from his statement in the mind of the receiver.

The relationship between the source of a message and what the receiver thinks he knows about the subject matter of the message may be crucial. When a receiver feels that his knowledge of a particular subject is fairly substantial, he may allow what he already knows to determine his response to new messages on the subject. But, if the receiver feels that he does not possess sufficient knowledge or that the subject is too complex or technical for his understanding, he may react largely in terms of the perceived characteristics of the message source. If the source appears knowledgeable and reasonable, his image may be the determining variable.

At times a receiver's reactions are based on the responses of other people. Desiring to remain or to become identified with a certain group, the individual may adopt the response of that group. In this case the group norm becomes the significant variable.

We have been simplistic in our description here, but you should realize that all these variables are always present and interacting, some to a greater degree than others. Hopefully we have been able to illustrate that any communicative transaction possesses its own peculiar complexion, depending upon which variables become paramount. Now we shall turn to a more direct examination of message effects as they occur on the level of public communication.

The Functions and
Effects of
Public Communication

A major assumption underlying all communication research is that communication is essentially purposeful and functional and therefore affects behavior. In keeping with this assumption the majority of research conducted by communication scholars analyzes and measures the effects of various kinds of messages. Recently some scholars have surveyed the proliferating findings of research and have noted with a certain dismay that nearly every generalization one would care to make about the effects of communication can be supported empirically. Regarding the effects of mass communication, Joseph Klapper writes:

> We have claimed, on the one hand, and on empirical grounds, that escapist material provides its audience with blinders and with an unrealistic view of life and, on the other hand, that it helps them meet life's real problems. We have hedged on the crime and violence question, typically saying, "Well, probably there is no causative relationship, but there just might be a triggering effect." In reference to persuasion we have maintained that the media are after all not so terribly powerful, and yet we have reported their impressive success in promoting such varied phenomena as religious intolerance, the sale of war bonds, belief in the American Way, and disenchantment with Boy Scout activities. It is surely no wonder that a bewildered public should regard with cynicism a research tradition which supplies, instead of definitive answers, a plethora of relevant but inconclusive and at times seemingly contradictory findings.[1]

Klapper's remarks apply equally well to all forms of what we have traditionally called *public address*. To paraphrase an earlier remark, we may say that, on some occasions, some speeches delivered by some

[1] "The Effects of Mass Communication," in *Reader in Public Opinion and Communication* (2nd ed.), eds. Bernard Berelson and Morris Janowitz (New York: The Free Press, 1966), p. 474.

men appear to have certain effects on some audiences.[2]   Obviously we must modify the rather common belief that public speech-making is always a potent persuasive force in society.

Yet we cannot conclude that public communication is without its effects or even that its force is always relatively impotent.   The history of the United States alone is replete with examples of the effectiveness of public-communication campaigns.   We can refer to the public agitation of various speakers surrounding the abolition movement and the fights for women's suffrage and for temperance or turn to historical accounts of the oratorical powers of such men as Wendell Phillips, William Jennings Bryan, John C. Calhoun, and Theodore Roosevelt.   We can point to the rhetorical prowess of the muckrakers, who early in this century aroused the citizenry to support much-needed social reform; or to the public controversy over the League of Nations, in which both President Woodrow Wilson and his opponents counted on public opinion to influence congressional voting; or to public speeches for and against Franklin Roosevelt's expansion of the Supreme Court; or to Harry Truman's whistle-stop campaign tour of 1948 to give further support to the notion that public communication can exert considerable influence in the affairs of man.   If we look abroad and to less democratic situations, we note the faith such men as Nikolai Lenin and Adolf Hitler had in vocal agitation and the uses they made of public-speaking situations to motivate and propagandize; or the innumerable occasions in some totalitarian regimes when citizens are called upon to publicly profess their shortcomings, proclaim their allegiance to the superiority of a certain way of life, and participate in various "educational forums."   Obviously, to say that public communication has no effect or little effect is to disregard considerable historical evidence to the contrary.

How then are we to understand the way in which public communication works in our society?   What can we hypothesize about the nature of the effects of communication?   What role does communication play in the overall scheme of man's activities, accomplishments, triumphs, and tragedies?   This section provides at least some of the answers to these questions.   The discussion which follows is based upon considerable research conducted by a number of scholars in various academic disciplines, but in no sense should we assume that the conclusions drawn are final.   As new findings accumulate, theoretical modification will become necessary.   Much has been accomplished, but much remains to be done in this area of study, which constantly demands new approaches, new methods of investigation, new hypotheses, and considerably more field observation than has yet been undertaken.

[2] Bernard Berelson, "Communications and Public Opinion," in *Communications in Modern Society,* ed. Wilbur Schramm (Urbana, Illinois: University of Illinois Press, 1948), p. 172.

A PHENOMENISTIC APPROACH TO THE STUDY
OF COMMUNICATION EFFECT

As we suggested above, the results of communication research clearly show that we must modify some of the common beliefs about the effects of public communication. One important modification is in the way we look at the relationship between communication and behavior. To be rejected is the notion of a one-to-one, direct relationship between a message and a certain behavior pattern. Such a conceptualization of the effect of communication is too simplistic; it rests on the assumption that a message travels straight to a receiver's mind without the interference of any intervening variables. We now know that a multitude of factors operate to influence the way in which a message is received and hence to determine the resulting effect of the message. The receiver's motivational and value systems; his identification with or his antagonism toward various reference groups; the social climate in which he finds himself at the time of message reception; and the people he comes in contact with before, during, and after he receives the message are all important variables in any communicative situation.

A more realistic way to view the effect of communication than by this so-called *hypodermic-effect* model is to adopt what Klapper calls a *phenomenistic* approach.[3] The assumption of the phenomenistic approach is that a public message is one among many variables, all of which act in conjunction to produce a receiver's response and behavior. Included in the phenomenistic assumption is the notion that any analysis of communication effect must be situational because the saliency, i.e., the prominence and force with which each of the variables may be operating, is likely to change from one situation to another.

Another problem in attempting to gauge the effect of public communication is that, just because our modern means of mass communication make possible mass exposure, one cannot assume mass reception. As Katz and Lazarsfeld point out, exposure is not so random, uniform, or total as originally believed.[4] It is instead a product of various economic, political, and social factors. Often those audiences selected as the target of a certain communication, because of lack of interest or predisposition, do not receive the communication either as intended or at all.

A further difficulty presents itself when we realize that effects may be

---

[3] Klapper, "The Effects of Mass Communication," p. 475.
[4] Elihu Katz and Paul F. Lazarsfeld, *Personal Influence* (New York: The Macmillan Company, 1955), pp. 15–30.

immediate or they may be long range. On only a few occasions is one able to notice any dramatic attitude or behavioral change immediately following a public speech. Roosevelt's fireside chats early in his first term of office, Nixon's campaign-fund speech in the 1952 presidential campaign, and the Kennedy-Nixon television debates in 1960 are somewhat unusual in that they produced fairly immediate and significant response. But, on most occasions, a public message is a part of a larger public dialogue, and, while the result of the dialogue (which may last a few months or many years) may be to affect behavior, it is difficult to assess the impact of any one particular message.

We can conclude that public communication plays a role in the affairs of men and society but that the precise role may not always be clear. Public messages occur amidst various emotional pressures, as a result of perceived human problems, and among numerous uncontrolled stimuli. We cannot know, let alone control, all the variables in such a social setting. Consequently, the analyst who attempts to determine public response to communication must necessarily draw inferences and ultimately rest his case on personal judgment. Rosenau, in his discussion of the effect of public opinion on foreign policy, makes the following observation, which holds for all analyses of the effects of public communication:

> If it means anything, influence denotes the *process* by which the behavior of one individual or group *modifies* the behavior of another individual or group. For influence to be operative, some form of interaction must occur between the influencer and the influencee. Thus, in order to identify influence and assess its potency, the researcher must examine both the behavior to which that influence may have contributed, and then he must estimate what the latter behavior might have been if it had not been modified by the influence. The measurement of "might-have-beens," however, is possible only through the manipulation of variables in controlled experiments, and, while there is an ever-growing body of reliable experimental data on the operation of influence in face-to-face situations, this method cannot be used to assess the opinion-policy relationship. One cannot manipulate the variables that would reveal which groups or persons in American society exercise influence over the formulation of foreign policy. Rather, the most one can do is to examine the behavior which appears to be a function of the opinion-policy relationship and then to deduce from that behavior those factors which seem to have been responsible for the influence in question.[5]

[5] James N. Rosenau, *Public Opinion and Foreign Policy* (New York: Random House, copyright 1961), pp. 10–11.

THE GENERAL EFFECTS OF
PUBLIC COMMUNICATION

Despite the difficulties of assessing the precise effects a particular piece of communication may have, we can speak in general terms about the functions and possible effects of public communication. As we recalled in the first part of this book, we learn about the world through sensory perception. From birth we receive numerous messages in various forms; some of these we attend to, assimilate, interpret, structure, and evaluate, until eventually we have a foundation of experience and knowledge upon which we operate. Verbal messages play an increasingly important role in our acquisition of knowledge and experience, so that by the time we are adults the verbal-symbolic dimensions of our world are important determinants of our behavior. In his essay on the effects of communication, W. Phillips Davison outlines three ways in which messages can lead to adjusted behavior:

1. They can report an actual or expected change in the environment or a previously unknown fact in the environment.
2. They can point out an existing feature of the environment and remind the individual that his needs would be served if he adjusted his behavior in a given manner.
3. They can bring to a person's attention a new way of patterning his behavior to his environment.[6]

The first function Davison points to is obviously an informative one. When we realize the limitations imposed upon us in terms of gaining first-hand information about the world in which we live, the importance of the informative function is readily apparent. In terms of total space, time, and experience, each of us lives in a very limited sphere of the world's activity. We cannot know everything about even the narrow confines of our immediate environment and locale, let alone about events happening throughout our state, or region, or nation, or in other nations, because we cannot be everywhere at the same time. Consequently we turn to the sense receptors of others for reports about what is happening elsewhere. Newspapers, magazines, television, radio, motion pictures, eyewitness accounts, second-hand reports and rumors (or hearsay) all present us with happenings throughout the world which we would not otherwise experience.

Not too many years ago a man's knowledge was fairly well confined

[6] "On the Effects of Communication," in Dexter and White, pp. 81–82.

to his own first-hand observations and the observations of his immediate neighbors. When news did arrive from other regions, it was less news than history. Today, because of the technological magic of mass communication, we can find out about insurrections, airplane disasters, royal weddings, military victories or defeats, election results, and the like from all over the world almost instantaneously. In one sense our world has expanded because modern communication techniques act as extensions of our own sense receptors; in another sense our world has been steadily shrinking as images from far continents pour into our daily life. Through mass communication man has the opportunity to be better informed today than ever before.

But we cannot talk about the informative aspect of public communication without also considering its potential for attitude formation because the two functions usually occur simultaneously. As we saw earlier, we do not receive all the raw data presented to us, but we select certain things to attend to, we ignore others, and we usually interpret what we do receive within a particular frame of reference. Similarly, the public-communication media also select certain aspects of the environment to report and very often project their own point of view on the information presented.

Lang and Lang give an interesting example of the projection of a point of view through television in their study of spectator reaction to MacArthur Day in Chicago, an event which occurred after the general was dismissed from his Pacific command by President Truman. The Langs compared the reactions and reports of persons who stood in various locations at Midway Airport and along the parade route in the Loop area with reports of persons who viewed the entire event on television. Examination of the reactions revealed a considerable discrepancy between the way activities were viewed in person and the way they were seen on television. The arbitrary sequencing of telecasting events, the selection of foreground and background chosen by television personnel, and the structuring of the situation through T.V. commentary combined to provide a more personal experience for the television viewer than for the on-the-spot witness. Furthermore, particular crowd shots shown on camera along with the commentator's remarks projected an image of overwhelming public sentiment in favor of MacArthur, which spectators who saw the events of the day in person did not experience.[7]

What was true of television coverage during MacArthur Day in Chicago is also true of every other public message. Newscasts, wire-service reports in newspapers, magazine commentaries, and all public speeches

---

[7] Kurt Lang and Gladys Engel Lang, "The Unique Perspective of Television," in Berelson and Janowitz, pp. 278–92.

and statements inevitably select and focus the information they present. Thus they present the ordinary receiver with an attitudinal structure to accompany the facts. Public communication has the potential for creating issues, for highlighting some issues at the expense of others, and for refusing to allow some issues to come to the public attention at all. Without the considerable mass-media coverage he received, Senator Joseph McCarthy would probably scarcely be remembered today. By the same token, Senator J. William Fulbright, chairman of the Senate Foreign Relations Committee, would not have been able to dramatize the considerable controversy over United States involvement in South Viet Nam as he did in 1966 without the extensive use of televised public hearings. And, too, television and newspaper reporting of various civil rights disturbances throughout the United States make public statements about the problems of segregation and integration salient and meaningful to the public at large. In short, we must agree with this statement by Sherif, Sherif, and Nebergall:

> Particularly in the complex and interrelated world today, mass media do provide anchorage points and definite limits of acceptability on many issues that ordinary citizens are in no position to learn about otherwise and in which they may have little psychological involvement.[8]

In addition to providing information and creating attitudes by focusing public attention on certain issues to the exclusion of others, public communication can arouse public opinion, reinforce attitudes which already exist, and cause attitude change. We can all think of instances when the reporting of certain events and the magnification of certain issues focused public attention on problems demanding solution. The danger of insecticides, the possible damaging effects of cigarette smoking, the high cost of dying, the lack of safety in automobiles, the increasing consumption of harmful drugs, the slum conditions in our major cities, and the increasing air and water pollution are all topics which have received considerable public attention through public discussion. Public communicators often count on public opinion to help them achieve a desired objective.

> An aroused public opinion was more effective in 1962, for example, in helping create a climate favorable to the recession of steel prices than any statutory tool. President Kennedy's televised explanations of his decisions on Berlin, nuclear testing, and the Cuban quarantine achieved

---

[8] Carolyn W. Sherif, Muzafer Sherif, and Roger Nebergall, *Attitude and Attitude Change* (Philadelphia: W. B. Saunders Co., 1965), p. 182.

on each occasion a new national consensus that discouraged any adversary's hopes for disunity.[9]

As we shall see in a later subsection, public communication is usually more successful in reinforcing attitudes which already exist than it is in changing attitudes. Studies which attempt to measure attitude change immediately following a particular message or even a particular campaign aimed at modifying attitude often report that no change occurred. But the concentration on immediate change often overshadows the slower, more subtle, but inevitable change in attitude which occurs as a result of many messages being received over an extended period of time. Lang and Lang report that, while mass media may not appear to change behavior during a campaign, behavioral changes do slowly take place between campaigns as new issues arise and party images change or fail to change. Since mass communication has the potential to make issues salient or to build and to change party images, they may exert a more extensive influence than classic voting studies reveal.[10] Berelson and Steiner provide us with a general summary of the effects of public communication:

> The more that people read or listen to communications on a given issue, especially in a concentrated fashion, then the less undecided they become, the more interest they develop, the more information they acquire, the more consistent their perceptions are with the messages being communicated, the more strongly partisan they become, the more closely they reflect the media emphasis on the subissues, the more likely they are to act.[11]

So far we have been discussing the effects public communication may have upon the receivers of the communication. In so doing, we have reflected the most prevalent focus of effect studies. But we should not overlook the influence a message may have on the communicator himself. If we examine our own experience, we may be able to recall times when we might not have undertaken a certain action if we had not made a verbal commitment to do so. We sometimes receive folksy bits of advice to the effect that if we say we can accomplish certain difficult tasks we can in fact do them; e.g., if we tell our friends we are going to quit smoking, it will be easier for us to actually do so. In terms of public opinion, we know that one of the sources of resistance to opinion change

---

[9] Theodore C. Sorensen, *Decision-Making in the White House* (New York: Columbia University Press, 1963), p. 46.

[10] Kurt Lang and Gladys E. Lang, "The Mass Media and Voting," in Berelson and Janowitz, pp. 455–72.

[11] Berelson and Steiner, *Human Behavior,* pp. 543–44.

is a statement a person makes about his beliefs or attitudes. If a person has committed himself to a position privately, he is usually more willing to change than if he has committed himself publicly. In the latter case, his reputation is at stake, and his attitude becomes all the more firmly held. In precisely the same way, public communicators become committed through the words they speak, and they may produce subsequent statements and actions with an eye toward remaining consistent. Government officials, for instance, are often cognizant of the need to appear trustworthy and to be consistent with former public policy declarations. Thus statements made by public communicators often become the parameters for later behavior.

Ted Sorenson, former assistant to President Kennedy, points out that, to avoid the appearance of confusion or deception, a President, when formulating a decision, often takes his own policies as precedents and considers his earlier statements binding. Sorensen provides a concrete example in his discussion of the decision-making process with regard to the possible United States response to the presence of Soviet missiles in Cuba. The blockade decision was not wholly developed during the seven days preceding its announcement.

> President Kennedy, on the morning of the first of those seven days, sent for copies of all his earlier statements on Cuba—on the presence of offensive as distinguished from defensive weapons—on threats to our vital interests—and on our armed intervention in that island. These earlier decisions made it unlikely that he would respond to the October crisis by doing nothing and unlikely that his first step would be an invasion.[12]

We may, then, assess the influence of public communication in terms of its effects on receivers and communicators alike.

THE NATURE OF PUBLIC OPINION

When we think of public communication and speculate about its effects, we usually refer to the impact such communication has on public opinion. But public opinion is an extremely vague notion which demands careful analysis in order to avoid several serious misconceptions. We often talk about the impact of public discussion as if the issues and problems being considered are received by a public that understands the significance and complexity of those issues. In other words we assume that those individuals constituting what we call a public operate within

12 Sorensen, *Decision-Making in the White House*, pp. 34–35.

a rationalistic frame of reference. But this image of public reception does not often square with reality. In fact, public opinion is more accurately thought of as emotion or sentiment, based on a few very general considerations rather than on careful thought. Each individual is busy with his own life, is confronted by problems which occur in his small world, is aroused by private ambitions and frustrations, and is intent upon maintaining satisfactory relationships with other individuals who populate his immediate surroundings. Consequently, most public issues rank no higher than fifth or sixth in terms of importance on an individual's list of things to attend to. We cannot equate public opinion with the total population of a nation, simply because not everyone is attending to the same things at the same time with the same intensity. Hence, only those individuals who happen to be aware of and hold opinions about particular issues under discussion constitute a public with respect to those issues.

Rosenau describes three strata of American society with regard to opinions about foreign-policy issues. We may certainly extend his description to cover domestic issues as well, and it may also be accurate for other nations.

At the base of a three-step pyramid, Rosenau places the mass public, making up about 75 to 90 per cent of the adult population. The mass public is generally uninformed either about specific issues or about foreign and domestic affairs in general. Members of the mass public tend to pay little if any attention to day-to-day developments; and, since they are uninformed, the opinions they do have are unstructured because they lack the cognitive and evaluative equipment with which to assimilate and understand the ideas and information. As a result, the response of the mass public is more emotional than rational, more mood than informed opinion. When the mass public does become aroused over such happenings as the launching of the first Sputnik or Soviet suppression of the Hungarian revolt, its response is impulsive, unstable, unreasonable, unpredictable, and susceptible to sudden shifts in direction. Even though the mass public is usually fairly dormant, decision makers often accept its opinions as the outer limits within which they may safely operate.

In the United States, for instance, political leaders often disagree greatly on such specific issues as taxation, housing, social welfare, and education. Similarly, a wide range of opinion often exists in local communities over such matters as fluoridation, sewage disposal, school policies, and commercial zoning. Nonetheless, no matter how much at odds various factions may seem, the majority of citizens share general convictions about such things as the values of property, equal opportunity, competition, individualism, and capitalism. These shared beliefs act as a sustained climate of opinion which limits the scope of the appeals practical opinion leaders and administrators can conveniently make.

The middle stratum of Rosenau's pyramid of public opinion, located near the top, is made up of the "attentive public"; that is, those individuals who maintain a fairly constant interest in public affairs and who are inclined to participate but lack the access or opportunity to do so. In contrast to the mass public, members of the attentive public are more faithful readers of newspapers and magazines, more constant and thoughtful receivers of newscasts and in-depth discussions of public issues, and in short make more effort to be aware of daily happenings and to gather information on the various points of view concerning an issue. Because members of the attentive public are more constantly involved in (in terms of attending to) public affairs, their opinions have more structure and depth than the opinions of the mass public. Even though the size of the attentive public is small, about 10 per cent of the population, this audience is a critical one for opinion makers and tends to offset the irrationality of the mass public.

At the top of the pyramid is the small group of individuals constituting the opinion-making public. In some cases the opinion makers may also be involved in the actual formulation of public policy; in other cases they may control access to various communication media. In either case their function is to present information, perspectives, and judgments to the public at large for its use in formulating opinions.

While the above three groupings remain fairly constant, in the sense that they hold true for the majority of issues that enter public discussion, numerous issues also evoke "attention groups," which arise out of the mass public. These unorganized segments are usually disinterested and passive, but they become aroused when an issue arises which seems to affect a common interest. Attention groups occur in great variety because of the numerous political, social, and economic affiliations which an individual may have in mass society. Rosenau describes the entrance of an attention group into public debate as sudden and impulsive; its interest is confined exclusively to a single issue, and other issues or policies do not affect it. Once its issue has been disposed of, the attention group loses its formal structure and becomes absorbed again in the larger mass public.[13]

When talking about the effects of communication on public opinion then, we must first determine which segment of the public we have in mind because one segment obviously responds differently from another.

In addition to identifying which segment of public opinion we are talking about, we must attend to the quality of the various opinions held

[13] We are indebted to Rosenau, *Public Opinion and Foreign Policy*, Chapter 4, for the basis of this discussion.

because opinion quality often determines the success or failure of a message. Direction, intensity, stability, and saliency are terms often used by public-opinion analysts to describe the quality of an opinion.

Direction refers to pro-con quality—that is, to whether a particular opinion approves or disapproves of the issue. Intensity refers to the degree to which beliefs are held; and stability pertains to whether the direction and intensity of an opinion will change in the future. The matter of stability opens the way for a discussion of the possible persuasibility of individuals holding opinions, which we shall discuss shortly. Saliency indicates the degree of importance an issue assumes in the mind of an individual holding an opinion on that issue. An issue is salient when it crowds out other items and becomes a focus around which a person may organize his thoughts or actions. Obviously, the more salient an issue, the more attention paid to it. And the intensity and stability with which a conviction is held determine to a large extent the effect messages relevant to that conviction have.[14]

We cannot often discuss the quality of one opinion without reference to a larger pattern of attitudes sometimes referred to as an *opinion cluster*. Opinions rarely occur in isolation; they are usually integrated with other opinions to form more total conceptualizations, or frames of reference, within which specific issues are judged. For instance, prejudice against one particular minority group may well be symptomatic of a larger pattern of prejudice against all persons whose mode of behavior or personal characteristics are significantly different from those of the person holding the opinion. An individual who strongly disagrees with a federal government program to establish medical care for the aged may also be unfavorably disposed toward the majority of government programs on the grounds that they are all insidious attempts to control a citizen's private life. In some cases religious beliefs are connected with political, social, and economic beliefs in a complicated but consistent network of attitudes. As we shall see later, it is much easier to change a fairly isolated opinion than to change one connected with a larger attitudinal system.

We can conclude from the above discussion that a concept of "mass public" does not faithfully represent what in fact exists. Rather than a public, there are multiple publics, some more actively concerned with certain issues than others, some more informed and rational than others, some more attentive and therefore receiving more messages than others. Instead of a public opinion, various opinions represent the several publics which may react to a specific issue.

[14] An excellent discussion of opinion quality can be found in Robert E. Lane and David O. Sears, *Public Opinion* (Englewood Cliffs, New Jersey: Prentice-Hall, Inc., 1964), Chapter II.

THE PATTERN OF COMMUNICATION FLOW

Another conception which has been discredited by research and observation is the notion of "the public" composed of many anonymous individuals who receive and react to messages directly, with no interaction among themselves. Such a notion posits a one-step pattern of communication flow in which the communicator speaks directly to his listeners, who respond directly to the communicator and his message. We already know enough about intervening variables to realize that the pattern is too simple.

Much evidence indicates that two of the most important variables affecting an individual's reception and interpretation of a message are his identification and affiliation with other people. One of the widely supported sociological generalizations is that the conceptual categories used by an individual to interpret and evaluate his words are primarily determined by the groups he relates himself to, usually called *reference groups*. Reference groups fall into two general categories. In familial, occupational, social, and recreational groups, group members maintain face-to-face contact. These are primary groups. Secondary groups are influential not because of face-to-face contact with other group members but because an individual thinks of himself as a particular kind of individual and derives his values from his ideal group rather than from his associates. For instance, even though a person's actual income places him in a middle-class economic bracket, his values and attitudes may be based on upper-class economic standards because he admires the wealthy and would like to be one of them.

These primary and secondary groups are called reference groups because members use group values, norms, and goals as referral points to determine their behavior and judgments. Reference groups provide the social space within which an individual moves; they influence his aspirations, determine his peer relationships, and identify those problems with which he concerns himself. In other words, reference groups help an individual achieve his social identity by telling him who he is and where he is and by providing him with a way of knowing reality.

We may also describe reference groups as positive or negative. A group operates as a positive reference structure when an individual adopts the values and attitudes of the group as his own. A group operates as a negative reference structure when an individual identifies himself against the aspirations and values of the group because he believes the group acts against his own best interests. A worker on the assembly line in an automobile plant, for instance, identifies himself positively with his local labor union, which is supposed to look out for his welfare, and negatively with management groups, which he thinks argue against his best interests at the bargaining table. A Democrat looks upon the Republican Party as a negative reference structure; a liberal identifies against conservatives, minority groups against an oppressive majority, and so on.

An awareness of reference groups is essential to an understanding of the effects of public communication because small, intimate groups often generate and reinforce so-called *private* opinions and attitudes. Furthermore the attitudes and opinions shared by a group are usually considerably more stable than those held in isolation. If attitudes do change under persuasive pressure, they are more likely to change jointly than individually. Katz and Lazarsfeld discuss the implications of reference groups for communication research in this way:

> The lesson is plain: No longer can mass-media research be content with a random sample of disconnected individuals as respondents. Respondents must be studied within the context of the group or groups to which they belong or which they have "in mind"—thus, which may influence them—in their formulation of opinions, attitudes, or decisions, and in their rejection or acceptance of mass media in influence attempts.[15]

We can no longer be content with measuring the effect of a communication upon the immediate, ostensible, intended audience; we must take into consideration the numerous reference groups which constitute hidden audiences and which exert considerable influence over individual behavior.

The fact that interpersonal and group relations act as anchorages for individual values and behavior—that individuals interact collectively to generate and maintain common ideas and patterns of behavior which are difficult to alter because of collective pressure—also carries implications for the pattern of communication influence. We can conceive of reference groups as networks of communication in which certain individuals have considerable prestige and influence. We have already noted that exposure to public communication is not random or constant; some individuals attend to public events and statements more than others. Thus, within nearly all primary groups, some individuals are opinion leaders. Who they are may change from issue to issue. Some are concerned with national affairs, others with local matters. Some have authority at one time and not at another. In any case they tend to be better informed than the average member of the group, are trusted by group members, and may be in a position of authority within the group. Such leaders become models for opinion within their group as they attend to communication

[15] Katz and Lazarsfeld, *Personal Influence*, p. 131.

media, pass on information gained to group members, make attitudinal statements about the information, and generally discuss public messages within the context of group experience.

Obviously, opinion leaders operating within the context of primary groups have more influence over personal attitude and behavior than do more publicly prominent leaders, who are further removed from the group. For one thing, all of us tend to trust people we know personally. For another, in the primary-group situation, where face-to-face communication not only is enhanced but also is difficult to avoid, the chances to gain reward for agreement or punishment for disagreement are immediate, personal contacts are more casual and less purposeful, and arguments can be tailor-made to fit each individual's frame of reference.

As a result of research on the flow of communication, the simple one-step pattern has given way to a two-step pattern, in which public leaders make statements which are then received by various opinion leaders, who in turn communicate to other members of their primary group. Rosenau believes that the two-step pattern is still an oversimplification.

> Even so well-established a concept as the "two-step flow" suffers from oversimplification and needs to be re-examined. At the very least it ought to be expanded to account for a "four-step flow" in which the news and interpretation of an event are first carried by, say, a newspaper; this is then read and adapted by opinion makers, who assert (step 2) their opinions in speeches on the subject that are reported (step 3) by the press and thereupon picked up by "opinion leaders" in the general public, who in turn pass (step 4) on the opinion through word-of-mouth.[16]

We could undoubtedly argue that the pattern should be enlarged even beyond the four-step flow model, though in some circumstances the pattern could be reduced. We are certainly safe in concluding that the extent and complexity of the pattern vary from situation to situation but that in any case the effect public communication has on a receiver never occurs in a simple one-to-one pattern.

INDIVIDUAL REACTION TO
PUBLIC COMMUNICATION

At this point we shall consider, at least in general terms, how an individual is likely to respond to public communication. We have already discovered that the social context and climate of group opinion have much

---

[16] Rosenau, *Public Opinion and Foreign Policy*, pp. 7–8.

to do with his response. But, to complete our analysis of effect, we must make some observations about individual behavior if for no other reason than to understand our own personal behavior better than we now do.

When we talk about personal behavior, we confront the problem of determining those motivational factors which cause us to respond the way we do to the multitude of stimuli around us. Psychological literature describes motivational states in numerous ways. It also categorizes and lists motivational factors in numerous ways. The problem is one of knowing which listing best suits our purposes, and at this point we find little if any help. Obviously physiological factors influence our behavior in the sense that we need to eat, sleep, eliminate, find shelter, and in general survive physically. Most of our motives, however, are called *learned motives;* that is, we acquire them as we interact with various social and cultural stimuli. The task of describing and listing secondary, or learned, motives is an especially difficult one.

> Since learned motives arise out of infinitely variable experience, lists of such motives must either be specific to particular cultures at certain points in time or so general as to lose much of their explanatory value. Furthermore, even with a given social situation, motives can be listed and classified at several levels of generality. . . . So it is difficult to maintain any particular level of generality as "basic"; the number and breadth of motives listed is arbitrary and depends upon the purpose of the classification.[17]

We shall not attempt to provide an exhaustive list of all those factors which may motivate human behavior. Rather, we shall provide the reader with a more general overview within which he can interpret his own specific behavior, and we shall try to relate that overview to behavior in situations in which an individual receives public messages or reports of public messages.

Let us begin by picturing the human being as a bundle of ongoing behavior patterns which have been formulating and developing throughout his life. These behavior patterns are not separate entities; they operate in conjunction with one another to produce the holistic behavior which characterizes human activity. At times various stimuli come into contact with the ongoing behavior patterns, and some of them are sufficiently strong to block normal behavior or to otherwise modify it so that the balance maintained by the individual's behavior patterns is upset. We may certainly classify communicative messages among those stimuli which have the capability of disturbing ongoing behavior. When imbalance occurs, the human strives to repulse the stimulus causing it,

[17] Berelson and Steiner, *Human Behavior,* p. 256.

or tries to adjust his behavior to redress the imbalance, just as a home thermostat triggers a heating system when a drop in temperature unbalances it.

The discovery that one of the very basic human psychological tendencies is the drive to maintain stability of environment, attitude, and behavior has led psychologists to develop the theories of balance and dissonance discussed in the first part of this book. The notion of cognitive dissonance is particularly useful to our understanding of the possible effects of communication because our attitudes form within cognitive frames of reference which organize, categorize, evaluate, and relate phenomena in the world around us so that they become meaningful. As human beings, we behave physically and attitudinally on the basis of our cognitive reality, i.e., in accordance with the way we see ourselves in our world. We react, in other words, on the basis of our image of reality.

When external and internal stimuli cause inconsistency, imbalance, or dissonance within our image of reality, one of two things happens—either we alter our behavior patterns or we reinterpret the nature of the troublesome stimuli in such a way that we regain cognitive balance. It is important to realize that we are dealing with cognitive representations of events rather than with the events themselves, which means that the reduction of cognitive dissonance through a cognitive change does not necessarily require any change in the actual events. One of man's essential characteristics is his ability to symbolize and structure his world to suit himself. We can say, then, that dissonant public messages which strike us with considerable force either result in a change in our cognitive-attitudinal structure and hence our behavior or cause us to modify the meaning of the message as we receive it so that our psychological balance remains unimpaired.

At this point, we shall consider another approach to the subject of attitude and attitude change in order to further assess the potential influence of public messages. In their provocative study of attitudes related to specific social and political issues, Sherif, Sherif, and Nebergall found the following to be true:

> An individual's attitude on an issue can be assessed adequately only if the procedures [for measurement] yield the limits of the positions he accepts (latitude of acceptance) and the limits of the positions he rejects (latitude of rejection), relative to the bounds of available alternatives defined by the extreme positions on the issue.[18]

[18] Sherif, Sherif, and Nebergall, *Attitude and Attitude Change*, p. 2.

In other words, the combination of acceptable and objectionable positions forms an individual's reference scale for judging specific issues. If an individual has a certain set of attitudes which are related to a social, political, or economic issue, those attitudes bring with them preconceived judgmental categories which influence the acceptance or rejection of pertinent public messages referring to the issue. Latitudes of acceptance or rejection vary from individual to individual. An individual may be strongly committed anywhere on an attitude continuum; in terms of politics, for example, one may locate his commitment, and with it his latitude of acceptance, at the extreme left or at the extreme right or in the moderate middle or anywhere between these points.

Generally, Sherif, Sherif, and Nebergall found that the more personally involved and committed an individual is on an issue, the greater is his latitude of rejection and the smaller his latitude of acceptance.[19]

> If the position of a communication does not diverge greatly from the latitude of acceptance, there is likelihood of an *assimilation* effect; it will be seen as nearer to the subject's stand. . . .
>
> If the position of a communication diverges so that it falls within an individual's latitude of rejection, the anchoring of his own position will result in a *contrast effect*, i.e., the communication will be seen as further away from the subject's stand.[20]

As a corollary, persons who are less committed on an issue are more likely to be influenced by public messages intended to formulate and change attitudes. And, when commitment is not strong, such variables as the perceived image of the communicator and the strategies of the message, such as the ordering of argument, style, and evidence, exert their influence on an individual's response.

We may now postulate three general hypotheses concerning human behavior in relation to persuasive communication. First, and obviously, the more directly a message arouses the receiver's attitudes, value positions, and identifications, the more they determine his response. Second, communication is likely to be very successful when it reinforces attitudes already in existence. It may play a significant role in formulating new attitudes where previously there were none. But it usually fails to change deep-seated attitudes already in existence. Third, a receiver often ignores, rejects, or distorts messages which run counter to his established attitude frame, and thus message impact largely miscarries. J. A. C. Brown reaches the following conclusion about the effects of propaganda:

[19] Sherif, Sherif, and Nebergall, *Attitude and Attitude Change*, p. 14.
[20] Sherif, Sherif, and Nebergall, *Attitude and Attitude Change*, p. 14.

It would appear that the main lesson to be drawn from our present study of propaganda is how very resistant people are to messages that fail to fit into their own picture of the world and their own objective circumstances, how they deliberately (if unconsciously) seek out only those views which agree with theirs.[21]

Brown's conclusion appears to be as true for other types of communicative messages as it is for propaganda.

Thus far in our discussion we have been using the term *attitude* to refer to several kinds and degrees of emotional commitment. Now we must turn to one further theoretical formulation in order to gain a more precise understanding of the levels of emotional commitment. In so doing, we shall view the process of communication influence from yet another perspective.

Brown, quoted above, in his very thorough survey of persuasion, provides a useful discussion of attitude formation. He describes three levels of attitude, which he labels "opinions," "attitudes," and "character traits." Opinions are characteristically topical, short-run judgments, held in connection with public-affairs issues. These beliefs often reflect an individual's social personality and are based on what the individual thinks he ought to believe. At the level of opinion, an individual is susceptible to change and responds positively either to reasoned argument or to propaganda.

Attitudes, as opposed to opinions, are more long lived, less socially determined, though they may reflect the values of a strong reference group, and more closely connected with an individual's basic character traits. Although attitudes can be altered, attitude change is often more apparent than real. What appears to be a radical conversion from fascism to communism may be a change on only the social level. Underneath, the converted may retain his basic attitude toward authoritarianism—an attitude satisfied within the confines of either communist or fascist ideology.

Character traits compose what Brown calls the nuclear personality. Character traits form early in life, become deep-rooted, and are the primary anchor points for an individual's system of adjustment. The nuclear personality is highly resistant to change because of the primacy of its formation and because it cannot be altered piecemeal but must be dealt with as a whole. Following Brown's ideas, we may picture the levels of attitude involvement in the following pattern:[22]

[21] *Techniques of Persuasion* (Baltimore: Penguin Books, Inc., 1964), p. 309.
[22] Brown, *Techniques of Persuasion*, pp. 37–57.

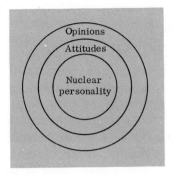

To rephrase one of our earlier hypotheses, the more public messages fall within the range of an individual's attitudes or nuclear personality, the more resistant the individual is to attitude change and the more he accepts or rejects messages in the light of already existent beliefs and prejudices. Public communication is effective in changing attitude only insofar as it can capitalize on already existent values, biases, and emotions to promote the change. If an individual experiences what appears to be an extensive revision of attitude, it is because his attitudinal frame of reference already has a tendency to change. According to Sherif, Sherif, and Nebergall, attitudinal change toward the direction advocated in a message occurs when the following conditions hold:

1. The object of evaluation (the message) is relatively unstructured; it permits a wide margin for alternative modes of interpretation and response.
2. The topic is unfamiliar to the subjects or is not highly involved in their scheme of priorities. In this case internal standards for judgment are uncertain or are not brought to bear at all.
3. The discrepancy between the individual's initial attitude and the communication is not near its maximum.
4. The communicator is acceptable in terms of the individual's reference-group ties. (Acceptance is especially great if the communicator is highly prestigious.)

The chances for attitude change decrease or there is negative change when the following conditions obtain:

1. The object of evaluation is well structured, indicating clear-cut differences and standards for evaluation. In other words there are few alternatives for response.

2. The topic is familiar to an individual and he is highly ego-involved in his position toward it.

3. The discrepancy between the subject's attitude and the communication is fairly great.

4. The communicator is not highly prestigious or is a member of an unfriendly reference group.[23]

The foregoing discussion reveals the problems involved in determining the precise effects of public communication and the reasons for apparent attitude change when such change occurs. The variables influencing individual or group response are numerous and interrelated, and communicative messages are just one influence among many.

CONCLUSION

We started our discussion of public communication by noting the differences between those messages exchanged among several individuals on a fairly private basis and those messages intended for wider public distribution. Then, by briefly surveying the historical development of public speaking, both in theory and in practice, we discovered that modern mass society and mass media have changed the nature of the rhetorical situation in distinct and important ways. An examination of the variables of public communication and of the way in which messages are disseminated and used by various audiences emphasized the complexities of the contemporary rhetorical transaction.

In the final analysis, even though public communication implies a broader scope of interaction than does a more intimate, interpersonal dialogue or a small-group discussion, we discovered that we must work our way back through the scene of group activity and through the possibilities and influences of the interpersonal situation to the individual dimension of behavior to account for the influence of a public message. The individual reaches his judgments, adopts his attitudes, and undertakes action on the basis of his perceptions of self and of the specific stimuli which affect him. Tracing influence from a source of public communication, through the various media which disseminate, amplify, diminish, and modify, through the web of social relationships surrounded and influenced by a climate of opinion, to the complex system of the individual's behavior potentials is not an easy task to say the least. In

[23] Sherif, Sherif, and Nebergall, *Attitude and Attitude Change*, p. 189.

many respects we have just begun the study of public communication in a mass society. We cannot yet accurately determine or describe all the situations in which the potency of communication is heightened. We have not spent enough time studying the long-range influence of public messages to realize their full capability for building and altering our image of reality. But we cannot doubt that public messages do play their part in determining human response.

ALLEN, FREDERICK LEWIS, *The Big Change.* New York: Bantam Books, Inc., 1961.

———, *Since Yesterday.* New York: Bantam Books, Inc., 1961.

ANDERSEN, KENNETH, and THEODORE CLEVENGER, JR., "A Summary of Experimental Research in Ethos," *Speech Monographs,* XXX (June 1963), 59–78.

ANDERSON, D. C., "The Effect of Various Uses of Authoritative Testimony in Persuasive Speaking." Unpublished Master's thesis, Ohio State University, 1958.

ARISTOTLE, *Rhetoric,* trans. Lane Cooper. New York: Appleton-Century-Crofts, 1932.

ARNOLD, CARROLL C., "Rhetoric in America Since 1900," in *Re-Establishing the Speech Profession.* State College, Pennsylvania: Speech Association of the Eastern States, 1959.

BAUER, RAYMOND A., "The Communicator and the Audience," in *People, Society, and Mass Communications,* eds. Lewis Anthony Dexter and David Manning White. New York: The Macmillan Company, 1964.

BECKER, CARL, *The Heavenly City of the Eighteenth Century Philosophers.* New Haven, Connecticut: Yale University Press, 1960.

BECKER, SAMUEL L., "Research on Emotional and Logical Proofs," *Southern Speech Journal,* XXVIII, No. 3 (Spring 1963), 198–207.

BERELSON, BERNARD, "Communications and Public Opinion," in *Communications in Modern Society,* ed. Wilbur Schramm. Urbana, Illinois: University of Illinois Press, 1948.

———, and GARY A. STEINER, *Human Behavior.* New York: Harcourt, Brace & World, Inc., 1964.

BROWN, CHARLES T., and CHARLES VAN RIPER, *Speech and Man.* Englewood Cliffs, New Jersey: Prentice-Hall, Inc., 1966.

BROWN, J. A. C., *Techniques of Persuasion.* Baltimore: Penguin Books, Inc., 1964.

CARTER, RICHARD F., "Some Effects of the Debates," in *The Great Debates*, ed. Sidney Kraus. Bloomington, Indiana: Indiana University Press, 1962.

CATHCART, ROBERT S., "An Experimental Study of the Relative Effectiveness of Four Methods of Presenting Evidence," *Speech Monographs*, XXII (1955), 227–33.

CORBETT, EDWARD P. J., *Classical Rhetoric for the Modern Student*. New York: Oxford University Press, Inc., 1965.

COSTLY, D. L., "An Experimental Study of the Effectiveness of Quantitative Evidence in Speeches of Advocacy." Unpublished Master's thesis, University of Oklahoma, 1958.

DAVIDSON, W. PHILLIPS, "On the Effects of Communication," in *People, Society, and Mass Communications*, eds. Lewis Anthony Dexter and David Manning White. New York: The Macmillan Company, 1964.

GIEBER, WALTER, "News Is What Newspapermen Make It," in *People, Society, and Mass Communications*, eds. Lewis Anthony Dexter and David Manning White. New York: The Macmillan Company, 1964.

GILKINSON, H., S. F. PAULSON, and D. E. SIKKINK, "Effects of Order and Authority in an Argumentative Speech," *Quarterly Journal of Speech*, XL (1954), 183–92.

GLENN, EDMUND S., "Meaning and Behavior; Communication and Culture," *The Journal of Communication*, XVI, No. 4 (December 1966), 248–72.

GREGG, RICHARD B., "The Rhetoric of Evidence," *Western Speech*, XXX (Summer 1967), 180–89.

HAIMAN, FRANKLYN, "An Experimental Study of the Effects of Ethos in Public Speaking," *Speech Monographs*, XVI (September 1949), 190–202.

HALL, EDWARD T., *The Silent Language* (2nd ed.). New York: Doubleday & Company, Inc., 1959.

————, and WILLIAM FOOTE WHITE, "Intercultural Communication: A Guide to Men of Action," in *Communication and Culture*, ed. Alfred G. Smith. New York: Holt, Rinehart & Winston, Inc., 1966.

HUIZINGA, JOHAN, "Play-Forms in Philosophy," in *Homo Ludens*. Boston: Beacon Press, Inc., 1955.

KARNS, C. FRANKLIN, "The Verbal Behavior of a Speaker as a Function of Certain Non-Verbal Aversive Stimuli Presented by an Audience in a Public Speaking Situation." Unpublished Ph.D. dissertation, University of Pittsburgh, 1964.

KATZ, ELIHU, and PAUL F. LAZARSFELD, *Personal Influence*. New York: The Macmillan Company, 1955.

KELMAN, K. C., and C. I. HOVLAND, " 'Reinstatement' of the Communicator in Delayed Measurement of Opinion Change," *Journal of Abnormal and Social Psychology*, XLVIII (1953), 327–35.

KENNEDY, GEORGE, "Two Problems in the Historical Study of Rhetoric," *The Pennsylvania Speech Annual,* XXI (September 1964), 20–21.

KLAPPER, JOSEPH T., "The Effects of Mass Communication," in *Reader in Public Opinion and Communication* (2nd ed.), eds. Bernard Berelson and Morris Janowitz. New York: The Free Press, 1966.

LANE, ROBERT E., and DAVID O. SEARS, *Public Opinion.* Englewood Cliffs, New Jersey: Prentice-Hall, Inc., 1964.

LANG, KURT, and GLADYS E. LANG, "The Mass Media and Voting," in *Reader in Public Opinion and Communication,* eds. Bernard Berelson and Morris Janowitz. New York: The Free Press, 1966.

———, "Reactions of Viewers," in *The Great Debates,* ed. Sidney Kraus. Bloomington, Indiana: Indiana University Press, 1962.

———, "The Unique Perspective of Television," in *Reader in Public Opinion and Communication,* eds. Bernard Berelson and Morris Janowitz. New York: The Free Press, 1966.

LIMB, BEN C., "Speech: The Life of a Diplomat," in *Culture and Communication,* ed. Robert T. Oliver. Springfield, Illinois: Charles C Thomas, Publisher, 1962.

MCCROSKEY, JAMES C., "The Effects of Evidence in Persuasive Communication," *Western Speech,* XXX (Summer 1967), 188–99.

MULLER, HERBERT J., *The Uses of the Past.* New York: Oxford University Press, Inc., 1959.

OLIVER, ROBERT T., ed., *Culture and Communication.* Springfield, Illinois: Charles C Thomas, Publisher, 1962.

REUCHELLE, R. C., "An Experimental Study of Audience Recognition of Emotional and Intellectual Appeals in Persuasion," *Speech Monographs,* XXV (1958), 49–58.

ROSENAU, JAMES N., *Public Opinion and Foreign Policy.* New York: Random House, 1961.

SAMOVAR, LARRY A., "Ambiguity and Unequivocation in the Kennedy-Nixon Television Debates," *Quarterly Journal of Speech,* XLVIII (October 1962), 278–79.

SCHLESINGER, ARTHUR M., JR., *A Thousand Days.* Boston: Houghton Mifflin Company, 1965.

SCHRAMM, W., and W. DANIELSON, "Anticipated Audiences as Determinants of Recall," *Journal of Abnormal and Social Psychology,* XVI (1958), 282–83.

SHERIF, CAROLYN W., MUZAFER SHERIF, and ROGER NEBERGALL, *Attitude and Attitude Change.* Philadelphia: W. B. Saunders Co., 1965.

SIDEY, HUGH, *John F. Kennedy, President.* New York: Fawcett World Library, 1964.

SOLA POOL, ITHIEL DE, ROBERT ABELSON, and SAMUEL POPKIN, *Candidates, Issues, and Strategies* (2nd ed.). Cambridge, Massachusetts: M.I.T. Press, 1965.

SORENSON, THEODORE C., *Decision-Making in the White House.* New York: Columbia University Press, 1963.

WHITE, DAVID MANNING, "The 'Gatekeeper': A Case Study in the Selection of News," in *People, Society, and Mass Communications,* eds. Lewis Anthony Dexter and David Manning White. New York: The Macmillan Company, 1964.

WHITE, THEODORE H., *The Making of the President, 1960.* New York: Atheneum Publishers, 1961.

ZIMMERMAN, CLAIRE, and R. A. BAUER, "The Influence of an Audience on What Is Remembered," *Public Opinion Quarterly,* XX (1956), 238–48.

Postscript

We have covered much ground in the preceding pages in providing the reader with information about speech behavior in social interaction. We discussed fairly reliable propositions, theoretical systems with their associated speculations and explanations, and recent developments pertaining to the individual's communication system, interpersonal communication, and public communication. The goal was to provide a descriptive analysis of the human-communication process on each of these levels. We described the processes of information collecting, storing, processing, recalling, and transmitting and interrelated the roles they play in the individual's communication system. In the area of interpersonal communication, we presented and analyzed aspects of the social bases of interpersonal communication, dyadic communication, and group communication in order to present the reader with information on the dimensions of face-to-face communication. The exposition of public communication focused on elements in our rhetorical tradition and in the rhetorical present; on several key variables of public communication including the communicator himself, the message, and the audience; and on several of the functions and the effects of public communication.

Since the descriptions within the three major divisions are incomplete and inaccurate representations of speech behavior in social interaction if taken alone, we devoted considerable discussion to the interrelationships that exist among the topics. In other words the divisions between each of the three sections are not absolutely definitive and clear cut because the subject matter does not exist that way in nature. One of the limitations of human description and textbook format is that they proceed linearly in a line-by-line, topical organization, while the subject matter itself is structured quite differently and manifests itself all at once in the real world. For example, communication codes have a definite place in Parts I and II; only a purist would relegate this topic exclusively to one or the other of the two perspectives. Throughout Part I we implied that the discussions were related to the subsequent discussions on interpersonal and public communication, and we made these implications explicit in Parts II and III. We discussed the interrelations of intrapersonal and interpersonal communication at considerable length in the section on the social bases of interpersonal communication; in fact, the whole section pertained to that interrelationship. We showed how interpersonal communication and public communication are bound together in several influential relationships which are derived from the nature of group norms, the societal climate of opinion, the attitude change in groups, and the many aspects of the rhetorical present. We treated the interconnectedness of public communication and the individual's communication system by considering how the cultural context, the nature of public opinion, and the pattern of communication flow provide, along with the several variables of public communication, incoming data or information which is processed by the mechanisms of the individual's communication system and which also influences the way in which those mechanisms function. Consideration of the reaction of the individual to public communication bound together Parts I and III at still another level.

By integrating these aspects of speech behavior in social interaction, we hope we have given the reader a sense of how far along the community of interested scholars is in its inquiry into the various aspects of this very complicated phenomenon. We hope we have fostered an impression of the ongoing process and incompletion of the research efforts in this area. The following reference to recent and current work in the several specialties underscores that impression and also provides the interested student with diverse foci for continued study.

Phillip Teitelbaum's *Physiological Psychology* (Englewood Cliffs, New Jersey: Prentice-Hall, Inc., 1967) presents recent research findings on sensation and signal transmission in the individual communicator. A fruitful stream of research into memory at the neurological level is currently under way. Especially great progress has been made in the investigation of RNA and in the relation of protein molecules to memory. These findings are popularized by Isaac Asimov's "Pills to Help Us Remember," *New York Times Magazine*, October 9, 1966. Our knowledge of the interpretation, or information-processing, phase of the individual's communication process is developing on several fronts. The idea of a governor, or cybernetic, which directs our development of symbolic processes and maintains our mental equilibrium is implicit in many of the theories in psychology, psycholinguistics, and linguistics. The works of Charles Osgood, Leon Festinger, Jerome Bruner, Eric Lenneberg, James Deese, David Ausubel, George Miller, Jerry Fodor, and Jerrold Katz in many current periodicals are pertinent here in connection with such topics as cognitive dissonance, mediation, thinking, learning, cognition, perception, and opinion or attitude change. In the area of verbal communication the works of Noam Chomsky, Sydney Lamb, Charles Hockett, Dell Hymes, Roger Brown, George Miller, John Carroll, Jerry Fodor, and Jerrold Katz may be helpful to the interested student.

In the area of dyadic communication pertinent material may be found in the books and works of Fritz Heider, John Thibaut and Harold Kelley, and Theodore Newcomb and Erving Goffman, and in the published articles of John Schopler, Marjorie W. Mathews, Howard Taylor, and Timothy Brock, to mention only a few. An overview of the large volume of recent experimental and theoretical works in the area of small-group communication is found in the introductory treatment of Clovis Shepherd's *Small Groups,* in paperback (San Francisco: Chandler Publishing Co., 1964). Basic and landmark theoretical contributions to small-group communication are in the books and published articles of Robert Bales, George Homans, Barry Collins and Harold Guetzkow, and W. C. Schutz. Up-to-date collections of articles are under the editorship of A. Paul Hare and Dorwin Cartwright and Alvin Zander, and a comprehensive survey of empirical research on the small group entitled *Small Group Research* has been compiled by Joseph McGrath and Irving Altman (New York: Holt, Rinehart & Winston, Inc., 1966). It contains abstracts of 500 studies and a bibliography of 2700 research reports. Fruitful journals to peruse in this area include *Speech Monographs, Journal of Communication, Sociometry,* and *The Journal of Personality and Social Psychology.*

In the area of public communication, *Reader in Public Opinion and Communication,* 2nd ed., edited by B. Berelson and M. Janowitz (New York: The Macmillan Company, 1966), and *People, Society and Mass Communications,* edited by Lewis A. Dexter and David M. White (New York: The Macmillan Company, 1964), both include a variety of essays typifying research approaches and giving data relevant to mass communication. M. L. DeFleur's *Theories of Mass Communication* (New York: David McKay Co., Inc., 1966) provides a good introduction to both the historical development and the theoretical study of mass communication. The works of Daniel Katz, Paul Lazarsfeld, Harold Lasswell, Wilber Schramm, Kurt Lang, Gladys Engel Lang, Gary Steiner, Raymond Bauer, Ithiel de Sola Pool, Joseph Klapper, George Gerbner, and K. W. Deutsch, among others, are significant contributions to an understanding of contemporary public communication.

Index of Names

Index of Subjects

Abstraction: linguistic, 105; perceptual, 105; process, 41–42
Achieved status, 151
Action group, 129, 130
Adjustment group, 129, 130
Adolescence, 100–101
Affective response, 160, 162
Ambiguity, 196–97
Amnesia, 25, 87
Antecedent ethos, 200–201
Anticipated audience, 213
Apathy, 146
Aphasia, 25
Argument, 206, 207
Arte of Rhetorique, The, 186
Athens, 183
Attention focus, 150
Attention group, 234
Attention mechanism, 47
Attentive public, 234
Attitude: assessment, 240–41; change, 208, 230–31, 242–43; formation, 229; preferences, 112; response, 201–2
Attitudinal frame of reference, 33–36, 40, 42, 43, 47, 48, 64, 65, 243
Attitudinal systems, 235
Audience, 209–15: analysis, 209–10, 215; beliefs, 211; commitment, 212; goals, 211; personal, 212; primary, 212; secondary, 212; size, 210; strategic, 212; values, 211; variety, 195–96
Audience response, 211
Authority figures, 36–37

Balanced role sets, 114, 116, 117
Barren dyads, 114
Barren role sets, 114, 115

Behavior, 158–62, 189: change, 125, 126, 231; individual's patterns, 239; interpretation, 161; norms, 114, 122; predictability, 122, 139
Belief systems, 35–36
Brain, 9, 15–20, 24, 25
Brainwashing, 21
Broken role sets, 119

Categorical memory, 49
Causality, 89
Casual group, 129, 130
Central nervous system, 8, 9, 14–16
Changing image, 203–4
Channels of communication, 143
Classical rhetoric, 182–92
Climate of opinion, 215–19
Closed-mindedness, 37–38
Cognitive balance, 28, 29, 34, 43, 44, 47, 51, 240
Cognitive dissonance, 29, 45–47, 54, 240
Cognitive structure, 23
Coherence, 45
Commitment: beliefs, 38, 39, 241; public, 231, 232
Communication: barriers in groups, 146–56; breakdown, 18; mass exposure, 226; media, 59–60, 180, 190, 192, 226, 228–31; process, 7; research 189–90; systems, 177–78; variables, 222–23
Communication effect, 224–26, 228: analysis, 227; communicator, 231; hypodermic, 226; immediate, 227; long-range, 227; phenomenistic approach, 226; public opinion, 234
Communication flow, 236–38: four-step, 238; one-step, 236; two-step, 238